3 8002 01732 866 9

LIBRARIES

WITHDRAWN

Reviews for *Mind Chi*

'When I read Mind Chi I said to myself, "It's about time." Mind Chi takes contemporary knowledge of the brain, the best thinking from Psychology and the wisdom of the ages and packages these in a format that allows access to their power. An eight minute daily dose of Mind Chi may not cure warts but it will certainly improve vitality, reduce stress and allow us to see the many blessings of life more clearly.'

Stephen C. Lundin PhD, author of the five million copy best-selling *FISH!*

'Leonardo had it, Edison had it, and now you can have it too. "It" is Mind Chi. This powerful book will show you how to cultivate, integrate and apply your mental energy for breakthrough performance in all walks of life.'

Michael J Gelb, author of *How to Think Like Leonardo da Vinci and Innovate Like Edison*

'Mind Chi is a novel, interesting, and practical way to boost your brainpower. Eight minutes a day is a worthwhile investment for anyone who's serious about personal development, well-being and happiness.'

Dr. Karl Albrecht, executive advisor, futurist, speaker, and author of *Practical Intelligence: the Art and Science of Common Sense*

'Although there are many parts of Mind Chi that are attractive to me, I believe you teach people how to conquer the No. 1 cause for forgetting: distraction. Eight minutes of uninterrupted focus not only begins the day but sets the tempo for each productive hour. Before the end of the day, you will be amazed at how much you have accomplished'

Scott Hagwood, author of *Memory Power*

'Vanda North and Richard Israel have crafted a tour de force that will transform lives. With passion, compassion, humour, and discipline, their calling is evidenced as a call to action … that your destiny matters. Buy this book, live its contents, and help others awaken to its dazzling delights!'

Dilip Mukerjea, author of titles in *The Creative Brain* series

D1513226

'Mind Chi gives you techniques you can immediately practice for long-lasting results'

Conni Gordon, best-selling author of the 4-step Instant Art Method

'Mind Chi is a leading edge compendium of practical exercises to optimise your mental energy. Applying the techniques on a regular basis gives the reader the potential to reach their goals and maximise the quality of their life as well as achieve greater levels of work performance.'

Helen Whitten, Managing Director of Positiveworks, UK, executive coach and author of Cognitive-behavioural Coaching Techniques For Dummies and Emotional Healing For Dummies

'This easy-to-read book offers real tips to help you make remarkable changes. Discover how to replace negative thinking, sharpen your mental acuity, strengthen your concentration and increase your energy. Mix and match the 50 Mind Chi Strategies for Success to create your own inner harmony. Control the mind and become the master of your destiny.'

Margo Berman, Florida International University professor and author of Street-Smart Advertising and The Brains Behind Great Ad Campaigns

'I am delighted to recommend Richard Israel and Vanda North's Mind Chi Program. I have known Richard personally for years and I can attest to his ability to find ideas 'on the cusp' and translate those ideas into workable programs. Mind Chi is a long overdue program which has finally arrived! I hope that you find it as helpful as I did.'

Bernie Cleveland, PhD, CEO, TeacherOnlineEducation.com

'Great Insight... In a challenging world Richard Israel and Vanda North's Mind Chi paves the way to be smarter about tackling life in the workplace. Mind Chi enables the readers to step outside themselves and see what they really need to see.'

Jeffrey Meshel, author of One Phone Call Away, Secrets of a Master Networker

'Not only have both Vanda and Richard successfully applied Mind Chi personally, but now they can transfer this to professionals and organizations for revolutionary success!'

Jamie Nast, author of Idea Mapping

MIND CHI

Re-wire Your Brain in 8 Minutes a Day

For Sarah Sutton,
whose extraordinary level of commitment to this project is unprecedented

Coventry City Council	
APL	
3 8002 01732 866 9	
Askews	Feb-2010
153.1	£14.99

MIND CHI
Re-wire Your Brain in 8 Minutes a Day

Strategies for Success in Business and Life

Richard Israel and Vanda North

CAPSTONE

This edition first published 2010
© Richard Israel and Vanda North 2010

Registered office
Capstone Publishing Ltd. (A Wiley Company), The Atrium, Southern Gate, Chichester, West Sussex, PO19 8SQ, United Kingdom

For details of our global editorial offices, for customer services and for information about how to apply for permission to reuse the copyright material in this book please see our website at www.wiley.com.

The right of the authors to be identified as the authors of this work has been asserted in accordance with the Copyright, Designs and Patents Act 1988.

All rights reserved. No part of this publication may be reproduced, stored in a retrieval system, or transmitted, in any form or by any means, electronic, mechanical, photocopying, recording or otherwise, except as permitted by the UK Copyright, Designs and Patents Act 1988, without the prior permission of the publisher.

Wiley also publishes its books in a variety of electronic formats. Some content that appears in print may not be available in electronic books.

Designations used by companies to distinguish their products are often claimed as trademarks. All brand names and product names used in this book are trade names, service marks, trademarks or registered trademarks of their respective owners. The publisher is not associated with any product or vendor mentioned in this book. This publication is designed to provide accurate and authoritative information in regard to the subject matter covered. It is sold on the understanding that the publisher is not engaged in rendering professional services. If professional advice or other expert assistance is required, the services of a competent professional should be sought.

Library of Congress Cataloguing-in-Publication Data

ISBN 978-1-9-064-6558-2

A catalogue record for this book is available from the British Library.

Set in 10pt Meridien by Sparks, Oxford – www.sparkspublishing.com
Printed and bound in Spain by Grafos SA, Barcelona

Who wrote *Mind Chi*?

Richard Israel is a consultant, speaker, trainer and author. Richard has forty years of experience and international expertise in sales training, leadership development, creativity, and memory training with a unique skill of applying cognitive science. As a pioneer in creating 'brain capital' he is sought after around the world. His work has increased the intellectual capital within organizations and enabled teams and individuals to achieve optimal performance. More than one and a half million people across four continents have been educated utilizing his material. He has consulted with companies in the retail, hospitality, airline, manufacturing and service industries, coaching them to achieve increased business results and discover new business opportunities.

Vanda North's life purpose is to assist people to rediscover and enhance their natural joy quotient. Her life has been dedicated to this end. From TV shows, to books, to setting up a global network, to training tens of thousands of people to living a joyous life! She concentrates on: improving stress management through 'Happiness & Wellness' classes; enabling learning through accelerated learning techniques, maps, memory, speedy-reading and info-intake methods (for both learning abled and 'dis'-abled); developing self leadership with communication, commitment and contentment; and now Mind Chi. Vanda travels the world delivering seminars and does adventure trekking, such as climbing Mount Kilimanjaro, to raise money for her local hospital.

Also by the authors

Brain$ell, Tony Buzan and Richard Israel

The BrainSmart Leader, Tony Buzan, Tony Dottino and Richard Israel

Business mapping, Vanda North

Get Ahead: Map your way to success, Vanda North

Get Ahead: Teen Learning Success, Vanda North

Grass Roots Leader: The brainsmart revolution in business, Tony Buzan, Tony Dottino, Richard Israel

How to Think Creatively: Using the 'TILS' 4-step technique, Conni Gordon and Richard Israel

Joy Journey, Vanda North

Sales Genius, Tony Buzan and Richard Israel

Shifting Gears: How you can succeed and lead in the new workplace – The technology of success, Susan Ford Collins and Richard Israel

The Spark, Vanda North

SuperSellf, Tony Buzan and Richard Israel

The Vision, Julianne Crane and Richard Israel

Your Mind at Work: Developing self-knowledge for business success, Richard Israel, Helen Whitten, Cliff Shaffran

Acknowledgments

From Richard:

Lois Feinberg for her love and understanding throughout the Mind Chi project; Susan Ford Collins for her counseling and partnership in marketing break-through concepts through the years; Conni Gordon for her wisdom and encouragement; Tony Dottino for sharing the vision in the important work we do; Kathy Shurte for her support from day one of the Mind Chi project in the United States; Lana Israel my constant cheerleader and inspiration; Helen Whitten for her continued belief in our work together; Gwen Carden who is the best PR agent one could wish for; Stu Elliott for his unconditional friendship; Dilip Mukerjea, the Superbrain and my model of the 'expert strategy'; Leon Cai for his support and hard work in marketing my materials in China; and of course my mother, Rita Israel who made this all possible. I would also like to thank all the 'brain stars', too numerous to mention in South East Asia, South Africa, Europe and North America who participated in the Mind Chi pilots that made Mind Chi possible.

From Vanda:

A big round of applause goes to all those who helped me to tweak Mind Chi by participating in my pilot phases, some of you were in workshops and some by email, those who were especially helpful were: Kate Boyd; Angelo Lam; Adrian Woods; Anne Jones; Maria De Ionno; Tony Muir; Kirsty Mawer; Pat Pollman; Alan Adair; Mike Collins and Bettina Jetter, I thank you enormously. Then there were my readers: Caro Ayre; Kim Cordes and Bob Chapman. You fought your way through many different versions, valiantly and honestly making suggestions for improvement. I hope you see the fruits of your labours and are proud of the result. Then I want to say a general thank you to everyone who has shared gems with me over the years that have now become a part of who I am and how I function. There is not room to name you all and there is always a special place of gratitude in my heart for you. And most importantly, those who have had to be by my side, my family and co-author! You have been my rock, my star, my joy, my sounding board and my sustenance. You are deeply appreciated.

From both of us:

We have been blessed! The role of mid-wife, coach and guiding light has been played by an angel who goes by the name of Sarah Sutton. From conception through the early 'formative years' of Mind Chi, she has been there. The book you hold, is here because of her dedication and expertise. 'Thank you' is just the tip of the gratitude-burg we feel.

Our team from Wiley, we thank for their dedication, patience, support and flexibility and are grateful for their graciousness.

To all that have ever attended our seminars – we thank you for the learning we received from you.

Special Mention goes to our mentor, Tony Buzan, who for the last twenty years was our teacher, coach, inspiration and friend and who encouraged us to fly.

Finally, a heartfelt thanks goes to Jamie Nast for her unwavering support, she is a true believer in mental literacy and a class act.

Contents

Mind Chi 50 Strategies for Success

GOALS

MANAGEMENT SKILLS

SALES

COMMUNICATION

JOB SMARTS

Mind Chi *Fast Track*

Here is a whistle-stop tour through the basic structure of Mind Chi – an overview of the benefits and features of the adventure you are about to start. A more detailed introduction follows, but here is what you need to know right now.

What is Mind Chi?

Mind Chi is your mental energy. Mind Chi shows you how to build, manage and direct your mental energy for increased success in business and life. It allows you to reinvent yourself with superior performance for changing times. Mind Chi provides you with a special present, to (re)gain control over yourself – your one oasis of security in this shifting season.

The benefits of Mind Chi

- fast and easy ways to improve your thinking
- change disruptive thoughts to supportive ones
- rapidly develop new positive habits
- mental processes that keep you stress free and confident

- upgrade your attention span, memory and belief systems
- have control over your feelings, thoughts and behaviours
- improve resilience and information management
- more mental and physical energy during and after your work!

Why is Mind Chi different?

1   Mind Chi builds four powerful change processes right into activities, seamlessly assisting you to make the changes you want; they are your **Mind Chi Vehicle** for change.

2   Mind Chi applies the latest research on how your brain/mind functions to how this information can actually make a positive difference in your life, via your **Mind Chi Program**.

Yes! These are BIG claims, and we believe you can do it!

3   Mind Chi comes with a built-in guide, **'Chi'** – your Mind Chi Mentor will help you achieve your goals and strengthen your willpower. 'Chi' will embed your positive, new **Mind Chi Meme**.

4   Mind Chi is a brain-friendly program, providing very 'simple' yet deeply profound processes that you can use to organize your thoughts and plan your life: your **Mind Chi Maps**. Mind Chi offers you control over yourself, your **B**ody, **E**motions, **A**ctions and **T**houghts in this present moment, using **Your Mind Chi BEAT**.

Make it Mind Chi-easy

- **Start today** – with eight minutes of Mind Chi a day for 28 days. You will gain a foothold of control and experience what is possible.
- **Solve a problem** with your Mind Chi Plan – use the 50 completed Strategies for Success, or write your own.
- **Attain your goals** – your Mind Chi Vehicle will take you there, ably assisted by 'Chi' your Mind Chi mentor.

Mind Chi philosophy

It is into the schools of Positive Psychology, Mental Wellness and Eudemonics that Mind Chi firmly fits. What is right about you and how can you have more of it? What processes and knowledge can assist you to direct your will to produce the outcomes you desire? How can you fix the (relatively) minor impediments and enhance the features you want? How can you flourish?!

That is what Mind Chi is all about!

Psst …

I can assist you!

Introduction to Mind Chi

Overview

Mind Chi is your mental energy
Benefits of Mind Chi
Mind Chi overview
It is all in your Mind Chi

Welcome to Mind Chi! Mind Chi offers you a simple and revolutionary way to improve your mental energy, regain control and achieve your greatest goals. Mind Chi is a synthesis of positive psychology, mental wellness and eudemonics (the study of happiness). The eight steps of Mind Chi are grounded firmly in established theories of memory, mind and motivational development and are the distillation of over eighty years' combined personal experience and development by the authors. The techniques are designed to improve your control, willpower and focus, and in so doing increase your success in business and life.

Mind Chi is your mental energy

Everything that you do, feel, express, experience and think is fuelled by your mental energy. Every thought, action or emotion results from the way you direct your energy. Are you using it for your own good or for your self-destruction? Are you using it to operate at your optimal level, or to function at your lowest level?

Mind Chi is your mental energy.

Mind Chi shows you how to build, manage and direct your mental energy for increased success and enjoyment in business and life. It allows you to adapt and reinvent yourself with superior performance in changing times. The concept of 'Chi' has its roots in Chinese culture and philosophy and will be a familiar concept to anyone who has seen or practised t'ai chi or qigong. Chi is related to, but not precisely the same as, the scientific concept of energy. In Mind Chi the Chi energy is a feeling and an attitude related to your willpower. Your mental energy increases in line with your level of attention and the strength of your intention. This is the basic premise of Mind Chi.

You need to know how to build, manage and direct your mental energy for your own well-being and success. It is all too easy to go through your life being unaware of how you are using this vital resource. You may feel that you are at the mercy of 'involuntary' responses – and you may be – but it doesn't have to stay that way. Mind Chi can allow you control over your body, thoughts, emotions and actions.

Mind Chi gives you a mind that works FOR you – NOT against you!

The decision, believe it or not, is yours!

Negative thoughts and actions generate further negativity – spreading a feeling of helpless gloom faster than the speed of Twitter. Negativity gives away the keys to controlling your will and volition. Mind Chi will show you that, just by thinking positively and appropriately, you (not anyone or anything else) can always be actively in control. Mind Chi is all about taking back the keys to your future and making sure you know when and how to use them.

The eight steps of Mind Chi encourage you to ask: what is right about me and how can I have more of it? How can I learn to direct my will to produce the outcomes I desire?

In just eight minutes a day you will learn to rewind your past, review your present, and visualize and plan a future of your choosing.

Over the course of 28 days this basic routine will be transformed into a life-enhancing habit.

About T'ai chi and Qigong

T'ai chi ch'uan is an ancient Chinese form of martial art. The Mandarin term means the 'supreme ultimate fist' and represents the fusion of 'yin and yang' and of many Chinese philosophies. It is one of the central pillars of Traditional Chinese Medicine (TCM) and is practised most commonly for the benefit of health and well-being. The coordinated body movements focus, cultivate and direct internal energy; the aim being to harmonize the mind, body and spirit, promoting both mental and physical well being through softness and relaxation. When practised correctly the movements (or Form) of t'ai chi appear rhythmical, effortless and as a continuous flow.

Qigong (pronounced, and sometimes spelt, ch'i kung) is a newer art; the name means 'air' or 'life-force' or 'energy'. Qigong also works with gentle movements and coordinates body and mind. With the practice of t'ai chi or qigong you become revitalized, relaxed, tolerant, self-confident, stronger and healthier in mind and body. Unlike most forms of exercise and sport, neither relies on strength, force or speed, making it ideal for people of either sex, young and old alike, whether strong or weak.

T'ai chi and qigong offer teachings on how to be healthy and to stay centred in a chaotic environment. Physical benefits include: improved balance, suppleness and posture; relaxation; better co-ordination; increased energy; stronger immune system; enhanced muscle tone and circulation; lower blood pressure and heart rate; prevention of osteoporosis and feeling more 'in tune' with your body. This is probably why t'ai chi has been practised since 1200AD and tens of millions of people are currently practising it daily. It has stood the test of time and numbers.

Benefits of Mind Chi

What results can you expect from Mind Chi?

Mind Chi helps you to improve your mental energy which, in turn, means that you increase your personal power and have a far better chance of obtaining the future that you want. Because you are able to manage your stress in a positive way, you will also benefit from overall increased good health. There is a direct correlation between your state of contentment and your state of wellness, so you will sleep better and feel more energized. This means that you will feel happier and more in control of each day. All that from an eight-minute-a-day routine!

The two key words that Mind Chi-ers report are 'control' and 'satisfaction':

Mind Chi becomes a way of life. It is a way of thinking and being that enables you to be all you wish to be.

- **Control** – in the sense that you will learn the Mind Chi BEAT: how to check your Body, Emotions, Actions and Thoughts, making you aware of how you are functioning. You can then choose to make any necessary adjustments to create a stronger feeling of control over yourself and anything that you may be facing.
- **Satisfaction** – comes first from seeing fast improvements in just a few days, which happens through projecting forward to visualize and plan your next 24 hours. You are more likely to gain positive outcomes and achieve your desired responses if you use Mind Chi to plan ahead.

Mind Chi will bring you many benefits, among them are:

1 *Balancing your work and life*: focusing on a healthy work/life balance. You will learn to 'work smarter' so that the really important things in your life can be given equal priority.

2 *Identifying your goals*: learning to visualize and plan for what you want. Mind Chi show you ways of visualizing and attaining your goals.

3 *Living 'in the moment'*: your Mind Chi BEAT – a simple method to check your Body, Emotions, Actions and Thoughts – encourages you to increase your focus and attention on the present moment and make the changes you need or want to.

4 *Being your best*: cutting-edge strategies for business success and personal happiness – improving communication skills; management techniques; health; self-concept and relationship issues. You will be able to give superior performance because you will have repaired small (or large) problem areas and achieved your goals.

5 *Enabling you to focus*: you will be able to cut out distractions and keep your attention where and when you want it.

6 *Improving faith in your memory*: learn how to remember what you want to remember and the causes of your 'forgettery' (absent-mindedness).

7 *Bringing quality to your relationships*: your professional relationships, and those with your family and friends will improve as your interpersonal skills develop and you become clearer about what you want and how you can achieve it.

8 *Increasing power and purpose in all you do*: which means greater job satisfaction, more effective outcomes and heightened enjoyment in all you do.

This is your life!

We think it is a good idea to make the most of it.

Mind Chi overview

Mind Chi is divided into four parts as follows:

Part 1   **Mind Chi Kick-off!** Part 1 will have you up and running with the eight steps of the Mind Chi Basic program – in no time. We introduce 'Chi', your Mind Chi Mentor and your Mind Chi BEAT to help you to gain immediate control of your thoughts. The Mind Chi Basic routine is explained in depth. The eight steps are completed in just eight minutes a day.

Part 2   **Mind Chi in Action.** As Mind Chi Maps are used throughout this book, we begin by explaining what 'maps' are and how they can be used. Part 2 shows you how to solve a problem or achieve a goal for your business and personal advancement. We explain the underlying process to you so you can either write your own Mind Chi Plan or use one of the 50 Strategies for Success included in Part 3. You will find two worked examples, a business and personal strategy on page 109.

Part 3   **50 Mind Chi Plans – Strategies for Success.** The focus of Part 3 is the practical challenges faced on a daily basis by those in business. We have used our combined experience to concentrate on the topics of most common concern – that will also improve one's efficiency and profitability.

Fifty Strategies are included and grouped under the themes of: Goals; Management; Sales; Communication; Job Smarts; Training; Health and Self-concept.

Part 4   **Mind Chi Plus.** Part 4 puts you at the wheel of your Mind Chi Vehicle and shows how it is engineered using a combination of Cognitive Behavioural Therapy (CBT), Rational Living Therapy, Robert Fritz's Structural Tension, Dr Jeffery Schwartz's 4 'R' Method and the sterling work of several scientists and researchers on how to improve your memory. In the Mind Chi Assistance chapter we include techniques on how to expand your thinking and overcome limiting beliefs, re-invent yourself and increase your self-esteem. Finally, we impart the Mind Chi Meme for you to take for yourself and pass to others.

Want to start the program immediately? Then go to **Mind Chi Kick-off!** (page 13) and learn the **Mind Chi Basic** routine (page 43).

Interested to learn first about the research behind the Mind Chi program? Go to **All in Your Mind** (page 9) and then to **Mind Chi Plus** (page 257).

Have a specific problem or issue? Select a Strategy for Success from the lists we have provided (page 135). But first familiarize yourself with the Mind Chi Basic routine and learn how to apply it to achieve your goal (pages 43 and 91).

Of course you may also read the book from start to finish. Mind Chi works whichever direction you choose to follow.

Mind Chi terminology

We have kept the names as descriptive as possible, so it 'does what it says on the can'!

- **Mind Chi Basic** – the eight steps of Mind Chi take eight minutes a day. This is the foundation of your program (page 43).
- **Mind Chi Plan** – a plan of action and a snapshot of the state of tension between your current reality, your BEAT and your future goal and preferred state (page 79). It includes your **Mind Chi Meme** (page 86), which is a positive-thinking phrase that will help propel you towards your goal. There are 50 Plans included in the book. They are your 'strategies for success' in work and life.
- **Mind Chi Applied** – when you apply Mind Chi to a plan of action you adapt the eight steps of Mind Chi Basic to the needs of your specific Mind Chi Strategy.
- **Mind Chi in Action** – nothing can change without action. Each Mind Chi Plan includes action steps and they should be followed in partnership with your Mind Chi Applied routine.
- **Mind Chi Program** – comprises the eight steps of Mind Chi Basic and Mind Chi Applied, your Mind Chi Plan and Mind Chi in Action (page 91).

Then there are four Mind Chi Methods to make it as easy as possible for you:

- **Mind Chi Maps** – a graphic portrayal of the information in a condensed and powerfully visual manner. Maps naturally improve your memory and usually increase your wish to be involved (page 73).
- **Mind Chi BEAT** – your way to increase your awareness of how you are currently functioning and be in control of your self in this moment. You learn to check and choose your responses at Body, Emotion, Action and Thought levels (making the acronym BEAT, page 39).
- **Mind Chi Vehicle** – a potent combination of four well-tested neuropsychological processes woven into the entire Mind Chi program to assist you to change (page 259).
- **Mind Chi Mentor**, called 'Chi' – the name for that voice that chatters away inside your head. 'Chi' will be encouraged to work with you for your greatest benefit (page 31).

We would love to receive your feedback. Log on to www.MindChi.com to share your views and for further Mind Chi resources.

These will be introduced to you in the next chapters and will soon become familiar.

The Mind Chi effect

There is a delicate balance between seeming to 'preach' and presenting concepts in a way that encourages you to strive for your best. Our intention is to help as many people as possible to become the best they want to be. You may be influenced by our techniques to a greater or lesser degree and it is our wish that they generate and inspire the highest ideals.

Once you have felt the benefits, share Mind Chi with others! This book is geared to the business community. That is, every one of you who does some sort of work (paid or not) on most days (well, we hope you get a weekend!). Nevertheless, the Mind Chi philosophy applies to

ALL humans, so share it with your children (please do – they really need to learn these concepts), with the 'older folk' – they too can really benefit and any person, in any endeavour who wishes for superior performance and increased satisfaction.

It is all in your Mind Chi

What is the difference between the 'brain' and the 'mind'? The debate is ongoing. The word 'brain' usually refers to the actual physical, chemical and electrical functioning of the grey matter in your head, whereas 'mind' is used to mean the cognitive functions, the intellect, consciousness and perceptions. However, as scientists delve ever more deeply into brain research, its greater intricacies are revealed, and the distinction between brain and mind begins to blur: it is no easy-to-follow, hard-wired 'machine'. In Mind Chi we use the words 'brain' and 'mind' interchangeably.

Even those who have been deeply immersed in brain research for years, who have some understanding of the brain's function and relationship to learning and effective performance, have been following with rapt attention the expansion of new frontiers, that cross the boundary between quantum physics and neuroscience.

Brain activity can now be mapped and scanned using PET (Positron Emission Tomography) scans, fMRI (functional Magnetic Resonance Imaging) readings and meticulous mapping; habitual behaviours can be seen *as they occur* in your brain. Even your thoughts can be 'seen' and interpreted accurately. Now, *that* is a statement with incredible ramifications! Further, it is realized that the 'plasticity' of your brain is far greater than initially expected: it literally rewires and remoulds itself in line with patterns of use. Your brain is a true 'learning machine' that adjusts as new information is received. It is designed to change and modify in line with your thoughts and direction. Two recent experiments to show this are: Pascual-Leone took some sighted people and blindfolded them for five days, he observed that it took only two days for the visual cortex to reorganize itself to process tactile and auditory signals; separately some chronic stroke patients were given two weeks of 'constraint-induced movement therapy' (CI) – where the arm that does work is kept in a sling and the 'useless' arm is given therapy and made to work – which it does, even after seventeen years of non use! The important point here is that your brain will always be able to reorganize and 'learn' new pathways because it appears that parts of your brain are not allocated to specific tasks, so you can – and do – use them as the need arises. Amazing!

The flexibility and enormity of the brain's ability to learn has immense implications for the effectiveness of Mind Chi and your ability to focus on and achieve your future goals. This offers great encouragement to keep learning new things all through your life.

You can and SHOULD teach an old dog new tricks.

The following information about your brain and mind will increase your awareness of the extraordinary power and potential you carry with you every day, possibly without too much consideration and appreciation. Your brain is truly miraculous.

About your brain

The human brain is quite different from animal or reptilian brains. What sets us apart is the neo-cortex (cortex means bark): the wrinkled outer surface of the brain that you 'see' and recognize. It makes up some 76 percent of the brain mass and is significantly larger than that of animals. This area is where the 'higher functions' mostly occur, the storage of language, thought, reason, consciousness and volition – those aspects frequently attributed to the 'mind'.

In the fourth century BC, Aristotle considered the heart was the centre of human function, whereas the brain was regarded as a form of 'cranial stuffing' or 'cooling'. This view has since been reversed: the brain is now known to be seat of intelligence, although the heart still features symbolically in our descriptions of memory, as in 'learning something by heart'.

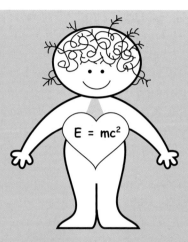

Arabic literature of the tenth century includes detailed descriptions of neuroanatomy, neurobiology and neurophysiology of the brain, and identifies several neurological 'disorders' and symptoms, including sleeping sickness, memory loss, coma, vertigo, epilepsy and love sickness.

Eleventh century orthodoxy said that vision occurs in the brain, rather than the eyes, pointing out that vision and perception are subjective in that personal experience has an effect on what people see and how they see. (This distinction is still misunderstood today. The phrase, 'I'll believe it when I see it!' should really be, 'I'll see it when I believe it!')

Following the invention of the microscope during the sixteenth century, studies of the brain became gradually more sophisticated and in the nineteenth century Camillo Golgi (1843–1926) developed a staining procedure that enabled the intricate structures of a single neuron to be revealed. At about the same time, work with brain-damaged patients suggested that certain regions of the brain were responsible for certain functions.

There have already been great advances in this century. PET and fMRI techniques now allow brain functioning to be monitored while a person performs an activity. Surgical advances mean that operations can now be performed on the brain while the patient is conscious. We stand at the portal of the 'last frontier' for exploration!

There is a long history of treatment based on empirical evidence for structural and functional abnormalities of the brain. These treatments were based on *observed* responses because scientists had no way (until recently) of accessing and observing the inner workings of the brain. Even today, we are only scratching the surface of the complexity of this structure. Many treatments have been judged as highly effective over time and those approaches which show successful results still survive.

We are now obtaining gradual insight into how processes occur in the brain, and so the scientific rationale behind the more successful treatments is becoming clearer.

- All the basic concepts of Mind Chi relate to verifiable brain functions.
- Many of the emerging explanations of how the mind works are reflected in the therapeutic concepts used in this book.

About your mind

The term 'mind' refers to the aspects of intellect and consciousness manifested as thoughts, perception, memory, emotion, will and imagination – your stream of consciousness. Your mind provides a model of the entire universe of your experience and insights.

The word 'mind' is frequently synonymous with 'thought'. You tell yourself that you will 'change your mind', or 'make up your mind'. In the privacy of your thoughts, no one could 'know your mind'. However, recently scientists have shown the physical evidence for thought and can program a computer accurately to 'read' what a person is thinking. This can happen remotely, so the person need not even be aware that it is happening. As a scientist recently said, 'There is no science fiction any longer, we are doing it all!'.

PART 1
Mind Chi Kick-off!

1   What is Mind Chi?

Overview

Mind Chi Basic
How can Mind Chi help you?
Mind Chi questionnaire
Making your Mind Chi commitment

Mind Chi Basic

When you learn to write a language you start by learning the letters of the alphabet. Once you have mastered these essential building blocks you move on to the next stage of learning to read and write. Mind Chi Basic has eight simple building blocks: eight one-minute activities that will take just eight minutes a day for 28 days. The benefits of learning these will enable you to achieve all you envisage for yourself in life.

Just as taking physical exercise will leave you more energized and in better physical shape, so too Mind Chi will leave your brain feeling recharged and raring to go. Mind Chi can be done at any time, in any place (with just a simple clock or watch to help you) and will benefit both your mind and body.

Why eight steps? Because the number eight has many positive connotations and connections. It is considered by many cultures to be a symbol of prosperity, wealth, continuity and the start of a new era. In China, the Beijing Olympics was orchestrated to begin on 8-8-2008 starting at 8:08 for exactly these reasons. It is also a number in the dynamic Fibonacci sequence of numbers, which has positive applications in mathematics, science and nature – and therefore life.

Why eight minutes? Because it is an amount of time that even the busiest people can carve from their day. It will not impinge on all the other priorities that demand your time. Further, it is the shortest amount of time in which to enable the powerful combination of the eight Mind Chi steps to have an effect. As it is an unusual amount of time (rather than ten minutes) it 'stands out' in the memory – which is important for learning.

Why twenty-eight days? Because it has long been held that 28 consecutive days is the minimum length of time that it takes for the brain to turn a new behaviour into a habit. (See Memory, page 16 to learn how the brain adapts to make the habit permanent.)

Mind Chi Program overview

There are two phases to the complete Mind Chi Program (see the map opposite):

1   **Mind Chi Basic** – It takes just eight minutes a day to complete the eight Mind Chi Basic steps. These will generate mental energy, improve your mental and physical functioning and kick-start your new Mind Chi habit and lifestyle. 'Repeat these steps for 28 days and you will create your foundation of self-control.

2   **Mind Chi in Action** – This is **What to do** and **How to do it**. Once you have mastered your Mind Chi Basic routine, you can direct your mental energy towards any aspect of your life. We provide you with 50 Strategies for Success, to overcome problems (such as Conquering Procrastination, page 94) and reach your goals (such

as 'Running effective meetings' page 160). We also show you how to write your own plan (page 79). Put your plan into action by applying Mind Chi Basic techniques to your Mind Chi Plan for 28 days – to achieve the results you want.

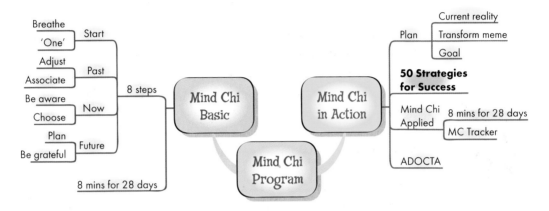

A map of the two phases of your Mind Chi Program (read out from the centre)

There are four powerful Mind Chi Methods to assist your success:

1 **Mind Chi Maps.** To present information to you in the most condensed, yet easily accessible manner, we have used maps. This graphic portrayal of information most closely mirrors the functioning of your brain and therefore allows easy storage of, and access to, data. Mind Chi Basic, Mind Chi Plans and Mind Chi Applied are all presented as maps. These maps convey the essence of the information and enable the relationships between the various aspects to be seen immediately. We encourage the use of maps in many of the Strategies for Success (page 135). A map works in natural partnership with your brain. For example, if you see several of your colleagues sitting round a table at a meeting, you might be able to recall who said what by linking to where they sat. Similarly, the map uses colour, image and association to help you to remember that which you often think you have forgotten.

2 **Mind Chi BEAT.** Mind Chi enables you to tune in to your **B**ody, **E**motions, **A**ctions and **T**houghts; together they form your Mind Chi BEAT (the acronym is based on the first letter of each stage). Your Mind Chi BEAT is at the heart of the Mind Chi process and it is a phrase that will appear frequently throughout the book. As you learn to be in control of your BEAT you choose also to be in control of yourself in the present moment. It closes the gap between what you have and what you want (BEAT, page 39).

3 **Mind Chi Vehicle.** This is a unique aspect of Mind Chi. We have carefully woven into the Mind Chi Program four very effective processes for change. They are Cognitive Behavioural Therapy (CBT); Structural Tension; the Four Rs and Memory Processes. These are introduced and their impact explained in Part 4 (page 257). All you need to know for now is that they have been built seamlessly into all aspects of Mind Chi to assist you to change with the greatest of ease.

I am 'Chi' and I am here to serve you as you wish!

4 **Meet 'Chi' your Mind Chi Mentor.** In Mind Chi you are introduced to your inner voice. We have called it 'Chi'. This well-informed guide can help you to develop your conscious awareness and transform negative thoughts into positive ones. This is a very important aspect of your Mind Chi success because 'Chi', your Mind Chi mentor, will help you to think positively and choose to discard old and outdated negative thought patterns ('Chi', page 31).

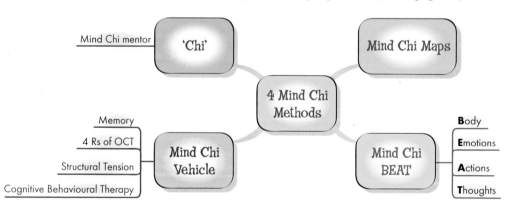

A map of the four Mind Chi Methods to assist your easy success

How can Mind Chi help you?

Mind Chi will help you to transform yourself from where you are and take you to where you want to be, literally helping to push you away from negativity and pull you positively towards your goals by completing your own Mind Chi Plan with the necessary actions and steps.

> Where you focus your attention is where you place your energy and that is the heart of Mind Chi.

Mind Chi is for those of you who are just trying to keep your heads above water in these rapidly changing times, as well as those of you who are managing and want to do even better!

The questionnaire on page 23 will show your current state of mind and the areas where Mind Chi can bring you immediate benefits.

We have worked in business and know how damaging the impact of stress and low energy levels can be. In our experience the severity of people's suffering and personal challenge has become critical and the common 'coping' strategies are often not positive (drugs, drink, burnout etc.). Our concern about the debilitating impact that these behaviours have on people's ability to fulfil their true potential has provided us with the sense of urgency to write this book now.

Where and when can you use Mind Chi?

Mind Chi can be used when and where you need it or as it fits in with your day. The eight steps of Mind Chi Basic are best done at the same time and place (if possible) so that you can make it an easy daily habit. You can also repeat any of the Mind Chi Basic steps as and when you need them through the day (e.g. to make sure you are staying positive or to get you back on track). The steps are done in your mind, so you can do them while waiting for an appointment, as a break, when you are feeling tense, or bored, or on your way to work or home.

How long does it take to master Mind Chi?

The eight steps to Mind Chi Basic can be mastered in one day or over an eight day period. Each step introduces you to one new skill (for one minute). These will build up until you can practice the full eight steps for a total of eight minutes. Each step is designed to lead quite effortlessly to the next. However, if you feel comfortable learning several or all steps together, then please proceed at your own pace.

Once you have learnt your Basic steps, commit to keeping up your routine for 28 consecutive days. You will then be well on your way to turning your Mind Chi routine into a habit and will be starting to reap real benefits. After 28 days you will be able to revisit the questions you answered on page 326 and see where you have improved. You have mastered Mind Chi Basic.

The next stage is to decide what particular aspect of your life you want to improve. You can either read through the 50 Strategies for Success (page 135) and select a Mind Chi Plan that is a priority for you, or begin by creating your own (page 79). Each Mind Chi Plan and Mind Chi in action will take another 28 days as you master a specific skill, overcome a problem or achieve a goal.

Simple concepts pack a big punch. There is a wealth of scientific knowledge and personal experience included in the Mind Chi Strategies for Success even though we have carefully crafted them to be easy to follow.

Why now?

Mind Chi is a program whose time has come; the paradigm shift that is occurring in business globally is unprecedented. We have experienced in our work – as never before – a burgeoning culture of stress, worry and uncertainty that is affecting millions, globally. There is a sad lack of joy, peace, happiness and satisfaction in our working and personal lives.

These are some of the aspects that are exacerbating the current situation (in no particular order):

- 'STUFF' – People seem, more than ever, to be focused on material gain. Only when they have achieved some level of 'success', do they realize that the new house, the bigger salary or faster car has not brought them the happiness they thought it would. So what will? More 'stuff'? (Later you realize that all that stuff needs cleaning, insuring, caring for and storing – bringing more worries and problems!) Mind Chi will help you to focus on the 'bigger picture' and remind you of what is really important to you.
- VALUES – Good old-fashioned 'values', 'ethics' and 'morals' are either changing, disappearing or being scoffed at. This makes it harder to achieve common consensus around how to behave, what is expected, how to act, what is right and who takes responsibility. Mind Chi reminds us all that the buck stops with each individual. We each have responsibility for our own actions and need to have the courage to speak up or change something that is wrong.
- CHANGE – Who would have imagined that we would be in such economic turmoil, with established corporations and well-known individuals finding the rug pulled from under their feet and the domino effect touching nearly everyone's lives? Redundancies are everywhere, 'recession' the word of the time and any form of 'security' a thing of the past. Mind Chi encourages us all to remain positive and to focus on the art of the possible. Change is a fact of life and a force of nature. As far as we know, the sun will rise again tomorrow and we can learn to always rely upon ourselves.
- ANXIETY – Global uncertainty in turn raises the level of worry for everyone. Can you keep up with the information overload, your work load, the demands of your family? Mind Chi is an effective tool for self-management and personal transformation in times of crisis

and difficulty. It equips you with coping strategies that will reassure you and give you confidence.

In creating the Mind Chi Program we wanted to craft a system that could assist you to manage your problems and achieve your goals, to help you control your part of the world (you!), no matter what else is going on about you.

About 'energy'

There is a substantial and growing body of research into aspects of 'mental energy'. As this is a relatively new concept the terminology is still being refined. Psychiatrist Jeffrey Schwartz uses the term 'mental force'; we also like the terms 'volition', 'free will' and 'willpower' (page 35), to denote the intentional direction of the energetic force within our brains and the resultant behaviour it produces.

Energy is defined as the capacity of a physical system to perform work. Scientists are able to measure the electrical energy usage of the brain. And it is a very greedy consumer! The brain makes up (approximately) two percent of body weight, yet your brain consumes 20 percent of your body's energy. Your brain consumes energy at ten times the rate of the rest of the body and if the energy is cut off for even ten minutes, the brain suffers permanent damage.

Really great athletes make performance appear almost 'effortless' as they achieve best results. You too will find that the more you build your Mind Chi capacity, the more you will be able to do, with less effort. An enviable state!

Mind Chi questionnaire

To give you an idea of how you are presently functioning and how Mind Chi can be of assistance to you, please complete this short questionnaire. (There is an additional copy on page 326 and at www.MindChi.com)

Instructions: Use a scale where 0 = none/negative and 10 = high/perfect*

Questions	Now	Later
1 How would you rate your energy throughout your work day?		
2 How much energy do you have at the end of a work day?	....	
3 How well are you sleeping?	....	
4 How would you rate your memory?	....	
5 How would you rate your concentration?	....	
6 How is your ability to make choices?	....	
7 How clear is your thinking?	....	
8 How positive are your 'inner thoughts'?	....	
9 How would you rate your self-esteem?	....	
10 How well are you managing negative stress?	....	
11 How satisfied are you with your work/life balance?	....	
12 How is your general health?	....	

What does this questionnaire reveal about how you are currently using your Mind Chi (mental energy)? Any response that is less than five needs your attention – now!

Name:_____ Date: _____

Dates: _____; _____; _____

Return after Mind Chi Basic and answer the questions again to note your progress.

*NOTE: This little comment pertains to all activities and is also a life philosophy!
We have used a scale of 0–10 because that is what most people find easiest to relate to. However, in workshops we prefer a scale of 0–100, as it provides a far greater level of refinement (e.g. a 93 score versus a 97 on a scale of 0–100 speaks volumes that a simple 9 on a scale of 0–10 does not convey). Please feel encouraged to use the 0–100 scale on any of the activities in Mind Chi (and in your life) if you would like to.

Making your Mind Chi commitment

How can you choose to change whenever you want to? You have the best of intentions, but somehow your old behaviour patterns tend to return. What you *don't* want seems to be more 'sticky' than what you *do* want. It is a common dilemma.

Making Mind Chi 'sticky'

Breakthrough news! Your brain is more malleable than was previously imagined. We now know that throughout your life it is evolving at a physical, chemical and electrical level. You 'rewire' your brain with every thought. Yes, *every* thought! This means that when you focus on 'why', 'what', 'when' and 'where' you want to change, you will have already sent a message that has started to change your brain.

Mind Chi combines the best of the behavioural change processes and the latest research about the plasticity of your brain and puts it altogether to make one 'super-sticky' program. All you need to do to change your habit pattern is to decide to take your first Mind Chi step!

Activity

Are you ready? Please answer these questions:

WHY do you want to make Mind Chi your new habit?

_____

_____

Decide WIIFM (What's In It For Me)? Think of your own reasons or look through the potential benefits from the questionnaire on page 23. Turn this into a clear benefit statement for yourself. For example, 'I want more mental energy to help me through my day'. Say it out loud! This is the **most** important of the questions and relates to your commitment and the 'stickiness' of your new habit.

WHAT will you do?
The eight steps of Mind Chi Basic (page 43) your starting point for change.

WHEN will you do your new Mind Chi habit?

_____

_____

Preferably find eight minutes during your day, at a break, lunch or during computer down time. Eight minutes is less time than it takes to make and drink a cup of tea! You can do the Mind Chi Basic in one sequence at any time, before you fall asleep, or first thing in the morning. It depends on you. Decide now that you will do it. Most important – decide *when* to start!

WHERE will you do your Mind Chi?

_____

_____

At home, at work, when commuting – the choice is yours. So far the most popular place has been in bed! And that is quite OK. You have to make the process work and be easy for you.

Your Mind Chi commitment

Stop and consider. Eight minutes a day, for 28 days – (the length of time it takes to have a cup of tea) – that is the commitment that you are asking of yourself – and the potential benefit is mastering a lifelong skill to allow you to be all you have ever wished.

Activity – Mind Chi sticky

So, on a scale of 0–100, how committed are you to putting just eight minutes aside each day for the next 28 days? (We use the scale of 100 here as we are talking about 100% commitment.)

0 _____ 100

> The best description of commitment is persistence with a purpose.

The purpose of Mind Chi is to enable you to achieve all your wishes in your business and personal life. It is to give you a program that you can apply to any area where you want to address a problem, improve your functioning and (re)gain control of yourself.

How committed are you? If you are not 100% committed, ask yourself:

What's stopping me from 100% commitment?

Your answer is critical to your success.

When you can build a benefit statement for yourself that is strong enough to make you want to carve out eight minutes a day to reap the rewards of change – then you will succeed.

Making a commitment

1 Before you think of making a commitment, contemplate deeply why you want to do this. What are the benefits *to you*? Write them on attractive notes and put the notes where you are sure to see them several times a day.

2 Think about the obstacles that may (or have) come up and plan a way to deal with each one now! Be ready; do not let them un-stick you.

3 Consider how important this is to you on a scale of 0–100. What would you put aside to make sure this task was done? If you haven't rated this with an importance of 100 percent, it probably won't be done! Might as well save your time and energy now.

4 When you do find something that you can give 100 percent to, then set a plan in action. Pick a start date and time. Pick an ending date to work towards. Create your action steps. Have a moment of celebration: a real point of recognition for the moment you are starting your plan. Feel its significance, that little quiver of anticipation, yes, even slight anxiousness. Then off you go.

5 Now, because this is a new habit, it is quite likely that in the first few days you may slip. *Do not give up* if you do. This is the mistake so many make. Simply observe, and ask, 'Why did I slip?' What safeguards could you put in place to prevent a further slip? Go for it one more day.

6 Use 'Chi' (your Mind Chi mentor, page 31) to heighten your awareness so that you pick up on the subtle signals of 'slippage moments' fast or before they happen, and can put into play the action you want, rather than the reaction you don't want.

7 Congratulate yourself when you do what you planned. Soon the new way will start to make its own groove and becomes less of a hassle.

Thinking you will requires both experiencing yourself as 'flying' AND the action of letting go of the branch!

8   Then suddenly you slip again! Smile to yourself and say well done for getting that far. Look at where and why you slipped up this time and fix that area. Keep on moving forwards, knowing that you *can* change. You will eventually re-wire your brain (page 106), eradicate all the little mind-games, distractions and subterfuges of your past thinking and you will be the triumphant holder of the cup of willpower (ADOCTA, page 99).

9   As you pump up your willpower strength you will discover that it is one of the greatest secrets to success, and it is Mind Chi-easy!

'I need to let go, to make this work!'

When you are ready … here is your commitment letter:

Dear Reader,

We want Mind Chi to be a success for you and we know that it requires 100% commitment to do **JUST eight minutes a day** for the next 28 days.

The only way that this will work is when you have:

- selected your real benefit,
- rated it as very important in your life,
- organized a time to do your eight minutes a day,
- felt your heart beat a little fast with anticipation, and
- signed this page with a witness who will help you hold yourself responsible.

We have your best interest at heart and that's why we wrote this book. However we must warn you that without 100% commitment you are probably wasting you time. That is the best advice we can offer before your start.

I, (your name) _____ , am making 100% commitment to complete the eight minutes a day for the next 28 days of Mind Chi Basic.

_____   _____   _____

Your signature   Witness   Date

Richard Israel   Vanda North

2 Meet 'Chi' – Your Mind Chi Mentor

Overview

What is the role of your 'Chi'?
Willpower and volition

You know that little voice inside your head? The one that tells you the good and the bad things to do? At the moment 'it' may often be a mischief maker or troublemaker, the voice that undermines you and stops you from doing good things. However, you will learn to befriend and control your inner voice and to use your self-talk to help you achieve all you wish.

We are calling your inner voice 'Chi' and will show you how to transform it into a Mind Chi mentor that can become a force for success and positive transformation.

To start with, become more tuned in to what your 'Chi' has to say. Is it more positive or negative in tone? Can you reason with it? From now on, encourage and coax your 'Chi' to do your bidding in a positive way. It is your most powerful ally and will become your greatest supporter.

What is the role of your 'Chi'?

'Chi' has many roles and wears many hats. Here are a few so you can start to appreciate how vital 'Chi' is to your well-being and success:

- It is your fresh thinking, your Mind Chi Meme (page 86) that allows you to realize new possibilities. It replaces the old, negative thinking that wears you down.
- It is available to you 24/7 as your best cheerleader (Chi-er leader!), supporter and friend.
- It is that little voice you hear constantly in your head, now working on your behalf.
- It is your intuition that knows your needs and wants, and understands your motivation at a deep level.
- It is a willing student, ready to be re-educated to provide you with positive and constructive advice.
- It helps you to act in your best interest when invited/encouraged to do so.
- It enables you to flip the switch of your 'free will' and 'free won't' (choosing what to do or what not to do.)
- It is there to increase your awareness of your Body, Emotions, Actions and Thoughts. We call it your Mind Chi BEAT (coming up on page 39).

> Your 'Chi' holds a very powerful position and you need to be on good terms with it to achieve the results you desire.

At first you will have to call consciously upon your 'Chi' to assist you, as you may have let it run wild for a while with no guidelines or direction. With more focused attention, your 'Chi' will learn quickly what you want and how to obtain your attention. If your 'Chi' has a habit of thinking negatively, the Mind Chi routine and Mind Chi Meme will gently re-educate your 'Chi' to become positive: your greatest asset instead of your worst saboteur (Chi, page 31).

How does your 'Chi' help?

You process information through your senses: hearing, seeing, smelling, tasting, and touching. All this information and the experience of all the events in your life are stored in your long-term memory, even though you may not consciously remember it all (Memory, page 276). Your memory is comparable to an immense library with millions and millions of books and files.

You have a constant stream of conscious thoughts every day. As a new thought enters your brain, your memory looks for the appropriate file to see if anything is similar to a previous experience, and how it relates – either positively or negatively – to your present reality or situation.

Fuelling these thoughts and absorbing all that is happening is your internal voice, your 'Chi', who is in charge of your filing system: looking up old files, refiling, and making up new files. Your 'Chi' is quite opinionated! It will tell you what it thinks and encourage or discourage your actions and reactions.

How to contact your 'Chi'

All the Mind Chi Basic steps will encourage you to become more aware of your inner voice. Tuning in may take a little practice, because it tends to chatter away so consistently and loudly, and you are so used to its noise in the background, you hardly pay attention to what is being said any longer. (It is similar to sitting alongside a chatty colleague whose voice you have learned to 'tune out' during a working day.)

Focus your attention and find how much of your inner chatter is to your detriment and how much for your welfare. Negative chatter is damaging. When it continues from day to day it becomes a habit that is highly destructive and renders you less than you can be.

Does your 'Chi' tell you that you are 'stupid' or 'dumb'? Or that you will make a fool of yourself if you speak up at a meeting? Or that you are unable to complete a project? When your 'Chi' is constantly undermining you, you will doubt yourself and perform to your lowest ability. Happily the Mind Chi Program allows you to correct this. Your 'Chi' when used consciously will boost your willpower and help you to choose to think realistically and constructively, to bring about positive reactions and results.

Survive or thrive with your 'Chi'

You use your willpower constantly through the day. Every thought is an act of will as you are selecting one thought, feeling or action over another. Much of the time this takes place in your para-conscious (not in your immediate awareness) as you choose water over juice, one bus route instead of another, this activity over that. You may pause to ponder the pluses and minuses of various options before you decide on one, but the process is fairly automatic and works well. Sometimes, however, you may come a bit unstuck if, for instance, you have a big hairy habit that takes you in the wrong direction (such as always being late). On these occasions you need your willpower to get yourself back on a positive Mind Chi track. (Willpower, page 35.)

On a scale of 0–10 ask yourself how you would rate the strength of your willpower? (It's tough to achieve, but anything less than 10 means there is scope for improvement.) Regardless of your score, your 'Chi' will help you to improve. Your 'Chi' helps you to recognize when you are distracted, taken away from your goal or focus. Your 'Chi' reminds you that you have the control to say yes or no: it is your 'free will' and your 'free won't'. It is imperative that you develop this skill. Left unchecked, a lack of willpower will leave you floating about at 'survival' level, rather than enabling you to thrive and achieve your wishes and desires – your full potential.

Let's start!

This is the pivotal point of the success or failure of your Mind Chi Program.

You have the choice to remain with and reinforce old habits that are not serving you or build new habits that will allow you to develop to your full potential.

Willpower and volition

Volition is a beautiful word that is rarely used. *The Concise Oxford Dictionary* defines it as, 'The act of willing or choosing; the act of forming a purpose; the exercise of will.' The term 'willpower' is often used to describe the same process. Volition and willpower are important Mind Chi characteristics that are strengthened with increased use.

There is now demonstrable evidence that conscious decision-making accounts for 20–50 percent of brain activity. Brain activity can be seen on fMRIs while tasks are performed. Many of your everyday decisions are made in the pre-conscious (para-conscious) mind, but readily brought into your awareness. Thus, your willpower (also referred to as conscious volition, intentionality, or self-control) is a force you can call upon when necessary – to help you to make a conscious *choice* to act in a certain way.

You tend to pay attention to your own willpower only when you are having problems applying yourself to a difficult task. The majority of the time you use it without even being aware of it, such as when you decide to make a phone call instead of an email, or vice versa.

Willpower is the most powerful force of human behaviour. When you learn to activate your willpower, or volition, you will reap the benefits of taking purposeful action and see more projects completed. But engaging volition isn't easy. It's at a higher attainment level than motivation. Motivation is the desire to do something; volition is the absolute commitment to achieving something.

To activate your volition, you must pass through a mental barrier. Research has shown that many people are motivated to achieve, but only ten percent are likely to overcome personal barriers to commit to the task in hand. Volition requires you to resolve an (often intensive) inner struggle between old habits and new desires to achieve what you really want. Having engaged your will, you will need the tenacity and commitment to deal with setbacks and persevere through the long, energy-intensive journey from a vision to its realization.

'Will I? or Won't I?'

The power of your will is like a muscle and, once you start to flex it, you will be quite delighted by how it responds. It is quite a heady feeling to know that you have control over yourself; you can do what you want, when you want. Your 'Chi' is at your command and it just becomes easier!

The branches of this WILLPOWER map show:

- *Volition* – to make the initial commitment, muster and direct your willpower into action.
- *Awareness* – your sensual perception, with no judgement, and being in the 'now'.
- *Attention* – now your awareness has brought something to your conscious attention you can selectively concentrate on it.
- *Choice* is now yours – your free will and free won't – you get to decide which you will or won't do! This ties in with the Mind Chi BEAT (page 39).
- *Intention* – the mindful selection of your possible choices, which will relate to your initial commitment. This takes you in the intended direction of your commitment.
- *Free will* – after you have made a commitment then your 'Chi' and Mind Chi Meme will assist you with all the other phases from awareness to intention (action).

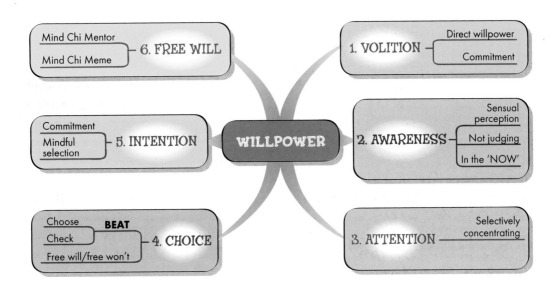

3 Mind Chi BEAT

Overview

Access 'NOW' through your Mind Chi BEAT

Your Mind Chi BEAT is the 'Open Sesame' to controlling your life. That is a strong statement and we know it to be true. Inspired by the very popular and productive 'talk therapy' called Cognitive Behavioural Therapy (CBT) or the more recent Rational Living Therapy, the Mind Chi BEAT will make you aware of how you are currently feeling and functioning and provides you with the choice to change as you wish (CBT, page 262).

Access 'NOW' through your Mind Chi BEAT

B.E.A.T is an acronym for **B**ody, **E**motions, **A**ctions and **T**houghts. The BEAT technique provides you with the precious gift of the present – living in the 'now'.

It is easy to lose contact with your awareness of the present moment because you are dwelling on something that has passed or are thinking about the future. But the 'now' is your only true point of control. You can do nothing about the past, it has passed. The only thing you can do is change your perspective about things that happened. You can't change the future by worrying about it; you can, however, plan and craft a direction and take steps now to make your preferred future a reality.

Your BEAT finger check

Tap your thumb against each of your fingers in turn to 'tune in' to what is happening to your Body, Emotions, Actions and Thoughts right now. We explain the BEAT process in depth on page 39 as part of Steps 5 and 6 of your Mind Chi Basic. In brief, all you have to do (and why not do it right now?) to become BEAT aware is:

Check – tap thumb	To begin the 'BEAT check'
Body – tap first (index) finger	Ask, 'How is my body responding now?' (Relaxed or uptight?)
Emotions – tap second (middle) finger	Ask, 'What emotions am I experiencing now?' (Calm or worried?)
Actions – tap third (ring) finger	Ask, 'What actions am I taking now?' (Directed or 'scattered'?)
Thoughts – tap fourth (little) finger	Ask, 'What thoughts am I having now?' (Supportive or undermining?)

The essential point is that once you are aware of your BEAT you can choose to change any aspect if you wish. What would be best for your well-being?

Do your BEAT 'finger check' at any moment when you want to shift your awareness from one state to another and one activity to another.

From this point of awareness you can change anything about yourself – and control your world, no matter what is happening. You can intercept at any moment to change the direction of your BEAT. See how important this is?

Mind Chi BEAT finger check

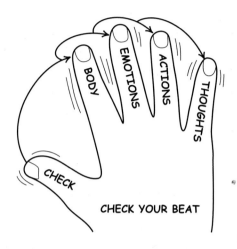

Use your fingers to do a quick BEAT check to 'tune in' to your state of mind and body

 When an event occurs, it has an effect on some or all aspects of your Mind Chi BEAT (Body, Emotions, Actions and Thoughts). In turn, these four aspects can impinge on each other. Without BEAT-awareness this can easily create a vicious circle where the negative situation gets far worse.

By becoming BEAT-aware, you can check and choose to change your reaction to a situation. You can retake control and create the outcome you desire. Now the vicious circle becomes a victorious spiral.

Self-control and willpower are the benefits you receive from your Mind Chi Program.

Here is an introduction to your Mind Chi BEAT through a cartoon.

4 Mind Chi Basic

The eight steps of the Mind Chi Basic process will take you only eight minutes a day. Mind Chi takes place in your mind. You don't need pens, paper or a computer, which means you can do it easily – at your desk, while you travel, at home or in bed. Try doing Mind Chi at different times of day to see what works best for you and your routine.

Initially you will need a timer, watch, clock or mobile phone with a second hand or a beeper setting, to alert you when the one minute time is up.

If possible, do the eight minute activities at the same time of day and in the same place each day. Select a time when you are not likely to be interrupted.

NOTE: If you are interrupted and need to stop your Mind Chi Basic before you have completed the eight steps, then start again with the Mind Chi Breath and continue where you left off.

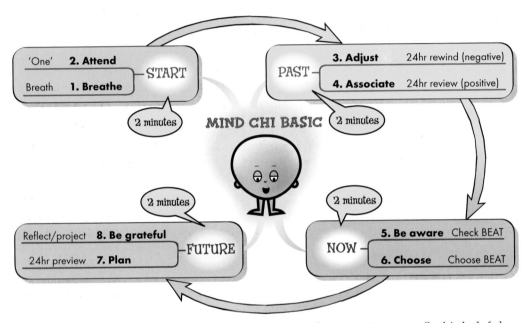

Here is a map summary of the eight steps. You may find it helpful to print the map (Sample pages, page 328 or from the website, www. MindChi.com).

The topic is the Mind Chi Basic, so it is in the centre of the map.

Begin at '10 o'clock' to **Start**: Steps 1 and 2; follow the 'clock face' round to cross over to 1 o'clock for **Past**: Steps 3 and 4; down to 4 o'clock for **Now**: Steps 5 and 6. Finally, over to 7 o'clock for the two steps to create your **Future**: Steps 7 and 8.

Mind Chi Start

There are two steps at the start of Mind Chi; they are concerned with regaining control over your breath and mind. They will increase your personal wellness by helping to reduce your feelings of stress and take up the reins to bring your runaway attention span under control.

If your mind is easily distracted or preoccupied with past or future events – events you can't change and events that might never happen – you become stuck. Instead of moving forwards you become lodged in inactivity or negative thinking. So, before you start, summon up a 'vision' inside your head of the 'you' that is *all you want to be*. Just stay with that experience and feel its impact for a few seconds.

Breath control is at the foundation of nearly all stress-relieving strategies, from yoga to modern sports psychology. The power of breath to improve the health of the mind and body has been known for generations.

Step 1: Breathe – to find inner calm and focus and increase your awareness of the present moment.

Step 2: Attend – to focus on your ability to strengthen your command of focus and attention. The vitally important 'One' exercise is deceptively simple and yet powerful in its impact. It allows you to practice refocusing at will. You can regard this Mind Chi activity as strengthening your ability to concentrate by improving mental conditioning. Focused attention is a prime element of intelligence.

NOTE:

As you are learning these Mind Chi Basic steps, you may choose to become familiar with just one step per day for eight days. Or you may feel ready to take on several or all at one time. Pace yourself as you feel comfortable.

Step 1: Breathe

When you are anxious or excited, you may find yourself feeling breathless. You may gasp, in an attempt to increase the flow of oxygen to your brain – which helps you to cope with your anxiety. For example, even the thought of public speaking will put many people into 'panic' mode. The Mind Chi Breath technique can be an effective tool in managing anxiety.

Breathing exercises have long been at the heart of many health and healing practices and appear to have numerous positive effects. Breathing deeply and from the diaphragm will give you more energy; reduce your mental and physical fatigue; increase the supply of oxygen and nutrients to cells throughout your body, especially your brain; ease the strain on your heart by increasing the oxygen supply; relax muscle spasms and relieve tension. Further, breathing exercises can partially compensate for lack of exercise and inactivity due to illness or injury and enable you to recover faster from stress and exertion.

The act of breathing is not the same as the art of breathing! The act of breathing is controlled by your autonomic nervous system (ANS) and fortunately for you, it occurs naturally, without your intervention. This is fine most of the time; however, there is a sting in that tail. When you are nervous or feeling under threat, your automatic reaction takes over with the 'fight or flight' response. This means you are either gearing up for attack, or you want to run away. Adrenalin levels increase and your breathing becomes shallow, fast and short. This is alright for brief periods of time, but if you live life in a constant state of stress you will develop a shallow breathing pattern that actually reinforces your stress state. Conversely, when you are naturally relaxed, you take deeper, fuller, longer and slower breaths. This type of breathing is health inducing. This is the type of breathing you will do in Step 1: Breathe.

Activity 1: Your Mind Chi Breath

PURPOSE

Step 1 of Mind Chi Basic shows you how – when stressed and breathing fast and shallowly, you can consciously alter your breath to become slow, deep and full. Controlled breathing will calm your nerves and undo the negative impact of constant stressors. You may find the Mind Chi Breath especially useful at moments when you are anxious or angry. Your Mind Chi Breath is a quick and effective way to safeguard and restore your health and reduce the effects of negative stress.

ACTION

Set your timer or look at the second hand on a clock for one minute, so you can concentrate on your breathing. Place one open hand over your belly and the other high on your chest.

Breathe in slowly and deeply, check that your belly hand moves in and out with each breath while your chest hand remains almost still. Breathe slowly and deeply, as if you were deeply relaxed or asleep.

One way to control your breathing is to count through each part of the Mind Chi Breath cycle. Count slowly for three seconds as you breathe in, hold your breath for the count of three seconds and breathe out for three seconds: nine seconds per cycle. (If you feel comfortable, stay empty – wait for three seconds to breathe in: 12 seconds per cycle.) Then start the cycle again. Continue for a full minute.

Instead of using a timer, you can just count seven Mind Chi Breath cycles of 9 seconds or five Mind Chi Breath cycles of 12 seconds = 60 seconds.

BENEFIT

Step 1 will reduce your negative stress levels, and improve the balance and harmony of your life. The depth, quality and rhythm of your breath are the keys to your health, well-being and positive performance. This simple activity has a great influence. It will create a positive shift in outlook in a very short time.

Step 2: Attend

How well can you attend? Attention is the ability to focus on a task and your ability to concentrate. Having full control over your concentration is central to your effective functioning in the world. Most people are frequently distracted throughout the day. In our increasingly frenetic world there is no rest from TV and the media; we allow phone calls and emails to interrupt our thoughts and the pace of technological multitasking leaves many people quailing in a fibrillating heap. But the main issue is that few people have ever been taught how to pay attention in the first place. 'Look at me when I am speaking to you!' was the cry from your teachers; so you learned to 'look' while your mind was everywhere else.

The Mind Chi Attention exercise will show you whether your thoughts are fragmented and what level of mind control you have currently. Practicing the 'One' activity will assist you to build your 'focused attention' and allow you to have the control to focus your attention for as long as you wish. To begin with you may find you have little control at all. The good news is that the exercise will quickly train your brain to concentrate more effectively. You will experience fast progress which will increase your motivation to keep going.

When you are concentrating, waves of electricity called the 'beta rhythm' are produced by your brain at a frequency of 12+ Hz. The 'One' exercise will tune up your concentration levels and increase your ability to focus your attention.

Activity 2: Your Mind Chi 'One'

PURPOSE

Are you easily distracted, especially when slightly bored? This tendency is a real disadvantage in business, when concentration on the task in hand is all-important; and in communication, where your colleague or client is expecting your rapt attention.

ACTION

Set a clock or timer to one minute and focus on the blinker or look at the second hand on a watch or clock as you silently repeat, 'One, one, one ...' to yourself.

As soon as a distracting thought intrudes, stop counting 'one' and change to 'Two, two, two ...' and so on. Increase the number each time you have another intruding thought, even if the thought is just on the periphery of your mind. This way you will keep count of how many intruding thoughts you have during the minute.

This seems so simple. However, the way it tends to work is something like this, 'One, one, one, ah this is easy – oops! – that was an intruding thought! Two, two, two, two, two, have I planned for today's meeting? – oh! This is harder than I thought. Three, three, three, three, three ...' and so on.

At the end of one minute note the number you reached. The goal is to be able to stay on 'one' without a single intruding thought for the whole sixty seconds.

BENEFIT

Step 2 will increase your attention span and improve your clarity of thought. These steps can be done whenever you feel the need to clear your mind, refocus or relieve stress.

Attention!

There are several kinds of attention:

- **Selective attention** – selecting a single aspect of a situation and ignoring all others, such as at a conference when you are striving to hear one person speak over the babble around you.
- **Divided attention** – where you are trying to focus on conflicting priorities, such as trying to concentrate on a serious telephone conversation whilst simultaneously writing an email. (Multiple and simultaneous responses are seldom effective, both usually suffer.)
- **Focused attention** – the ability to know how to concentrate on the subject of your choice (even if you find it boring) for an extended period of time. It is easier to pay focused attention to matters that interest you. However, you require your focused attention 'muscle' to work whenever necessary, even with activities that may not be on the top of your high interest list!

Mind Chi Past

Steps 3 and 4 make your memory sharper and fine-tune your awareness of how negative or positive your thoughts really are, so you can choose and direct them consciously to become more positive and well-motivated.

By taking these two minutes each day, while your memories of the past 24 hours are still fresh, you gain control over their impact on your future. You will learn to put the negative into perspective and tease the 'lessons' from the experience. Most importantly, you will focus on all the things you did that were helpful and successful and start to build your positive memories. By building up a memory bank of positive thoughts, you are creating an antidote to moments of self-doubt; which means that when you feel less than positive your 'Chi' can remind you of all your positive deposits and bolster your self-confidence.

The process of memory is a complex and fascinating one that still continues to baffle and challenge scientists. Memory begins when the mind consciously, through one or more of your senses (sound, sight, smell, touch and taste) takes in some information or an experience. This is known as sensory memory. (Less well-known is *proprioception memory* – the sense of knowing where your body is – which allows precise movements to be repeated; as when playing a musical instrument, typing, swinging a golf club, driving etc.). When you pay attention to an experience, your senses transform each element into short-term memory. Your short-term memory lasts only a few minutes. The key is to be able to transfer short-term memories into your long-term memory bank in a way that the information can be readily recalled on demand.

Long-term memory is the largest component of the memory system; its storage capacity is virtually limitless, so there is no need to worry about running out of memory space as you age. There are two important aspects to effective long-term memory. These are encoding and retrieval. Encoding is the ability to organize and store information into your mental filing system. Both encoding and retrieval are assisted by a) paying *focused attention* and using your senses to create associations between facts or information you have in your memory files already and b) rehearsing information using a process called 'spaced repetition' (page 278).

Step 3: Adjust

In Step 3: Adjust, you will be practicing and strengthening your memory and adjusting the influence of your negative memories in the process.

Think of your memory as a computer – your input can be through keyboard, mouse or any number of USB devices. Your RAM stores things in the short term (and is typically a few gigabytes in size) and your hard disk stores your long-term memory via a series of interpretation programs. Your hard disk memory capacity is almost limitless.

However, sometimes our memory habits will distort information, recalling some types of information more readily than others. (For example, when given three compliments and one criticism many people will take the criticism to heart and downplay the compliments.) Step 3: Adjust will improve your ability to recall information more accurately simply by focusing on the experiences of the day and reassessing aspects that felt negative or unhelpful.

The 'adjustment' here is that having recalled the past 24 hours and focused on the negatives – you then *adjust* to think 'what could I have done differently?' 'What will I do next time?' 'How can I adjust my thinking/actions/emotions to be better next time?'

Your memory will accommodate your adjustments and will begin to recall the lessons learned more easily. Your brain will learn that it needs to pay more attention to achieving positive outcomes during each day. It also means you will live each day more consciously and work towards reducing the negative and increasing the positive, because you know your daily review exercise is coming up.

Activity 3: 24 Hour Rewind (Negative)

PURPOSE

Looking at the negative or unhelpful aspects of the past 24 hours might be uncomfortable because negatives often carry more weight in the mind and have a tendency to overshadow or 'erase' the positives. By looking at the negatives more closely, you may find the situation more balanced than you realize. You can discover any inherent lessons and ask yourself what you might do differently another time. Choose to rewind and adjust your approach to the past.

ACTION

Set your timer for one minute so you can concentrate on your recall of the day. Rewind the past 24 hours as if you were replaying a movie of your day. It helps to close your eyes when conducting this review as it cuts out any external visual distractions. Particularly look for times when:

1   You were hijacked emotionally by your thoughts or reactions – you may have found yourself thinking about an emotionally charged issue over and over again such as, 'My supervisor really seems to have it in for me'.
2   You got caught in an unhelpful repetitive pattern of behaviour – such as eating comfort foods when you felt stressed.

Note each unhelpful memory by counting it on a different finger of your non-dominant hand (i.e. your left hand if you are right-handed, and vice versa). Then at the end of the minute brush them off your non-dominant hand as if removing some dust, symbolically releasing those negative and unhelpful thoughts. By metaphorically brushing them away, you let them go. Tell yourself, 'the past is past'.

BENEFIT

Step 3 will make you more aware of your negative thoughts and therefore able to reduce their power; you will then be able to adjust your thinking and have more positive energy/Mind Chi available throughout the day.

Step 4: Associate

To associate is a function of the brain that is automatic. Associations focus on strengthening the basic function of your brain and memory. You will find that as you start to remember one thing, it associates with another and helps you to pull up the other memories.

You tend to associate in two main ways (Blooms, page 76).

1   A 'bloom' of associations: from a central topic you bloom out associations (like petals on a flower) so you might say 'butterfly' and Vanda might respond with: 'change; beauty; brooches; mother, joy and bananas'. All words are directly related to the central stimulus of the word 'butterfly' in a way that is *unique* to her. Your words would be your own particular associations showing all your memories, connections, experiences and thoughts relate directly to the central topic.

2   A 'flow' of associations: here one word triggers the next and that one the one after it, in a more linear fashion. Starting with 'butterfly' Vanda might say; 'wings – plane – travel – holiday – adventure – Mt Kilimanjaro…' one word causing an association with the next, moving outwards from the central trigger, in a flow. Unlike a 'bloom', the final word may have no direct association with the first.

However, if you wish to store, retain and recall with the greatest efficiency, then taking care with your associations will pay dividends.

> MEMORY TIP: If you do NOT have pen and paper to hand and you want to recall your ideas, then think of your front door at home and use your imagination to attach (associate) the thought in some fun, exaggerated, multi-sensory and dramatic way to your front door. If you have more than one thing to recall, open your front door and imagine attaching the next idea to the first thing that you see, like a picture hanging on the wall or a coat stand. You can, of course, write them down as soon as you have pen and paper.

Activity 4: 24-Hour Review (Positive)

PURPOSE

Step 4 is similar to step 3, but this time you will look back over the past twenty four hours and recall what *positive* and *successful* things occurred. As you recall and review your day, teasing the happenings from your mind, you will experience how each event links, connects and reminds you of another. The more associations you create, the more you are reinforcing the behaviour that you want to repeat.

ACTION

Set your timer for one minute so you can concentrate on your appraisal. Review the past 24 hours as if you were replaying a movie of your day. It helps to close your eyes when conducting this review as it cuts out any external visual distractions. Particularly look for times when:

- You had a small success, acted or felt the way you wanted, 'I successfully completed that report on time', 'I kept calm all through the meeting'.
- You had a peak experience – moments of happiness, contentment or joy, such as, 'I was so pleased with how my presentation went at the meeting'.

Note each positive and helpful memory, by counting it on a different finger of your dominant hand (your right hand if you are right-handed or vice versa). At the end of the minute, gently squeeze your dominant hand to symbolically reinforce your positive memories and successes.

BENEFIT

Step 4 will give you a chance to applaud yourself on how well you have used your Mind Chi over the past 24 hours with successes and positive thoughts. This will directly increase your self-esteem and energy.

When you have completed Steps 3 *and* 4, become aware of whether you had more positive or negative memories. Simply observe. The important thing is to help your self to have a better day tomorrow. Step 7 will help you to make this a reality.

Success filing: it's especially important to acknowledge and file your creative success. These seemingly tiny, minor decisions – consciously made – are actually profound choices that lead to major changes that you want. What plans or projects did you create? What new methods or systems, such as a new way to store your clothes or organize your work did you invent today? Susan Ford Collins, *The Joy of Success*.

Associations

Associations can be strengthened by:

- Making sure the association process is fun or turning it into a game.
- Visualizing – allow your imagination to be creative.
- Using actions to connect your associations together.
- Charging them with positive emotion and making them multi-sensory.
- Keeping things simple – only two things connected and in sequence.
- Exaggerating and using the bizarre and ridiculous.
- Practicing – this strengthens the association.

Eight times World Memory Champion – Dominic O'Brien – uses journeys to create memory associations. He has many 'mental videos' of places he knows and he associates what he wishes to remember with a place on the journey.

Mind Chi Now

Steps 5 and 6 will increase your ability to live an aware and positive life, choosing not to be hampered by the past, or overly shaped by the future. The term 'awareness' usually refers to the present moment (the power of 'now'). It is also akin to the popular psychological concept of 'self-awareness'. However, for thousands of years it has been a core component of Buddhist philosophy, that of developing 'mindful awareness'. This means the capacity to observe your inner experience in a 'fully aware' manner without 'attachment'. In simple terms this means not holding on too tightly to past feelings; allowing yourself to 'let go' of past hurt, disappointments, needs and feelings, in order that you can fully experience this present moment.

Normally when you observe something, the left cortex of your brain gives you a running commentary; this is your 'Chi' in action. Mindful awareness requires you just to 'stare' and appreciate, receiving information via all your senses, without judgement. Over the years this kind of awareness has been given many names, Adam Smith, a leading philosopher from the eighteenth century, called it 'the impartial and well informed spectator'. It is the ability to witness your actions, thoughts and emotions as a disinterested observer.

Your 'Chi' is a willing guide to help you to increase your awareness of 'now' so that you can check your current reality of your Mind Chi BEAT.

Step 5: Be aware

Awareness is the ability to think consciously; to feel or perceive what is happening *now*: it is the mind's point of focus at any given moment. If you were asked to become aware of your right foot, you could do so in an instant: immediately the feeling of your right foot comes into your conscious thought. Your right foot has been there all the time but there was no need to be aware of it (unless it was being tickled!).

Becoming aware can also be triggered by events occurring outside your body, as in the case of someone walking into the room while you are reading. Your senses will pick this up and you become aware of that person.

In the Mind Chi Awareness activity, your awareness is brought to four very specific aspects. By asking a set of questions regarding your **B**ody, **E**motions, **A**ctions and **T**houghts, you focus your awareness on them at this moment in time. Together they form your Mind Chi BEAT (the acronym is based on the first letter of each stage, see page 39).

> Pay attention to your Mind Chi BEAT. It is at the heart of the Mind Chi process.

After you have completed 28 days of practice you will find that you are increasing your sensitivity in the four BEAT areas and will notice subtle signs of being either 'on form' or 'out of sorts'. By focusing on your Mind Chi BEAT you will be able to increase your awareness and then adjust and change your state of being to become more constructively directed and in control of you.

'Are you aware?'

Activity 5: Check Your BEAT

PURPOSE

To change consciously requires you first to have awareness; and then to introduce new directed thoughts. Activity 5 will train your conscious mind to become aware of your mind and body, by asking four important questions.

ACTION

Set your timer for one minute so you can concentrate on this activity. Bring your attention to the present. Sit quietly for this minute, and tune in by asking yourself and responding to these questions.

1   What is my *Body* experiencing NOW?
    I have a bit of a headache and my neck feels tight.
2   What *Emotions* am I feeling NOW?
    I am worried and feel under pressure and stressed.
3   What are my *Actions* NOW? (Or, what was I just doing?)
    I was gathering some data for a report.
4   What *Thoughts* am I having NOW?
    I am battling with all of my priorities, which should I do first?

This is the Mind Chi BEAT check. Use it to help increase your self-awareness so that (in the next step) you can make rapid, positive changes to your Body, Emotions, Actions and Thoughts. By focusing your awareness on the here and now, you will begin to live more fully and consciously 'in the moment'.

BENEFIT

Step 5 will bring your awareness to the present moment to help you check how you are currently functioning. Once you have acquired this awareness you can successfully gain control over your reactions to any situation you face.

Step 6: Choose

Every step of the Mind Chi Program is designed to enable you to gain (or regain) control over yourself and your life.

This Mind Chi step focuses on how you choose to use your mental energy. It will make ALL the difference; it is the realization that at this very moment YOU are in control. Nothing and no one else – just YOU! So, take this minute to make sure that you are taking control and *choosing* what you want to experience *now*.

When you bring your awareness to your Body, Emotions, Actions and Thoughts, ask yourself: 'Are they functioning at their best for my productivity and happiness?'

If not, then take the next Mind Chi step to consider what and how you want to change.

You will experience a whole new level of functioning and satisfaction with yourself as you hold the reins of self control. The result is exhilarating and liberating.

Activity 6: Choose Your Beat

PURPOSE

Feeling a lack of control is one of the greatest stressors that you can face. For example, when it seems that everything 'out there' has it in for you. 'Choice' is the point where you choose to regain control and is of critical importance.

You are already aware of your current Mind Chi BEAT (although you may not know it); and you can, at this moment if you so choose, create a *different* BEAT. You can change your Thoughts, alter your Emotions, slow your Actions and consciously release the tension in your Body. You can make a choice to regain control over yourself. This will enable you to handle any external situation with far greater ease.

ACTION

If your Mind Chi **BEAT** is not what you want it to be, then set your timer for one minute so you can concentrate on choosing the BEAT that would be most productive for you. In doing so you will realize that you *do* have control over your **BEAT** state.

Look at each one of the four areas, how would you choose them to be? For example:

1 **B**ody: My head feels clear and my neck relaxed.
2 **E**motions: I feel calm and focused.
3 **A**ction: Keep writing my report.
4 **T**houghts: I have selected this as my top priority.

BENEFIT

Step 6 is a MOST crucial skill, which is directly related to the 'negative' and 'positive' findings of Steps 4 and 5. If you learn to manage and direct your Mind Chi BEAT state you can do and be what you really want. This is another area where your 'Chi' may assist. Let your self-talk heighten your awareness of 'now', correct the negatives, enhance the positives and create a self-directed future.

Accentuate the positive

Before you can direct change in your life it helps to look on the positive side of life.

1   This is where your 'Chi' can be most helpful. Ask it to bring your awareness to your negative thoughts and words. Becoming aware of what you say and think will take you nine tenths of the way to positive change. Why are you saying or thinking in the negative? Is it necessary?

2   Consider your options. Might it be better to say nothing than to say something negative? Can you make a constructive suggestion rather than a complaint? Can you find some aspect of the situation to compliment?

3   Be kind to yourself. Negative thinking/talking/being may well be tied up with your self-concept. Ask yourself how you can start to bolster your view of yourself, then you may find that you do not feel the need to be so negative. When you start to be more positive, you will probably feel better about yourself as well (Growing self-esteem, page 250).

4   Do not fuel negativity. Speak to positive people about positive things. Build yourself up, not tear yourself down. Focus on growing a positive environment about you. Banish cynical remarks from your conversation. (Only listen to the news once a day.)

5   Give your mind 'homework' to hone your positive thinking. If you begin thinking negative thoughts, then focus on coming up with four positive things to counter-balance each one.

6   There are many shades of positive. Consider it as a whole continuum, from slightly positive to overjoyed! Experiment with the shades of positive, put one on and see if it suits you. Practice feeling comfortable at the joy-filled end of the spectrum.

7   Tie this together with developing your 'attitude of gratitude' and enjoying work, and soon you may find that you have developed a positive addiction.

POSITIVE CONTINUUM

Mind Chi Future

The final two steps in Mind Chi Basic are designed to help you to develop a 'realistically positive' attitude. Even when there are problems to be dealt with, it doesn't mean that all is bleak. Problems are surmountable and there are always good moments amidst the not-so-good. Taking stock of what IS good helps you to have the necessary energy to face the rest. That is the 'glass half full' outlook on life.

This is an important stage – especially for those who habitually think that the worst is going to happen. You don't have to think that way, so use Step 7 to plan your next 24 hours and accentuate the realistic and truthful positives which you want to have happen.

Step 7: Plan

When you give your 'Chi' a sense of direction and a plan to go towards, you automatically increase your momentum. As any truly successful person knows, planning is the secret to success. It is a powerful tool that will assist you to accomplish everything from a simple activity to your life's purpose. Step 7 will enable you to plan more effectively. Step 8 will encourage you to tune in to your successes and feel gratitude for all that you have achieved, and for the on-going process of improvement. The success of both these stages is dependent upon your attitude and state of mind.

Research has shown that if you take a positive approach to living, your health is better than average and you will live longer! The University of Texas found that people with an upbeat view of life were less likely than pessimists to show signs of frailty. They speculated that positive emotions may directly affect health by altering the chemical balance of the body.

When you are optimistic, your brain creates endorphins, which are natural painkillers: *gamma globulin* for fortifying your immune system, and *interferon* for combating infections, viruses, and even battling cancer. Your brain can combine these and other substances into a vast number of tailor-made prescriptions for whatever ails you.

Attitudes are your established ways of responding to people, events and situations. You have learned these based on your beliefs, values and assumptions. Attitude drives your behaviour and can show in your body language. If you plan to think upbeat thoughts, you can send out a message that everyone around you will understand. You will receive feedback such as, 'You certainly appear to be on top of the world today.'

Success is not dependent upon education, intelligence or title; anyone can choose what their attitude will be at any time. It is a question of adjusting your thinking. The next two Mind Chi processes will help you to take control and responsibility for your thoughts and attitude – so that lasting adjustment and success will follow.

Activity 7: 24-Hour Preview

PURPOSE

Your mind responds to your future thoughts in the same way as it does to past or current thoughts. By taking time to plan and project how you want to be in the future, your brain will start to react, think and act as if you have already made those events happen. Remember the saying, 'Be careful what you wish for, it just might happen'? It is true. Every time you think a thought, you increase the likelihood of it actually happening. You have formed a 'future memory' (page 98) within the plasticity of your brain. This is why Step 7 is so important.

ACTION

Set your timer for one minute so you can concentrate on **pre**viewing the next 24 hours of your life. Now create a movie of your next 24 hours as you would like it to be. (It helps to close your eyes when conducting this preview as it cuts out any external visual distractions.)

Take a few deep Mind Chi breaths. Visualize (experience in your mind) all the people you may see, the activities or events you may do. Focus specifically on how your Body feels when you preview each event. Make is a multi-sensory event; what Emotions you will experience; what positive Actions you will be taking; and the quality of your Thoughts. You are projecting forward your Mind Chi BEAT so that your memory understands that that is the way you wish to respond.

Make sure that your preview is a positive projection of the way you *choose* things to be, and how you want to have responded to them. This is your chance to set your future attitude and outcomes.

BENEFIT

Step 7 will build your energy and the ability to craft your positive activities and responses to the day ahead. This lets your 'Chi' know what you want and helps you to make it so!

Step 8: Be Grateful

'Gratitude unlocks the fullness of life. It turns what we have into enough, and more. It turns denial into acceptance, chaos to order, confusion to clarity. It can turn a meal into a feast, a house into a home, a stranger into a friend. Gratitude makes sense of our past, brings peace for today, and creates a vision for tomorrow.' – Melody Beattie (author)

Gratitude, thankfulness or appreciation can be for what you have received as well as what you may receive. Psychologists have started to measure gratitude and have crafted eight aspects: appreciation of people; possessions; the present moment; rituals; feelings of awe; social comparisons; existential concerns; and behaviour which expresses gratitude.

There is a real payoff for being grateful; extensive research has shown that you will sleep better, experience less negative stress, feel more 'in control' of your life and environment and will be happier! Gratitude is shown to be 'uniquely important' in coping with life transitions and appears to be the attitude most likely to improve your overall well being.

Gratitude is like a muscle, so start to get it to work better for you by taking a few minutes, once a week, to write down things for which you are grateful. It is free and you can find out for yourself whether it works. You have nothing to lose and a great deal to gain.

The power of gratitude

Vanda selects special stones from her beach and paints them with happy faces. She has sold these 'gratitude stones' to raise money for her local hospital charity. She suggests that you place one by your bed so that last thing at night and first thing in the morning, you will see it and it will help you to smile as you think of the happy things in your life. It is a good way to start and end your day. (Further resources, page 323.)

Activity 8: Mind Chi – Reflect and Project

PURPOSE

To appreciate what you have achieved and received there needs to be a time for reflection and being grateful. The final Mind Chi Basic step is to wrap yourself in a cloak of gratitude. When you take this last minute to reflect on everything for which you are grateful, you cull the positives and successes from the last 24 hours as well as projecting your gratitude into the next day.

It allows you to bring into your conscious awareness the good things that are happening daily in your life. It closes the eight minutes with a smile and leaves you with a positive attitude to go about your day.

The purpose of the Gratitude step is to put you into a mindset where you find that you do have positive, good things happening to you in many areas of your life. When you are grateful for what life offers you, you reinforce new behaviours as well as the new thought patterns. By shifting the focus away from the negative aspects of a situation you are able to see the positives more clearly. This in turn puts you into a state of mind where your 'antennae' will notice more of life's opportunities and benefits.

ACTION

Set your timer for one minute so you can concentrate on your GRATI-TUDE. It helps to close your eyes as it cuts out any external visual distractions. As you think over both now and the upcoming 24 hours what things pop in to your mind? 'I am so grateful that …' Or, 'I feel so fortunate that …' Taking just one minute to complete your Mind Chi eighth step with all that you have to be grateful for, sets you up with a wonderful attitude to be receptive to even more areas of gratitude!

BENEFIT

Step 8 will energize your mind to appreciate all the wonders that have come and will come your way over the next 24 hours. This increases your chance of making them a reality; additionally you feel better right now!

Mind Chi FAQS

Q **I have such a hectic day, when can I do my Mind Chi Basic?**

A Even with the busiest day, you have to go to bed sometime! If you have not been able to create time for eight Mind Chi minutes during the day, then start Mind Chi Steps 1 and 2 as you lie in bed. If you can, do Mind Chi 3 and 4 as well (the unhelpful and positive reviews of the past 24 hours) as it is still fresh in your mind. Then, when you wake up the next morning, do your Mind Chi Breath and continue where you left off.

Q **What if I miss a day (or two)?**

A Just carry on! If it happens, smile and say, 'I choose to continue today' and extend the Mind Chi Basic days on your diary (Tracker, page 329). In order for a new habit to 'stick', it is preferable to continue the practice for 28 consecutive days – but if you were to miss a couple of days, just add those days on at the end.

Q **Must I do Step 3 – the 'unhelpful/negative' review?**

A Yes, because you have much to learn from the 'negative' or 'unhelpful' review. It brings any negativity to your attention and will help you to improve management of your 'Chi' self-talk. Negative ('unhelpful') body reactions, emotions, actions or thoughts are depleting your energy. By increasing your awareness of them, you think of coping strategies and start to put them into action as you plan your next 24 hours, before too much energy has been wasted!

Q **Can I use the Mind Chi BEAT throughout the day?**

A Yes! Please do. It is such a powerful way to check in to what is happening inside you, allowing you to grab the reins of control and respond in the way that is least damaging to your body and leads to the most efficient use of your energy.

Q Why do I do the Mind Chi eight steps for 28 days?

A Because it takes 28 days to create a new neural network or habit. After this you may find that you are naturally doing some of the steps as they are needed throughout the day: especially the Mind Chi Breath (page 46) and your Mind Chi BEAT (page 39).

Q What can I expect once I have practised my Mind Chi Basic for 28 days?

A Mind Chi Basic is the foundation of the Mind Chi Program. In 28 days you will have regained control over yourself. You will be able to:

1 Negate the effects of negative stress by using the Mind Chi Breath.

2 Focus your concentration as and when you desire through Mind Chi 'One'.

3 Check and choose your BEAT (Body, Emotions, Actions and Thoughts) to gain control over yourself and your reactions.

4 Balance any negative memories from the past 24 hours and harness the joy of your successes.

5 Project what you do want to experience in the future and remember all the things for which you are grateful, enabling you to live the life you choose.

All that from your commitment of just eight minutes a day – what a return on investment!

Support to help you complete the Mind Chi Basic 28-day routine

- An excellent form of support is to have a Mind Chi buddy so you can do the Mind Chi Program together. Having someone to answer to can help ensure that you complete the daily activities. Plus you will share your progress tips and, most importantly, offer each other moral support.
- Support can also take the form of a friend who is simply willing to listen and encourage you along the way.
- Set yourself personal goals. Mark the 28 days of your Mind Chi Basic from 1–28 on a calendar. As each days passes – and you complete your activities for that day – note it on your calendar. This way you can see your progress. (Mind Chi Tracker, page 329.)
- Tune in to your self-talk and encourage your 'Chi' to encourage you to make time to incorporate eight minutes into each day.
- Write out all your reasons and the benefits of completing your Mind Chi Basic. (Remember to ask WIIFM?: ('What's In It For Me?' – your Mind Chi radio station!) Make several copies and post them around the house: in your bedroom; bathroom; kitchen and back of the front door and in your office: on your computer; planner or wall. You need to keep reminding your 'Chi' and yourself as you build this new habit.
- Keep a small card in your wallet or purse with all the WIIFM reasons listed on it. At various moments during the day, take time to read it. This reinforces your intentions to master Mind Chi Basic, reminds your inner voice and strengthens your commitment too. Your persistence will pay handsome dividends that you will enjoy from now on.

'Chi' using the supports above

PART 2
Mind Chi in Action

5 Mind Chi Maps

Overview

About maps
How to map
Map applications
Map terminology

The use of maps in your Mind Chi Program is one of the four enabling Mind Chi methods. We have included them to make the whole Mind Chi process as easy for you as we can. Mapping ideas, in whatever way works for you – by hand or on the computer – is the best technique there is to organize your thoughts and maximize the flow of your mental energy.

About maps

A map emulates the workings of your brain. It uses the basic brain and memory function of association and it uses the skills of both the left and the right cortex. It is like a direct line to you mind and, as such, aids all your thinking processes.

Maps have been around for thousands of years. Cavemen in Africa used pictorial maps before the birth of language. Since the 1950s maps have become more sophisticated and commonly used in both business and education. Technology has spread the acceptance of mapping by creating map software, for which there are numerous suppliers.

Many of you will use some form of mapping technique already. For those of you who are unfamiliar with mapping, or who would like some additional ideas, here is a quick introduction to this magnificently simple and profound process.

You will see that we have used a form of map to graphically illustrate the Mind Chi Basic, 50 Strategies for Success and Mind Chi Applied; in fact we used maps to organize and write this book. The maps provide the essence of the information.

How to map

Mapping is easy:

1   Turn a blank sheet of paper sideways (landscape) and draw an image of the idea, problem, concept or feeling you want to explore in the centre of the page. If you prefer, use a combined word and image (a 'wimage'!). An image is important as it helps to activate more of your brain's responses.
2   Next draw several 'arms' or branches growing out from your central image, long enough to hold a four letter word (approximately). These empty branches will stimulate your brain to want to put something on them (your brain loves completion!).
3   As you think of key topics triggered by the central word/image or 'wimage', write them down as key words or as very short phrases. Use capital letters, and make sure you write ON the line. The concepts are **IMPORTANT** and the underlining and capitals will remind you of that.
4   As you think of further ideas related to the initial topic, add further branches to your map, making a bare tree-like structure. Your brain

will start to 'bloom' with associated ideas and actions and your thought processes will 'flow' outwards. Your map will capture the process, so that you have a permanent record of your thoughts and state of mind.

5   If you find you grind to a halt, add doodles and images on and around your words; add some extra empty lines; get creative with colour. Your brain will soon provide more words! Voila! You have mapped!

Map applications

The uses for mapping are limitless. They speed up your thinking process to make whatever you are doing more efficient and more enjoyable. Use mapping to make yourself Mind Chi-efficient.

We have created maps to illustrate each of the 50 Mind Chi Strategies for Success in Part 3. They are designed to show the dynamic tension between your current reality and the movement towards your desired goal.

Throughout the book we recommend using bloom, mini-, multi-, mega- or full maps as the best way to motivate yourself into action. This Mind Chi Method reflects the way your brain operates and is therefore the natural way to assist you to manage and direct your thinking.

You will soon discover the benefits of mapping for yourself. Maps can:

- Dramatically improve your memory!
- Eliminate non-crucial words (usually some 80–95 percent of most business texts) so you are able to separate the wheat from the chaff.
- Help you to compare details.
- Show you the key points of your argument.

- Organize and convey your thoughts with authority and ease.
- Clarify complex situations.
- Allow your thoughts to be refined.
- Assist difficult decision making.
- Enable you to organize your thoughts fast.
- Improve your ability to make natural and effective presentations.
- Increase your creativity.
- Help you to manage information overload.
- Enhance your time management.
- Build understanding, relationships and negotiation skills.
- Make you want to *just get on with it*!

Mapping terminology

All levels of map have the same basic structure, that of a radiant hierarchy (from the centre outwards) and, without the words or images, look like the bare branches of a tree. However, various mapping terms have specific meanings, summarized here for your reference:

- **Bloom** – When you put a word/image ('wimage') in the centre of your new map and capture associated key words on the branches you have drawn, you are creating a 'bloom' of associations that are based on your own unique experiences. Your thought 'bloom' reflects the development of a flower: just as petals open and bloom from the centre of the plant, so too your thoughts open and bloom from the central topic on your page. This technique is particularly good for clarifying your thoughts; aiding communication; understanding MIS-understanding; developing negotiations; and defining abstract feelings – especially in close relationships. A 'bloom' of thoughts will show you (and others) the aspects that are of greatest importance to you. A 'bloom' tends to de-personalize the subject – useful if emotions are running a bit high – and can greatly enhance levels of mutual understanding.

- **Flow** – The process of 'flow' is used to generate ideas, think creatively, and help you become unstuck. It helps you to look at the world from a different perspective. As you consider one of the words on your map, your thoughts will 'flow' to another associated word which you may choose to capture on a connected line. The second word now inspires a third thought, which leads to another and another. Allow your thoughts to travel four or five levels outwards from the central topic. It is highly likely that you will find that your thoughts are far removed from the initial word. That is the whole idea. It is a pathway to creativity.

- **Extendo-map** – When you combine your bloom and flow of ideas the result is an extendo-map. It usually extends to four or five branch 'levels' and helps to open up some creative new ideas.

- **Mini-map** – This is a small map that is usually created very fast. It is a map that can be created 'on-the-run': an 'organize-your-thoughts-as-you-go' map. It is useful to keep mini-maps for each of the people with whom you work closely, to keep track of ideas and information you will want to share. When something occurs that you want to communicate, just pop a key word on the appropriate mini-map as a reminder to yourself. Mini-maps are also an excellent way of making notes before or during phone calls or quick meetings, to ensure that you cover all the things you intended.

- **Multi-map** – A multi-map is made up of many mini-maps on the same subject. These are useful to review over time, especially if you want to see how your thoughts and reactions are changing; or to clarify your thinking on a complex issue or difficult decision. Multi-maps are useful for exploring a situation from several perspectives, or examining what might happen in various scenarios.

- **Mega-map** – Large enough to cover a whole wall and designed to capture a 'mega' quantity of information. Mega-maps can be used with great success when revising for exams or when summing up complex product information that needs to be conveyed clearly. It is an invaluable tool for exploring the crucial relationships between a mass of apparently disparate information. (Several people are in jail because of maps – that is; the detectives pieced together the clues, solved the crime and found the culprits using a mega-map!)

- **Full map** – A complete map on a single subject is known as a full map. It can be created by hand or using mapping software on the computer. There are many computer mapping programs available; most can be trialled for 21 days so that you can find out whether they suit you.

The great advantages of a full map done on a computer are:

- The ease of sharing information with co-workers.
- The quantity of information can be extensive, without paper size problems!
- Hyper-linking reports/spreadsheets/files – all information managed from ONE place.
- The facility to correct and spell-check.
- The same information can be re-organized and re-presented for a different audience.
- They can be linked to diary systems.
- They can be used to keep track of a global team working on a project.
- They look more 'professional' and can easily incorporate clip art.
- They can even be worked on live on the web.

You are invited to use some form of mapping in many of the Mind Chi Plans; the Strategies for Success (page 142) frequently refer to this powerful process as a step towards solving a problem or achieving a goal.

6

Create your own Mind Chi Plan

Overview

Mind Chi Plan creation
Mind Chi Meme

Can you immediately think of an area that you would like to 'fix' or improve in yourself? If you have issues you want to address, look at the map of Strategies for Success in Part 3 (page 135) to see the topics we have covered. Have we covered your concern? If you select one of the 50 topics, then this chapter will help you understand how they are constructed and how to amend one if necessary. If your desired topic is not there, this chapter will tell you how to create your own Mind Chi Plan and craft your personal Strategy for Success. Each **Mind Chi Plan** is a tried and tested Strategy for Success: the '*what*' of your new goal. It includes:

- **Your Current Reality and Mind Chi Goal** – your situation now and the outcome desired.
- **Your transformational Mind Chi Meme** – a positive self-talk phrase for you to focus on in support of your goal (called a meme as it makes copies of itself).
- **Your current Mind Chi BEAT** – analysis of how you are currently functioning at Body, Emotion, Action and Thought levels.
- **Your preferred Mind Chi BEAT** – analysis of how you want to feel at Body, Emotion, Action and Thought levels.

Mind Chi Plan creation

Following is a blank Mind Chi Plan – your key to future success. We will explain each element so you can see how and why the plans are constructed as they are. Turn also to the 50 Strategies for Success (page 135) where we have already filled in the plans for you.

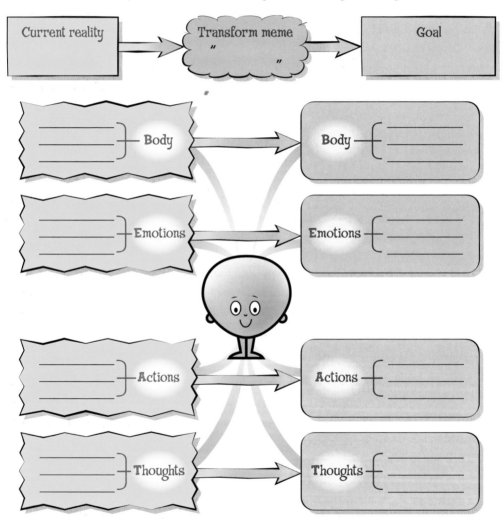

The Mind Chi Plan template

The Mind Chi Plan

The Mind Chi Plan is a reflection of the structural tension that exists between what you have (your current reality) and what you want (your future goal). In order to turn one state into the other, a process of *TRANSFORMATION* needs to take place in the 'now': the centre point of your life. Your new Mind Chi Meme is written in this box, to focus and direct your attention towards your goal.

On the left side of the plan add your Current BEAT (Body, Emotions, Actions and Thoughts): all the things that you may say, experience, feel, do and think – now.

On the right side add your goals BEAT: all the things that you want to say, experience, feel, do and think – in the future.

At any one moment you are changing your now and creating your future. This point of transformation assimilates the power your inner voice 'Chi' and flexible focus (being able to look at your current reality and then look at your goal). Attuning what you think and say to your future goal will propel you forward (in the direction of the arrows). The Mind Chi Program will help you to transform yourself to create the future that you really want.

Your Current Reality and Mind Chi Goal

You probably have a clear picture either of what you want to move away from (a problem area) or of what you want to move towards (a goal). In the top, left-hand box write the undesired state and in the top, right-hand box write the desired state. This is your Mind Chi Goal. This is a short, positive statement that encapsulates the desired outcome. For example: *'To be the best sales person in the team this quarter.'*

You need to choose and write your own Mind Chi Goal to fit your specific and personal plan. You can use one of the Strategies for Success supplied and simply update and amend any aspect that does not ring true for you.

As you observe both your current reality and your future goal you will already start to feel the push from the negative side and the pull from the positive side as those arrows pull you from left to right. (If you feel 'stuck' use your Mind Chi Breath activity to help you to relax and focus on your new goal – page 46.)

The phrase **TRANSFORM MEME** is placed between the two extremes to remind you that you are transforming yourself. Inside the box is the inspirational phrase that you will use to reinforce your intention to reach your goal.

> **Flexible focus** is the dynamic process used to propel you towards your ultimate goal. Your current reality will keep changing, whereas your Mind Chi Goal will remain a constant target. As you change, you need to keep updating the current reality BEAT on your plan. The structural tension pulls you closer to your goal and you will become aware of your progress. Keep flexible; keep feeling that push from the negative side and the pull from the positive. Let yourself stay in the Mind Chi flow towards success.

Your current reality BEAT (left column)

Fill in at least three descriptive words on each branch of the left column to describe your current feelings in relation to your Body, Emotions, Actions and Thoughts. Three words encourage you to give each aspect considered thought.

Take some time to really feel the reality of your current situation. Make yourself aware of how much you want to be 'out of there'. Now you are experiencing the negative push, exacerbating the desire to push yourself away from that situation.

Your goal BEAT (right column)

Fill in at least three descriptive words on each branch of the right column to describe how you would ideally like to feel in relation to your Body, Emotions, Actions and Thoughts. This is your desired future state of being. The reason for selecting at least three means that you have given each area considered thought.

Consider carefully, what do you really want? How would your Body function; how would you feel Emotionally; what Actions and Thoughts would you want to have achieved when you reach your goal?

Please note the considered use of the word 'when' you have achieved your goal. There is no question of doubt; no 'if'. By noting these words 'as though' you are experiencing the state of having achieved your goal *in the present*, you are reporting what it is like in your new reality.

Take some time to make sure the words convey what you really do want. Keep them positive. Put them on, as if they were of the finest material, feel them slip over you and make you smile. Luxuriate in the experience at a multi-sensory level; make it as real as you possibly can. Feel the pull of the positive goal. Remember that as you do this, it *is* real in your brain, you have already, at one level, 'made it so'!

Notice that there are arrows between each Body, Emotion, Action and Thought branches. These set up and reinforce the dynamic and structural tension between the two states of present and future (page 265).

In the centre of your Mind Chi Plan is an image of your 'Chi' to remind you that all of this is directed by your willpower and your volition; supported by your Mind Chi BEAT for your well-being NOT your destruction.

Word selection

To assist you to describe your Body and Emotional 'haves' for the current reality (left side) and 'wants' for the goal (right side) please see the lists below. Think about the best you will experience and put those words on the appropriate branches on the right side of your map. Negatives should appear only on the left side of your map. These may be a part of your current reality but have no place in your desired future.

Body – Negative

Allergies	Diarrhoea	Listless	Sluggish
Alopecia (hair falls out)	Diverticulitis	Munchies	Smoking
Altered sense of taste/smell	Dizzy	Nail biting	Stiff necked
	Drinking	Nausea	Sweaty
	Eczema	Nervous cough	Tight jawed
Anorexia	Exhaustion	Palpitations	Tummy ache
Asthma	Fidgety	Rapid breathing	Tics
Breathlessness	Flatulence	Recurrent infections	Twitchy
Butterflies in the tummy	Headachy	Self harming	Tired
	Heartburn/ Indigestion	Shaky	Tight chest
Constant hunger	Heavy Limbed	Shingles	Tinnitus
Constipation	Languid	Sleepy	Weary
Craving	Lethargic	Slothful	Yawning

Emotions – Negative

	Cantankerous	Irritable	Unbalanced
	Concerned	Keyed up	Unconcerned
Aggravated	Cross	Lazy	Unconfident
Anguished	Depressed	Messed up	Uneasy
Angry	Dissatisfied	Moody	Unhinged
Anxious	Distressed	Nervous	Unstable
Apathetic	Disturbed	Overwhelmed	Vexed
Apprehensive	Droopy	Rigid	Weak
Awkward	Frustrated	Snappy	Weighed down
Beleaguered	Grouchy	Suffering	Worried/
Besieged	Indifferent	Timid	Wound up
Bored	Indolent	Traumatized	
Bothered	Insecure	Troubled	

Body – Positive

Adaptable
Animated
Anticipatory
Assertive
Assured
Balanced
Bright
Bubbly
Calm
Cheerful

Comfortable
Composed
Confident
Controlled
Dignified
Durable
Easy going
Energetic
Enthusiastic
Excited
Flexible

Focused
Hardy
High spirits
Jovial
Keen
Keyed up
Lively
Motivated
Open
Passionate
Pleasant

Poised
Positive
Prepared
Refreshed
Relaxed
Resilient
Satisfied
Self-assured
Self-confident
Strong

Emotions – Positive

Accommodating
Affectionate
Appreciative
Ardent
Blissful
Buoyant
Carefree
Caring
Charming

Cheery
Content
Delighted
Eager
Ebullient
Ecstatic
Enchanted
Encouraging
Expectant
Exultant
Fortunate

Glad
Grateful
Happy
Happy-go-lucky
Hopeful
Joyful
Jubilant
Light hearted
Loving
Managing
Merry

Optimistic
Pleased
Secure
Tender
Thankful
Thrilled
Upbeat
Warm
Wholehearted

Mind Chi Meme

Your new mode of positive Mind Chi thinking is crucial to your Mind Chi success. There is a new term that is becoming increasingly popular; it is a 'meme'. A meme is a nugget of information which can be replicated in your own mind and shared with others. It is important to provide your 'Chi' with an upbeat and encouragingly life-changing phrase that reprograms your self-talk and supports your new Mind Chi habit. This will gradually replace any old and negative self-talk that was holding back your progress.

Some care needs to be taken as you craft this phrase as you are giving a command directly to you brain. The phraseology is important and needs to be expressed in the correct 'brain language'. (Practitioners of NLP and hypnotherapy will recognize the importance of these guidelines, now supported by scientific research.)

1   The first part of your thought must be expressed as 'I' (you may add your name here as well if you wish extra emphasis);
2   The next word must be 'choose', because you need to let your mind (Chi) know that it is your choice.
3   'Choose' is followed by 'to';
4   The final part of your Mind Chi Meme needs to be the desired outcome.

For example: Mind Chi Meme: *'I choose to improve my negotiation skills.'*

NEVER write what you *don't* want because your brain cannot process a 'not'. (Always write what you *do* want to have happen!)

We will show you how this works. Promise, right now, that you will not think about what you are not to think about. OK? So do NOT think about a blue elephant in a pink tutu … and?? Dancing in your head right now is a lovely blue elephant and if you put a cross through him, he is still there; or if you change him to green, he is STILL there!! So, you see – your brain cannot do a not!

A meme is a nugget of information which has a powerful influence – as it replicates itself in your mind and even in the minds of others

Where were you? Ah, yes, express your desired outcome in positive, measurable and specific terms.

Be careful of statements such as 'I choose to be slimmer' – where does that end? It is potentially life-threatening. You might have to take your goal up a level. What is the greater goal than being slim? To be radiantly healthy or to be your perfect size? Yes. Good! (Perfect size, page 118)

To sum up, your Mind Chi Meme says: 'I choose to … (positive outcome)'.

Authors' Mind Chi Plans

The following two Mind Chi Plan examples were used by the authors to help write the book – and to keep us in shape whilst writing. We have elected to keep the two Mind Chi Plans for several months to keep us focused on our long-term goals.

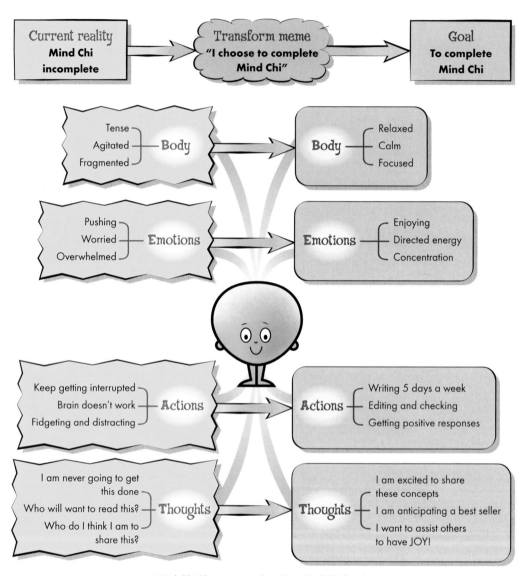

Mind Chi Plan to complete the *Mind Chi* book

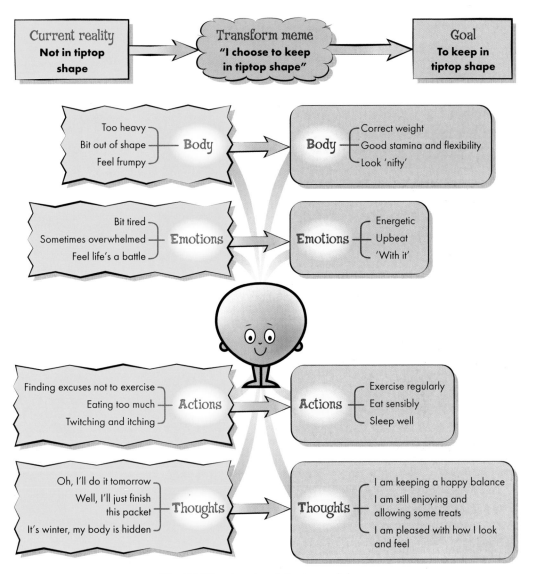

Mind Chi Plan to get and stay in good shape

Keep your Mind Chi Plan in view

Keep your
Mind Chi Plan
within your sight
and in your
mind!

Put your completed plan somewhere you will see it every day: your bathroom mirror; refrigerator; desk; computer or in your planner or notebook: somewhere you are bound to see it EVERY day. When it floats into your vision, stop! Really look at it for a minute, feel the tension between where you are and where you want to be. Ask yourself where you are on your Actions and what steps you need to take next. Use your flexible focus to experience the negative push from the current reality side and the positive pull to your goal.

7 Mind Chi in Action

Overview

Mind Chi planning in action
ADOCTA and tracking progress
Two worked examples:
• Making decisions
• Achieving your perfect size

Mind Chi planning in action

To turn a Mind Chi Plan into your new reality you need to put Mind Chi *in action*. This means applying your plan to the Mind Chi Basic – 8 minutes a day routine and taking an action step:

1   Apply your Mind Chi Basic routine to your plan for 28 days, following the guidelines on page 79.
2   Identify what practical actions and steps you need to take to move from your current reality to reach your desired goal.
3   Take one of those steps every day.

Start

Step 1: Breathe – Activity: Your Mind Chi Breath
Remains unchanged – focus on your breathing for one minute. (Page 46.)

Step 2: Attend – Activity: Your mind Chi 'One'
Your Mind Chi 'One' activity is replaced by your positive Mind Chi Meme. Repeat your positive phrase for one minute. (Page 48.)

Past

Step 3: Adjust – Activity: 24-hour rewind (negative)
Rewind your day in relation to your goal and adjust any negative thoughts by deciding what you can do differently in future. (Page 52.)

Step 4: Associate – Activity: 24-hour review (positive)
Review your day in relation to the helpful things you did to move success-fully towards your goal and use your senses to create memory associations. (Page 54.)

Now

Step 5: Be aware – Activity: Check your BEAT
Remains virtually unchanged. Check your BEAT in relation to actions that take you towards your Mind Chi Goal. Become aware of any aspects you need and want to change. (Page 58.)

Step 6: Choose – Activity: Choose your BEAT
Remains virtually unchanged. Choose to change any negative reactions in your Body, Emotions, Actions and Thoughts to positive ones that will take you towards your Mind Chi Goal. (Page 60.)

Future

Step 7: Plan – Activity: 24-hour preview
Preview the next 24-hours in relation to your goal and your meme. Experience it 'as though' you are living it now. This will pre-program your 'Chi' to think positively, act and be in ways that will take you nearer to your goal. (Page 64.)

Step 8: Be grateful – Activity: Reflect and project

Reflect on all the positive thoughts and steps you have achieved in relation to your Mind Chi Goal. Be grateful that your meme is taking you in the right direction and that your 'Chi' is aiding your willpower to focus and reach your goal. (Page 66.)

Repeat your Mind Chi Applied routine for eight minutes a day for the next 28 days to make your new Mind Chi Goal your new way of being. As you get used to your Mind Chi routine you can do it all in your head as four 2-minute sections, to make it easier.

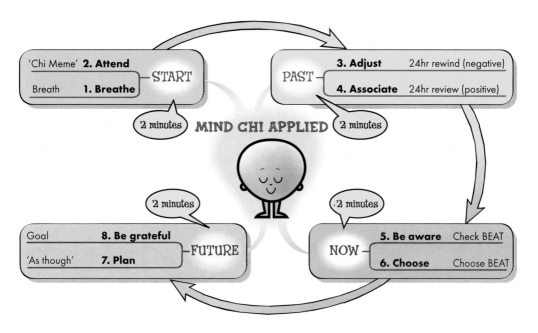

Mind Chi Applied map, showing how to adapt Mind Chi Basic into a plan of action

Now you have crafted or selected your Mind Chi Plan, you need to use your Mind Chi Basic routine and apply it to your Mind Chi Strategy to achieve your goal. Take an Action Step each day until you reach your goal.

Following is a 'worked example' showing how Mind Chi can be applied to 'Conquering procrastination'.

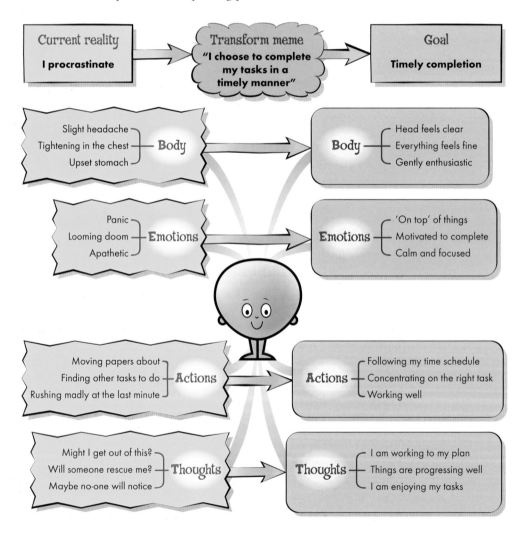

Mind Chi – Start

Visualize your Mind Chi Plan as completed before you begin your Mind Chi Applied steps for the day. As each day passes you will move closer towards your goal and your current reality will change. Keep it updated to keep experiencing the positive pull towards your goal.

Conquering procrastination – 'see' yourself going through your day 'as though' you already are a person who completes tasks in a timely manner. (Pages 94 and 150.)

Step 1: Mind Chi Breathe – If you are finding that the breath work is enjoyable and beneficial (and you can make the time) do a few extra minutes. If it feels comfortable, increase the time for each part of the cycle: breath in for a count of four or five seconds, hold for the same time, out for the same time and stay empty for the same.

Conquering procrastination – step 1 stays the same as Mind Chi Basic (page 43), there is no specific application to the goal.

Step 2: Mind Chi Attend – Now that you have greater control, direct your attention towards your desired outcome, using the Mind Chi Meme that fits with your goal. Repeat your Mind Chi Meme during your minute. (You can also develop the habit of repeating your meme whenever you have a spare moment. Over a cup of tea; waiting for a phone to connect, or for the computer to boot up.) Be sure to repeat your Mind Chi Meme at least four times every time your thoughts sabotage your progress.

Remember that these two steps are useful to repeat whenever you want to be razor sharp: before going into a meeting, as you make a presentation, or just starting your day.

Conquering procrastination – your Mind Chi Meme is, 'I choose to complete tasks in a timely manner'. Say this, sing this, think this, as often as you can and definitely for the one minute of focused attention in step 2 of your Mind Chi Applied routine.

Mind Chi – Past

Steps 3 and 4: Adjust and Associate – As you think about your goal, check anything about your BEAT (Body, Emotions, Actions, Thoughts) that has been unhelpful or undermining during the past 24-hours. Brush off your non-dominant hand to symbolically brush away the negativity and to encourage your brain to let it go.

Ask yourself, 'How did I feel, physically and emotionally?' 'What did I do or say?' 'How did I act?' Rewind so you can learn from your answers and decide what strategies you might put in place that will enable you to listen to your inner 'Chi' sooner, heighten your awareness and put your free will into action. You may be pleased to discover that you caught yourself and put your new behaviour into action (this is noted on your 'success', dominant hand as well).

The idea is to build your success into a neural pathway in your brain until the new behaviour becomes natural. Spend your two minutes of Mind Chi Past, reviewing, re-living, re-enjoying and re-minding yourself of all the successes that you have accomplished over the past twenty-four hours in relation to your goal. Squeeze your dominant hand to encourage your brain to remember those successes.

Conquering procrastination – what specifically did your 24-hour review show to you in light of your 'timely manner' meme? What unhelpful things happened? Did you: ignore your priorities? Or think, 'Oh I can leave that a bit longer'? These were unhelpful thoughts, so now you observe this, what can you learn and how might you adjust yourself tomorrow? Were there any successes that took you towards your goal? Even small ones count! A step in the right direction is acknowledged and can be 'caught' by squeezing shut your dominant hand.

Mind Chi – Now

Steps 5 and 6: Be aware and Choose – These two steps can be done together. You can either increase your awareness of where you are now and then choose to change your BEAT if/as necessary, or you may prefer to look at each aspect: Body, Emotions, Actions and Thoughts separately and then update your BEAT choice for each in turn. Do whichever suits you best. (Refer to page 58 for a reminder of these steps.) Completion leads you to the final two steps.

Conquering procrastination – the NOW steps, 5 and 6, stay almost the same as your Mind Chi Basic routine. You can do your BEAT finger check regularly during the day, to check in to your state of mind and body when you are doing (or not doing) tasks in a timely manner.

Mind Chi – Future

Steps 7 and 8: 'As though' and Be grateful – Here you will find another slight adjustment from the original Mind Chi Basic in that you are specifically projecting into the next twenty four hours 'as though …' you already have achieved your goal: you have changed your habit and now you are living your life in this new way. How does this work on the next day? You will gradually learn to respond and act from this new perspective. Set your mind to create new and positive synaptic connections and let your brain be your willing slave to make your vision of the future become real.

The eighth step is very important, your gratitude. To have an 'attitude of gratitude' is a wonderful way to live. Cover yourself with appreciation for all you have and will have to be grateful for. Make no distinction between what you have now and what you are working towards. Just feel your gratitude, express it, and revel in it. You understand the idea! It feels marvellous and means that you complete your Mind Chi Applied with a big smile on your face.

Conquering procrastination – experience yourself completing your tasks in a timely manner and at multi-sensory BEAT levels. Your Body is free of negative tensions; your Emotions are calm; your Actions are purposeful; your Thoughts are preparatory; you see the project complete; and you hear your colleagues thanking you for good and timely work.

Creating future memories

Think of what you did yesterday. It's not a difficult thing to do, you simply went back into your memory and recreated events of the last twenty-four hours. Your memory stores the past and it can also store what you are planning. This is called 'future memory'. Think of something you intend to do tomorrow. Use your imagination to come up come up with a goal. For example, make a business presentation that results in a new contract. That thought is now stored in your 'future memory'. This is an extremely powerful Mind Chi thought process because you are pre-setting your future intention. Running this new thought pattern through your mind several times, prior to the presentation, sets you up for success.

Acting as though something has happened tunes you into your future memory and this makes your goals much easier to achieve. Few use this unique mental asset, except when planning or rehearsing an important event, such as a conference, a talk or a wedding. Then a good deal of future planning, stored as future memory, takes place. There are even rehearsals where the groups act as though the occasion is actually happening.

From time to time you probably use 'acting as though ...' to sabotage yourself. Do you worry and fret about things in the future that may (but most frequently don't) occur? When you do this you are creating a 'future memory' of what you do not want to happen. Now you know that any instruction is 'real' to your brain, you also know that it is an extremely detrimental activity. Ask your 'Chi' to help you stop yourself from doing any worrying from now on. Instead, focus on considering scenarios and planning possible responses for each, which is good forward planning.

There is a phenomenon, especially well recognized in sport, where mental rehearsal actually improves physical performance. There was also a case where a prisoner of war, who had played golf and who was denied access to a course or clubs, actually 'thought' himself into becoming a better player. When he returned to the game after the war, his handicap was much lower. This capability has also been demonstrated by a classical pianist who progressed to professional performance standard after years in prison. He had 'practiced as though' he had an actual piano. You can see how powerful your future memory and acting 'as though' can be to assist you and your 'Chi' to create the life you wish.

ADOCTA and tracking progress

We provide you with two additional processes to support you on your Mind Chi path: One is ADOCTA. Like any doctor, this will make you aware of what is going on inside you. It is a simple acronym for a process that allows you to see that, 'if you do *this* then *tha*t is likely to happen'. Staying aware of the cause and effect of your actions will keep you on track and solidify the reasons for your daily Mind Chi Applied steps. The second is your Mind Chi Tracker, to keep you motivated to complete the 28 days that will create a new and positive habit.

Call ADOCTA

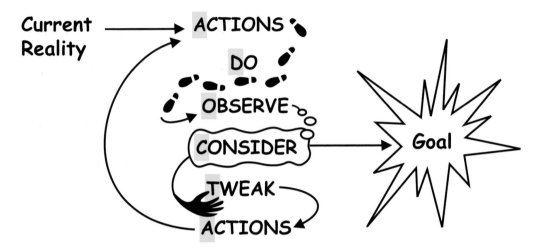

Your prescription for success: ADOCTA in action

ADOCTA might be just what you need to prescribe success with your goal. After you have crafted your actions and steps, you need to use your flexible focus to constantly assess where your current reality is now and then keep the tension towards your goal. This journey is not a straight line and ADOCTA allows you to make the amendments quickly so you keep heading towards your goal without too much wasted time and effort.

This process will start you on your virtuous positive spiral. You start with:

A = ACTIONS – write out each of your Action Steps. Think of someone who has already achieved your goal or imagine yourself there. Hold that image for inspiration.

D = DO something – take one Action Step (big or small) towards your goal.

O = OBSERVE the outcome of your Action Step. See what happens, remain impartial. This can involve others or just yourself and your 'Chi'.

C = CONSIDER alternative actions. Will they take you closer to your goal? Did you achieve your expected result?

T = TWEAK in preparation for your next action, what do you need to amend?

A = ACTIONS – remind yourself where you are headed and take your next step.

Continue this iterative process until, at your *Consider* stage, you decide that you have reached your goal. This is an important stage. Change your 'C' to *Celebrate*, you have completion. Well done! When you really understand ADOCTA you have the prescription for success with any endeavour. This is how your brain learns, adapts and changes. The only failure possible is if you quit before you have attained a goal you want. Many successful people say that it was 'that one extra push' that let them achieve where others didn't.

Making up your Action Steps

A map is very helpful when creating a plan of action as it conveys the essence of what you need to do. Plan small, doable steps and take one every day, even if it is only to speak to someone about your intentions. This helps to keep your goal uppermost in your mind and structural tension will pull you towards it. Your brain will be constantly searching for information, assistance, people, opportunities and gems to move you closer. (There are two worked examples at the end of this chapter.)

Your plan of action needs to be detailed and should follow the SMART principles (i.e. it needs to be Specific; Measurable; Achievable; Relevant and Time-based.) This acronym is used in project management, as a way of evaluating the objectives or goals for an individual project; and in performance management, where goals and targets must be fulfilled. Your plan is a crucial element in achieving your goal and must be included. You will need to make conscious progress towards it every day. Each sequential step is intended to take you closer to your goal.

How do you arrive at these steps? You make them up! Yes, here the power of your creative brain kicks in. Now you are using your mental energy to its full potential. The steps must be goal-directed so that your 'Chi' is given a positive direction and a clear outcome to aim for.

For example: in the Mind Chi Strategy 'Conquering procrastination', you would need to make up a series of actions and steps. These might be:

Actions: Start to build your 'timely manner' philosophy:

Step 1:	Look at all the tasks/commitments that need to be completed in the next three months.
Step 2:	Write the completion dates in your diary/planner/computer.
Step 3:	Make a 'my completion' date one week (as appropriate) ahead of each date.
Step 4:	Notice if there are any overlaps or conflicts of dates.
Step 5:	Write each step for each completion and calculate how long each will take.
Step 6:	Work backwards in your calendar so you know when you need to begin, etc.

Actions: Take control of the time-stealers:

Step 1:   Decide how 'perfect' the result needs to be.
Step 2:   Set your watch to be 5 or 10 minutes fast.
Step 3:   Turn OFF your phone and emails for increasing time
            blocks (for as long as you are able) etc.

As soon as you DO take action you will need to OBSERVE what happened. Did the step turn out the way you hoped?

Look for overlaps and conflicts. If you find one, OBSERVE this step and decide how it will need to be amended.

CONSIDER what to do. Once you have decided how to correct your action you can TWEAK the steps as necessary.

In order to make your goal a lasting habit, keep repeating the process for 28 complete days until new neural pathways have been fashioned. (Some goals require longer – such as writing this book – just keep the plan in view and continue to take Action Steps until the goal is achieved.)

ADOCTA will start you on your virtuous and positive spiral, rather than the vicious circles of negative thinking.

Mind Chi Tracker

When you start a new Mind Chi Plan, write it in your diary. Note the start date, count 28 days and circle or highlight that date as your completion date. Allow for a few extra days in case they are necessary. Many people prefer to begin on a Monday as it feels easier to make it part of the routine on a working day.

Each week, on your 'anniversary' start day, do a weekly check. Ask yourself honestly, 'How am I doing?' Notice any special things that have happened. What have you achieved? Do you need to revise your Mind Chi Goal or Plan in any way? Is it working as you want it to? Do you need any extra guidance or assistance? Mark, note or check off the days, count down (or up!) so that you are keeping the activity uppermost in your mind.

On a daily basis, for 28 days in a row, you will be considering your past experiences and, based on the awareness and learning you have gathered, create the future that you would like to experience wilfully.

We have created a special Mind Chi Tracker calendar and matrix for you on pages 329 and 330 (or visit www.MindChi.com to download copies) to help you to track your daily progress. After you have done the 8 steps of Mind Chi per day (either the Basic or the Applied), place a number between 0–10 (or 0–100) in the appropriate box to show what progress you are making. Zero would mean that you have made no progress (or even slipped back); 10 means that you really 'lived' your new Mind Chi way. You are working towards having several 10s in a row.

1   Fill in the date you begin on the top row.
2   Write the dates into each of the boxes in the top left corner.
3   Note the 28th day and circle or highlight it.
4   As you complete each day, place a score (from 0–10) in the box to represent how well you feel you performed. (Use a smiley/ unhappy face or thumbs up/down scale if you prefer.)

Mind Chi Tracker – Date begun: 27th April

Monday	Tuesday	Wednesday	Thursday	Friday	Saturday	Sunday
27 (Day 1) **7** Started!	28 (Day 2) **6**	29 (Day 3) **7**	30 (Day 4) **8** Better	1 May (Day 5) **3** Bad day!	2 (Day 6) **8** Took time!	3 Took the day off!
4 (Day 7) **8** Determined	5 (Day 8) **9** Very pleased	6 (Day 9) **8** Holding on	7 (Day 10) **6** Oops, went back-wards!	8 (Day 11) **8** Re-focusing	9 (Day 11) **8** Better	10 (Day 12) Didn't complete
11 (Day 12) **8** Push for the third week	12 (Day 13) **8** Getting steady	13 (Day 14) **9** Half way there	14 (Day 15) **8** Sleeping better!	15 (Day 16) **6** Lost con-centration	16 (Day 17) **9** Energy at end of day!	17 (Day 18) **9** Enjoying this!
18 (Day 19) **7** Tough day	19 (Day 20) **9** Back up there	20 (Day 21) **10** Woo Hoo!	21 (Day 22) **9** Feel good!	22 (Day 23) **10** Confidence rising	23 (Day 24) **10** Lovely!	24 (Day 25) **10** COMPLETE MC Basic Enjoyable
25 (Day 26) **10** Positive addiction!	26 (Day 27) **10** Part of my life now	27 (Day 28) **10** (Just in case!) Needed the extra days!	28	29	30	31

Remember that on a journey all sorts of unexpected things will happen to throw you off track and sabotage your best efforts. This is where sticking to your commitment is paramount. The secret is persistence. Ask yourself, what is the problem? How can I solve it? Find a way round it? Fix it (don't ignore it – it will come back to haunt you), and move on!

If you need help in building your willpower, see page 35. If you hit an 'awkwardness gap' (page 107), just keep going.

As with all journeys, you may like to keep a journal, either electronically or in a special book, to remember where you were and to see how far you have progressed. One thing we have observed is that once the new way becomes a norm you forget where you started. This is good in one way but prevents you from giving yourself the well-deserved pat on the back for the advancement you have made. The journal is a lasting and positive reminder.

Building new habits

It has long been held that 28 days is the time it takes to create a new habit. Scientists can now show the synaptic connections in the brain and how the myelin sheaths (that cover some axons) build to facilitate speed of thought in a certain direction. That is the good news, where a 'new habit' becomes easier and does not require so much energy. The 'bad' news is that it takes a further six months to convert the plasticity of your brain to 'rigidity' where the habit is 'permanent'. This is why we suggest that Mind Chi becomes a way of life. Repeat the Mind Chi Program every day, but change your goals over time. To make the specific new skill become permanent, use spaced repetition (Memory, page 278) and your new good habit will stay with you for life.

When you have completed 28 days of Mind Chi and have Applied yourself to achieving your Mind Chi Goal, make sure that you have some form of celebration! Tell some associates as that helps to reinforce the continued new behaviour. Reward yourself. Wallow in how good it feels to have control and to have built your power of commitment. You will probably feel inspired to start a new Strategy for Success!

The awkwardness gap

Developing any new skill requires practice, adjustment and perseverance to gain the skill. There is no straight line of progression from start to completion.

In developing your volition and completing your commitment there will be times when the process feels awkward and you may find yourself in a 'dip' – seemingly unable to progress any further. The dip is known as the 'awkwardness gap'. It is the 'oops!' factor – a hole you may fall into and need to pull yourself out of. It is awkward because it feels unfamiliar and your brain likes safety and familiarity.

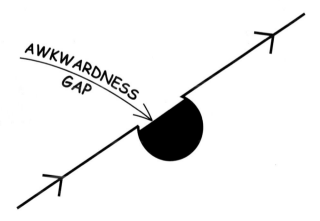

The awkwardness gap

Imagine you are a self-taught golfer or tennis player who decides to have a few lessons from a professional to improve your game. The pro tells you how to hold the club or racket and shows you how to correct your grip. Immediately if feels awkward and you want to revert to your old way. However, if you want to improve, you need to learn to adjust your grip and keep practising.

To progress, you will need to focus your awareness (check your Mind Chi BEAT), adjust to the situation, choose to pull yourself *out of* the gap *towards* your goal, and see yourself as though you have achieved your outcome.

Making it permanent

Now you know that it is, indeed, Mind Chi-easy!

Woo hoo! You have achieved your first Mind Chi Plan. You can now be confident that your new mind pathway has become a highway and, with maintenance, it should remain permanent. Wonderful! Now that you understand the process you will feel comfortable applying it to anything you want to achieve.

Two worked examples

We present two worked examples for you here, so you can really see Mind Chi in action.

We have selected a business strategy: 'Making decisions', and a personal strategy: 'Achieving your perfect size'. However, if you are feeling comfortable with the process, by all means zoom on to Part 3 and get started with your own strategy for success!

By this stage you will have completed your 28 days of the Mind Chi Basic routine and already be experiencing the overall positive effects. You are ready to tackle an area that you wish to improve. You have great trouble choosing a plan and so decide that 'Making decisions' is the one. Ha! A step in the right direction – you have just made a choice!

Read the Mind Chi Plan carefully to make sure that each element of the BEAT is true for you now and for what you want to experience. If you want to make amendments, then either go online and download a blank plan, or use the one provided on page 333, and amend it. It is important that the words are right for you and really repel you (left column) and attract you (right column).

Making decisions

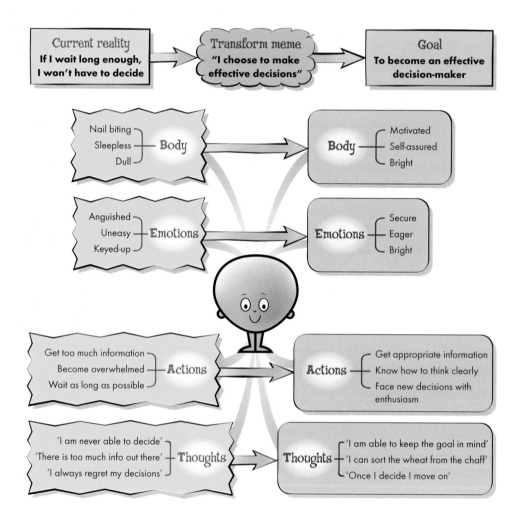

Mind Chi in action

Use a map (page 73) to help assess your decision-making choices. Depending on the seriousness of the decision you need to make (and the amount of time you have to make it) you might do all or some of these steps:

1   Start with a quick, mini-map of your thoughts and feelings. What are your options? What are the consequences (if you know them) of those options? What are your gut reactions and feelings? Put this map aside for a while and when you look back at it, does anything else pop into your mind?

2   Do your homework. Do you need to speak to people before making your decision? Do you need to do research? Decide on an appropriate level of preparation. Please note the word 'appropriate',;there will always be new information coming and you have to decide when to cut and run. Decision making is made harder if you feel you need to know *everything* before choosing your action.

3   Are others also involved in your decision? If yes, what are their opinions? (Even if they cannot be met, the fact that you are considering them is important and may bring up something that you had not thought of.)

4   When there is a very big decision to be made, and where big emotions may also be involved, try to make time to create a mini-map per day/week/month to capture your 'gut' feelings – and then review them all for consistent reactions.

5   For complex decisions you may also want to put on a 'weighting scale' – here you can assign a value (from minus 100 to plus 100) to each aspect and then add them all up and see what that says about your order of priorities.

6   If one or two decisions seem to be equally OK, then toss a coin! Yes! As soon as it lands observe closely your gut reaction. If your heart leaps, you have a winner! If you instinctively groan, then rethink. There is great wisdom in the right cortex of the brain that can 'see'

the whole picture and sends you a 'feeling'. It is wise to listen to that inner voice, your 'Chi' speaks!

7   Decide and commit! Yes, the world will change and maybe in hindsight you could have decided differently, but know that you did the absolute best you could at the time and with the knowledge you possessed. So go with it and be happy!

8   Be aware that to NOT make a decision IS still a decision – with its own consequences. There is NO escape. You will ALWAYS be making decisions, even if you think you are not!

Mind Chi Applied

Steps 1, 5, 6 and 8: Should still be done. They remain the same as for Mind Chi Basic.

Step 2: ATTEND – Repeat: 'I choose to make effective decisions'

Step 3: ADJUST – Rewind and adjust any times that you ducked a decision.

Step 4: ASSOCIATE – Review and associate all the times you decided well.

Step 7: PLAN – Preview the next 24 hours as though you are a super decider.

Perform your daily action steps using ADOCTA to refine your actions until you know you have become an effective decision-maker.

28 days of Mind Chi in action

Prepare your plan and make several copies to place where you will see them numerous times every day:

Day 1

- Start your Mind Chi Tracker (either electronic or by hand) and mark your 28 days (plus a few days, just in case!).
- Read over the Action points opposite the plan to give you a 'starter for 10'!
- Make sure that the Mind Chi Meme (the phrase that your 'Chi' will now say to support and encourage you) is right for you, for example 'I choose to make effective decisions'.
- Modify your Mind Chi Basic routine to become Mind Chi Applied. For 'Making decisions', it would be modified as follows:

Step 1: BREATH – The same as Mind Chi Basic (page 43).

Step 2: ATTEND – Focus on your Mind Chi Meme: 'I choose to make effective decisions'.

Step 3: ADJUST – As you rewind your past 24 hours, look particularly for times when you postponed or ducked out of making a decision, no matter how small. For example a colleague says, 'Shall we meet on the 13th or the 21st?' and you say, 'Oh, I don't mind, you choose!' Rewind that to observe it, count it, and brush it off your non-dominant hand at the end of the minute. (You want to increase your awareness to be able to improve in the future, not berate yourself.)

Step 4: ASSOCIATE – As you review the past 24 hours, look particularly for times when you made a positive step towards improving your decision-making ability. You might say, 'Oh, actually the 13th would be better for me'. Well done! Now count that on your dominant hand at the end of the minute, squeeze that success into your memory. When you squeeze your hand in future, you will associate the action with being known as a good decision maker.

Step 5:   BE AWARE – Check your BEAT, both in general and with specific thought to moments when you were involved in any form of decision making.

Step 6:   CHOOSE – Choose your BEAT for now, to make good decisions.

Step 7:   PLAN – What opportunities does the next 24 hours hold for you in the decision-making department? Will you make even the easiest decisions such as tea or coffee? Will you pick up your dry cleaning on the way in to work, or going home? Give yourself points! Notice how many decisions you do make, and flex and build that memory. Experience yourself making bigger and better decisions that might occur in the next 24 hours using multi-sensory memory triggers.

Step 8:   BE GRATEFUL – Your joy-filled last step is to be filled with gratitude for all that you have done and will do to improve in becoming an effective decision maker.

You might want to give yourself a score (from 0–10 or 0–100) for how you felt you did overall and mark that on your tracker.

Day 2

Having worked out the way you will shape your Mind Chi Applied to 'Making decisions' all you need to do now is to decide when and where you will do it each day. (This may be the same time and place as when you did the Mind Chi Basic.) Now DO it!

During the next 28 days how are you going to prepare for that big decision you have to make? Let's say your decision is whether and where to move house. NOTE: some BIG decisions may take longer than the 28 days; just extend the whole process until the desired result is achieved (as in this case when one of the authors moved house!).

You may want to start to map your overall actions and steps. Map out the crucial aspects, such as: price; location; size; ambiance; critical (and flexible) features and some 'wild' alternatives. Then sign up with various estate agents in the appropriate areas.

Make sure that you are taking some action step towards your desired goal every day. Remind yourself of the negative of the current reality and keep yourself inspired with the multi-sensory rapture of the attained goal.

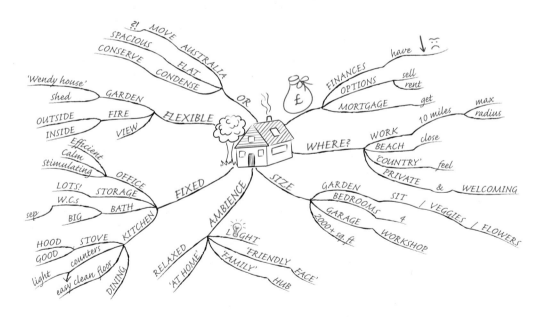

A map of the desired house helps when sifting through all possible alternatives

Day 3

Perform your Mind Chi Applied steps and give yourself a rating on your tracker.

Decide how many possible houses you will search the internet for, and when and for how long you will do that. Contact the appropriate agents and set up viewings (group them for the weekends and evenings).

Day 4 onwards

Keep repeating the appropriate steps; this is where the ADOCTA is so helpful. As long as your goal remains the same, then decide on an Action, Do it, Observe what happened, Consider if it took you closer to your goal (or not), Tweak as necessary and select the next Action that you need to Do.

In the case of the house selection, there was also the issue of financing which ran parallel and integral to the final decision. As the selection process was narrowed, greater emphasis needed to be placed on that issue.

Refer to your research; remind yourself what you need to do. What others might be involved in the decision? A quick glance over the map keeps all aspects in your mind.

Keep performing your Mind Chi Applied routine and note your result each day on the tracker.

Day 24–26 (or whenever you experience the following)

Let's say that you realize that you are 95% of the way towards achieving your goal. Whoopee! And beware!! Sometimes that last push to complete the final 5% can be where you can quit: 'Oh I am nearly there, that's good enough!' What actions do you need to take to complete? Give yourself the satisfaction of the wonder of completion. Take those closing steps.

Keep performing your Mind Chi Applied routine.

Day 27 (or whenever the goal post is right there)

What finalizing steps might you need to take? Plan them into your day.

Perform your Mind Chi Applied with extra emphasis on Step 8 – being grateful for all you have achieved.

Day 28

Is this a habit that you feel you may need to review to make permanent (see page 278) or have you achieved what you want?

Celebrate with something that makes you really realize that you have succeeded and achieved a new level of personal and professional functioning.

(Author Postscript: the perfect house was found and is now being greatly enjoyed!)

Achieving your perfect size

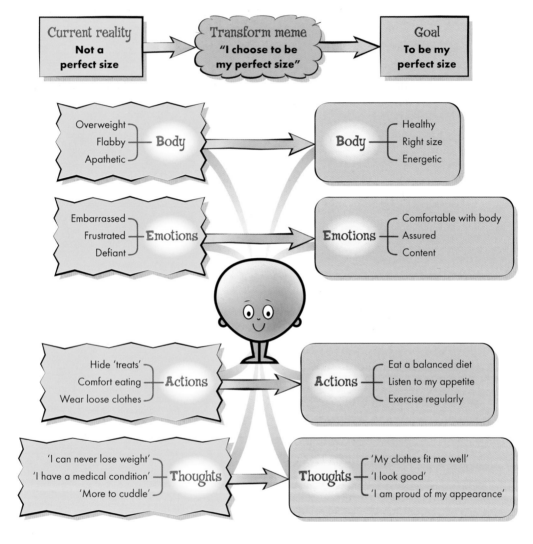

Please note that we carefully did NOT call this strategy 'Become Slimmer' or 'Lose Weight' because these are loose, non-specific goals with the danger of an unhealthy outcome.

Mind Chi in action

Numerous things can affect your 'perfect' size. It does not stay constant throughout your life. Only a *very* small proportion of people are overweight because of disease or the side-effects of medicines. Recent research (although this science is still very young) has NOT been able to prove a 'fat gene', only that the reason people are overweight is because of their lifestyle.

There are only three factors to consider:

1   What you put into your body.
2   What you do with your body.
3   Your Mind Chi direction.

Let's look at each of those.

What you put into your body

- The more sugars, carbohydrates, 'empty' calories and fatty or preserved foods you eat, the more weight you will put on. If your diet has fresh fruits, vegetables and lean meat or fish you are less likely to put on weight.
- How often and how much do you eat? Many people tend to 'graze', losing the delight of the feeling of being 'hungry'. Try three meals a day; eating them when you feel hungry.
- Develop 'delayed gratification'. If you keep busy, or do something physical, you will often find that your 'hunger' disappears!
- Help yourself by using a small plate (especially at 'all you can eat' restaurants). A simple rule is eat 20 percent less for every 20 years of your life – as long as you are maintaining the original level of activity.
- Most importantly, eat SLOWLY. Your appetite is a bit slow at informing you of sufficiency! If you eat very fast you are more likely to say, 'Gosh, I am STUFFED!' Put your knife and fork down and talk (with your mouth empty, please) to your table companion (pet, teddy bear).

What you do with your body

- Just as longer car journeys use more petrol, so too the more active you are, the more calories you burn. If you want to eat that dough- nut, you must walk fast for an hour to burn it off!
- The ONLY way to lose weight is to burn MORE calories than you eat. That is it!

Your Mind Chi direction

- Your motivation to overeat is complex, as 'hunger' is often a ruse feeling for missing love, attention, satisfaction or confidence. The 'hunger' is momentarily satiated by food, (drugs, nicotine or al- cohol) but the subsequent 'low' afterwards requires you to crave MORE the next time. That causes a very negative downward spiral. Becoming aware of what is really happening is already a big step in the right direction.
- Enrol your 'Chi' to assist you. Make a commitment to your new size, with a new outfit as the reward. Your volition (willpower) will take you there. Tell those closest to you of your goal, so they are your supporters.
- What are your habitual triggers? The phone ringing triggers the need for a chocolate? The end of a day requires several glasses of wine? It is 1 p.m. and time for lunch?! Use delaying and distracting activities until your trigger melts away.
- It is very important that you use moderation and still enjoy life! So, if it is your birthday, have that piece of cake and plan to run a bit further the following evening. Keep flexible and at the same time, steadfast in your direction.

Your Mind Chi in action

As before, look carefully over the Mind Chi Plan for 'Achieving your Perfect Size' to be sure that the BEAT of the current reality and goal is what you have and want to experience. If it is not, then amend it. It is important that the words work well for you.

Having prepared your plan and made several copies which you have placed where you will see them numerous times every day, you are now ready to begin the Mind Chi Applied routine and put your Mind Chi in action.

This is how it goes:

Day 1

- Start your Mind Chi Tracker (either electronic or by hand) and mark your 28 days (plus a few days, just in case).
- Read the action points opposite the plan to encourage you.
- Make sure that the Mind Chi Meme (the phrase that your 'Chi' will now say to support and persuade you) really suits you. 'I choose to achieve my perfect size', 'I choose to be the healthiest version of myself possible'.
- Prepare your Mind Chi Applied for Making Decisions by:

Step 1: BREATHE – The same as Mind Chi Basic (page 43).

Step 2: ATTEND – Your Mind Chi Meme: 'I choose to achieve my perfect size'.

Step 3: ADJUST – As you rewind your past 24 hours, particularly look for times when you did not follow the guidelines you have given yourself. A colleague brought in doughnuts and you ate three. Just observe and consider what will you do next time? Just have one. Count this on your non-dominant hand and brush off any bad feelings as your minute ends.

Step 4: ASSOCIATE – As you review the past 24 hours, particularly look for times when you made a positive step towards achieving your perfect size. In the scenario above, you took three doughnuts, then realized what you had done and offered them to your desk mates. Bravo! Now you can count that activity on your dominant hand and associate that behaviour with your increasing success of attaining your perfect weight.

Step 5: BE AWARE – Check your BEAT, both in general and with specific thought to moments when you were involved with food (or empty calorific drinks, such as alcohol).

Step 6: CHOOSE – Choose your BEAT for now. Keep your meme in mind.

Step 7: PLAN – What opportunities do the next 24 hours hold for you to work towards your perfect weight? Look at both where you can restrict as well as work off what you put in! Experience yourself at a multi-sensory level looking super in that new outfit.

Step 8: BE GRATEFUL – And your joy-filled last step is to be filled with gratitude for all that you have done and will do to become your perfect size.

You might want to give yourself a score (on a scale of 0–10) for how you felt that you did and mark that on your tracker.

Day 2

1   Having worked out the way you will shape your Mind Chi Applied to 'Achieving your perfect size' you need to decide when and where you will do it each day – and then, DO it!

2   What is your realistic goal and size? You may want to start to map your overall actions and steps on Day 2. Over the next 27 days how are you going to help yourself to become that perfect size?

3   Tell your closest associates your goal so they can become your coaching team to success. Further they won't inadvertently derail you with 'Oh I bought YOUR favourite doughnuts in today!'

4   Make sure that you are taking some action step towards your desired goal every day. Remind yourself of the negative of the current reality and keep yourself inspired with the multi-sensory rapture of the attained goal.

Day 3

1   Perform your Mind Chi Applied and give yourself a rating on your tracker.

2   Put away your dinner plate and choose to eat from a smaller one. Prepare a bag of celery or carrot sticks to take into work. Park further away from any door you need to go through and walk.

3   Notice any areas that were a problem yesterday and consider what 'coping strategies' you can put in place.

4   Do some extra activity, even if it's low level. Start the good new habit.

Day 4

1   Perform your Mind Chi Applied and give yourself a rating on your tracker; how are you doing?

2   What physical activities can you do? Sign up for a salsa class, or join a walking group; something that you will enjoy so it is not a chore.

3   Realize that if you don't buy it, you can't eat it! Make sure there is *no* ice cream in the freezer; *no* bags of crisps sitting about; *no* cakes and biscuits or chocolates as easy nibble food.

Day 5

1   Keep repeating the appropriate steps. This is where the ADOCTA is so helpful: as long as your goal remains the same, then you decide on an Action, Do it, Observe what happened, Consider if it took you closer to your goal (or not), Tweak as necessary and select the next Action that you need to Do.

2   Refer to your research, remind yourself of what else you could do to make it as easy for yourself as possible. A quick glance over the map keeps all aspects in your mind.

3   Keep performing your Mind Chi Applied routine and note your result for this day on the tracker.

Day 6

1   Catch and tweak a 'food trigger' today. What activity automatically makes you want to eat (when you don't really need to)? Plan a buffer – a way to distract yourself, or delay your response for 5 minutes, then 10 minutes, and build up until the trigger has lost its power.

2   Perform your Mind Chi Applied and repeat your Mind Chi Meme as many times as you can throughout the day.

Day 7

1 One week has passed! Allow yourself a look at your weight on the scales. Note it on your tracker after you have completed your routine. Just observe. (Remember: muscle is heavier than fat.)

2 Allow yourself a *non-food* treat (if you have been good!).

3 Visit the shop with your desired outfit and admire it. Speak to the attendant about your goal. Feel the material, catch the new aroma and imagine yourself in it.

Day 8

1 Tune in with extra care to the messages from your body. Are the 'hunger' signals real? Is there another hunger that might be under the physical one? Sit quietly and consider (or map) what that might be.

2 Complete your Mind Chi Applied routine and note progress on a scale of 0–10 on the tracker. There is seldom a straight road to success, the important thing is to *just keep going*. Whatever the obstacles, find a way round them. If you forget for a couple of days, just continue the next day; if you have a weak moment and eat some 'rubbish' go for a brisk walk that evening; if you are under stress and just sit in front of the TV all evening – be extra energetic the next evening.

Day 9

1 Thank your 'Chi' for all the assistance you have received so far and consider what you might do to help further. Have a 'conversation' with your 'Chi', maybe as a letter – 'Dear "Chi", How can I assist you to help me with this strategy of achieving my perfect size?' Then start to write a reply from 'Chi' – we know you are making it all up and you might be happily surprised with what you create!

2 What is the next stage of refinement in what you put IN and how you burn it up? Now your 'perfect size' volition is working, you can step up one notch.

3 Complete your Mind Chi Applied routine and record your progress on your tracker.

Days 10–24 (or whenever you experience the following)

1 Let's say that when you come to the *Consider* step of ADOCTA you realize that you are 95 percent of the way towards achieving your goal. Whoopee! And beware! Sometimes that last push to complete the final 5% can be where you quit – 'Oh I am nearly there, that's good enough!' What actions do you need to take to complete? Give yourself the satisfaction and the wonder of completion – completion, in this case, getting ready to purchase your new outfit.

2 Note exactly ALL the calories you consume today.

3 Keep performing your Mind Chi Applied routine.

Days 25–6 (or whenever the goal post is right there!)

1 What finalizing steps might you need to take? Plan them into your day.

2 Perform your Mind Chi Applied with extra emphasis on Step 8 – being grateful for all you have achieved.

Days 27 and 28

1 This will be a habit that you will want to review to make permanent (Memory, page 278).

2 You are changing your whole lifestyle and many traps wait to pull you back. You may wish to do another 28 days or certainly to hit the 'spaced repetition' reminders (page 278).

3 If you have achieved your goal of your perfect size, have a celebration; take a good friend as you go to purchase your new outfit.

4 'Achieving your perfect size' is one of the more difficult of the strategies. You may have been on a diet 'rollercoaster' for years. The difference with Mind Chi is that it provides you with brain-friendly tools to succeed. You logically understand that what you

> Knowing you can trust your volition to serve you well is a heady experience.

put in must be burned off and you have the mental constructs (with the aid of your 'Chi') to shift your thinking and way of being. Be gentle with yourself, but as long as the goal remains the same, keep your ADOCTA working and you *will* achieve.

5 When (notice the use of 'when' *not* 'if') you have achieved this strategy, you will know that you have the volition to succeed and that you can achieve any goal you wish. This is one of the best feelings you can experience.

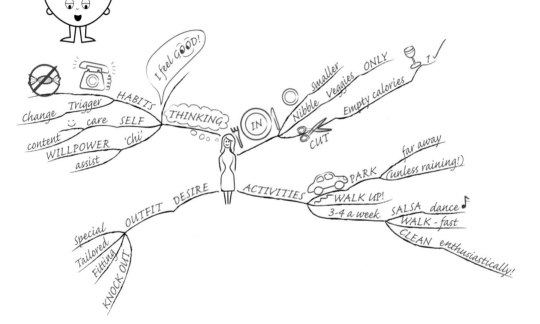

A map of the actions you will take towards achieving your perfect size

8 Mind Chi Change

Overview

The emergent worker
The new security
Stress at work

As we write this book the world is facing unparalleled change. Every aspect of the corporate world as we have known it, financial systems, methods of employment, styles of communication and forms of technology, is transforming before our eyes. What the outcomes will be are not clear but what we do know is the new world of work will be very different from the one we are leaving behind.

How the changes are impacting on you will depend on your personal circumstances. Nevertheless, you will still need a vocation, to make time to play, enjoy relationships and cope with the daily chores. The Mind Chi process can help you to cope and function more effectively than you thought possible as you adjust in the face of this global paradigm shift.

Ask yourself: do you have the necessary skills and knowledge that the occupations of the future will require? Such as being able to cope with information overload by learning to read at one thousand (plus) words per minute, or enhancing your creative thinking so that you can work smarter and adapt to technological change? Your Mind Chi Program will assist you to thrive as the world of work evolves. Old thought patterns will need to be replaced with new ways of thinking – in just about everything. A new style of worker is appearing, known as the 'emergent worker', who updates skills and knowledge to meet the demands of tomorrow's jobs.

The emergent worker

As an 'emergent worker' you will:

- work with new values and expectations,
- want to be rewarded for a job well done,
- expect honesty and fair play from your employers,
- be mobile and flexible, moving from company to company as you work on projects with teams that form and then disband,
- continue to upgrade your skills, knowledge and earning ability,
- understand that you are a brand and be able to sell yourself,
- keep up with cutting-edge technology and use it to your advantage, and
- build a personal network, keep it current and stay connected with it.

In order to achieve all of this, you will need to retrain your brain. You will need to discard outdated ways of thinking. The paradigm shift you are encountering will require new ways of thinking not only about the world you are entering but also about yourself. Mind Chi is designed to assist you with this major transition.

The new security

During the post-war years many employees associated 'the corporation' with security. A job meant a job for life and large businesses looked after employees and their families all their working life – often into retirement. Modern job security lies not within the corporation, but within yourself. Security relates to your ability to think – creatively, flexibly, efficiently – to provide for yourself and to keep on learning.

The purpose of Mind Chi is to provide you with improved mental processes and directed control to make this shift towards secure thinking in a way that is profitable to you. How you think about your self, your team, your boss or your company will determine your ability to thrive – in any circumstance. You will need to have the confidence to think for yourself and not let others do the thinking for you. Another essential skill is your ability to change your focus of attention rapidly, from the big picture to fine detail and back again.

As the financial markets flounder around the globe, so the international currency has changed from money to knowledge. As a knowledge worker the smarter you are, the greater is your value. Learning new skills and knowledge is the new security.

Opportunities to learn, earn and grow

Learning is a continuous state of mind that will last throughout your career and into retirement. Learning keeps you young, and is easier today than ever before owing to the explosion of information that is now readily available on every subject imaginable. The Internet has revolutionized the playing field when it comes to accessing information. Once, what was the privilege of an elite few is now available to anyone, anywhere at just at the touch of a button.

Life-long learning increases your earning potential as well as your growth and development with your organization. Companies pay for expertise. The more you ensure that you remain expert and well-informed in a relevant area, the more highly you will be valued.

In order to learn to manage the ever-increasing overload of information that bombards you every day, it is important to develop the essential process of learning, so that you can discern what is important to you and what is not.

Stress at work

The price of stress to companies has now reached epidemic proportions and costs billions annually in staff changes and absenteeism as overloaded employees suffer from disillusionment, burnout, illness, and substance abuse. The cost to the individual is just as great. Stress can potentially ruin your health (mental and physical), your relationships and the whole quality of your life.

In *Shifting Gears*, authors Collins and Israel explain three different working gears you are presently using on a daily basis:

- In First Gear you are learning new skills and acquiring information.
- In Second Gear, known as the productivity gear, the cry becomes, 'Do it quicker and cheaper'.
- In Third Gear you have a chance to reflect and be creative.

Unfortunately, business is generally obsessed with Second Gear thinking. This constant pressure results in a stressful working environment affected by growing absenteeism and ill-health. To be effective you need to be able to work in all three gears: to learn, work hard, and have time to reflect and create. Using Mind Chi as a work tool will enable you to develop a more balanced approach and a greater chance of creating a stress-free working environment.

Change:
The ONLY
constant!

A quiet revolution in the health field is well underway with the growth of health clubs, an increase in consumer information regarding the contents of food, and the advent of government programs into the dangers of obesity, smoking and excessive drinking. Mind Chi compliments and enables these initiatives by enabling you to control and direct your energy towards improved physical and mental health in a balanced and healthy way.

NOTE: Beware of extremes. Working-out or losing weight to the point of obsession and extreme weight loss creates negative 'Chi' energy that feeds negative thinking and your own internal self-destruction!

PART 3
50 Mind Chi Plans – Strategies for Success

Mind Chi has been developed from established personal development techniques and from the latest research on brain function, and is the result of our combined years of business, training and life experience. At its core is the knowledge and understanding that only by gaining control over yourself and applying a positive attitude and constructive actions will you achieve whatever goals you wish to set. Yes, you will also need information, assistance and new processes to bring about positive change; then remarkable things can happen. When you develop command over yourself, you will also create the belief and desire at a profound level that you can improve and achieve all the things you wish.

The 50 completed Mind Chi Plans: your Strategies for Success (plus any others that you write for yourself) are based on the Mind Chi principles. This provides the understanding that you will achieve progress in any area of life where you are willing to direct your mind's 'Chi' to go forward tenaciously in a positive direction.

The really good news is that you can achieve all that you imagine possible!

By following the Mind Chi Program you can choose to change habit patterns that have not been working in your best interest by replacing them with positive, self-directed practices that will lead you towards the outcomes you wish to achieve.

Following are 50 Mind Chi Plans for tackling the challenges faced most frequently by business people around the world. They are not intended to be all-encompassing; they cover a wide selection of disciplines that are appropriate in practically all business environments.

The map (next page) shows how the 50 strategies have been organized.

- First choose and highlight the topics that you consider important for your self-improvement.
- Next, add any additional personal goals not contained in the 50 Mind Chi Plans and then prioritise your choices. (For example,

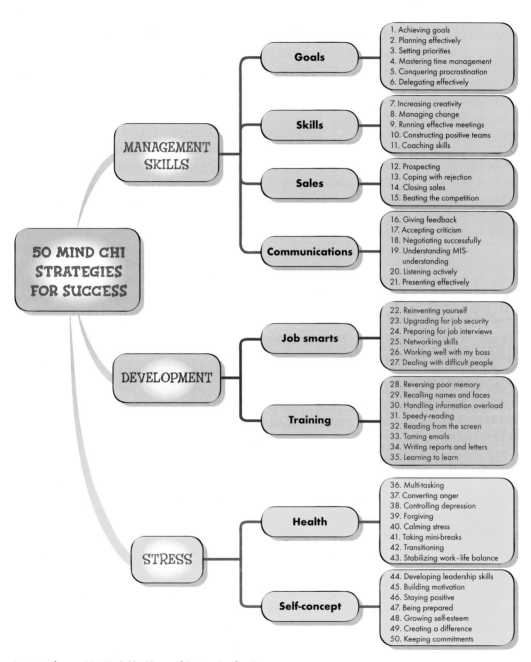

A map of your 50 Mind Chi Plans of Strategies for Success

perhaps you will first select 'Mastering time management', because it will have a positive impact on many of your other Mind Chi Goals, making it a high leverage Mind Chi Plan.)

- After prioritizing your list, off you go!

Mind Chi in action

Look carefully over your chosen Mind Chi Plan to be sure that the BEAT of the current reality and goal is what you have and want to experience. If it is not, then go online and download the plan (or use the blank on page 333) and amend it. It is important that the words really repel and attract you.

Having prepared your plan and made several copies which you have placed where you will see them numerous times every day, you are ready to begin the Mind Chi Applied routine and put your Mind Chi in action. (There are two worked examples starting on page 109.)

Mind Chi applied

Each Strategy requires you deliberately to amend the Mind Chi Applied routine. It remains the same as your Mind Chi Basic routine – but focused on your specific strategy.

- Step 1: BREATHE – Stays the same as the Mind Chi Basic (Breathe – page 46).
- Step 2: ATTEND – Repeat your Mind Chi Transform Meme for the minute, instead of counting (Attend – page 48), without distraction.
- Step 3: ADJUST – As you rewind your past 24 hours, particularly look for times when you did not follow the guidelines you have given yourself. Count these on your non-dominant hand and brush off any bad feelings as your minute closes (Adjust – page 52).

- Step 4: ASSOCIATE – As you review the past 24 hours, particularly look for times when you made a positive step towards achieving your goal. Count them on your dominant hand and, at the end of the minute, squeeze your fist to tell your memory to associate that behaviour with your increasing success of attaining your goal (Associate – page 54).

- Step 5: BE AWARE – Check your BEAT, both in general and with specific thought to moments when you were involved with your goal (Aware – page 58).

- Step 6: CHOOSE – Choose your BEAT for now, take care of yourself (Choice – page 60). Additionally check and choose your BEAT whenever you are performing your new Action Steps.

- Step 7: PLAN – What opportunities do the next 24 hours hold for you to work towards your goal? Experience yourself at a multi-sensory level 'as though' you are there (Plan – page 64). It is crucial for you to experience being or doing your goal, as the brain perceives this as 'real' and acts accordingly.

- Step 8: BE GRATEFUL – Your final joy-filled step is to be brimming with gratitude for all that has occurred and will occur to help you achieve your goal (Be grateful – page 66).

At the bottom of each Mind Chi Strategy page you will see 'Chi' reminding you to do your Mind Chi Applied for the 28 days to make your goal a reality.

You might want to give yourself a score, on a scale of 0–10 (or 0–100), or a comment for how you felt you did and mark that on your Mind Chi Tracker (example – Page 105, and blank Mind Chi Tracker – Page 329).

Also perform your daily action step(s) using ADOCTA! Refine your actions until you achieve your goals by experiencing the Structural Tension between them and your current reality. Use your 'flexible focus' to keep updating what you have now and what you want.

9 Goals

1   Achieving goals

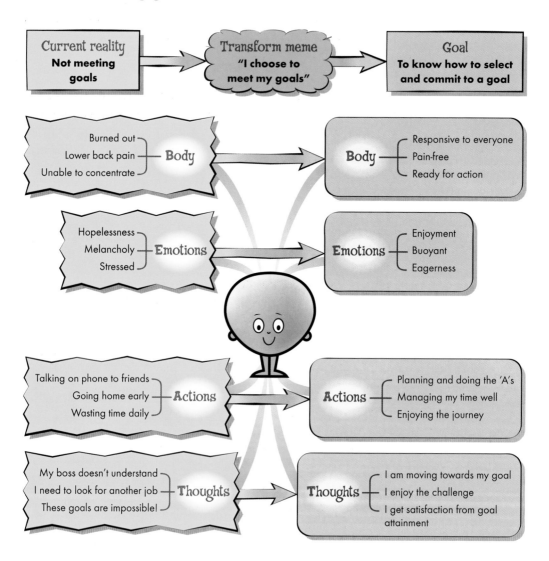

Mind Chi in action

First you must decide upon your next goal, as nothing will happen without one. Some goals are set by others: by the company or department you work for; others you are able to decide yourself. Either way, goals help direct activities through a planning process that includes an action plan with action steps. These need to be practical and realistic. To reach a goal, you must be 100 percent committed to it. Without your full commitment, you reduce your chances of total success. Here are a series of questions to help build your commitment:

1   Do you fully understand the benefit and/or reasons for reaching this goal?
2   Do you know all the action steps that need to be taken?
3   Have you the required energy, resources, people, support, time and money?
4   Have you other conflicting goals and/or priorities?
5   Do you have the persistence and focus needed?
6   Have you the necessary skills and/or knowledge?

Make your goal a reality with Mind Chi Applied!

The answers to these questions determine your likelihood of attaining the goal. Now you can decide what to do next: this could be to quit, change the goal, ask for help, change your priorities, learn new skills or start to make your action plan. If you choose to 'drift' where others lead you, your chosen goal is to not be in control of your own future. (Planning, page 143; and Prioritizing, page 145.)

You will need to create Structural Tension (About Structural Tension, page 265) in order to reach your goal. Ask yourself, 'Where am I now?' (Say 1800 units left of 4000 need to be sold in five days. What action steps must you take to reach your goal?) This flexible focus develops the psychological pull for goal attainment.

2 Planning effectively

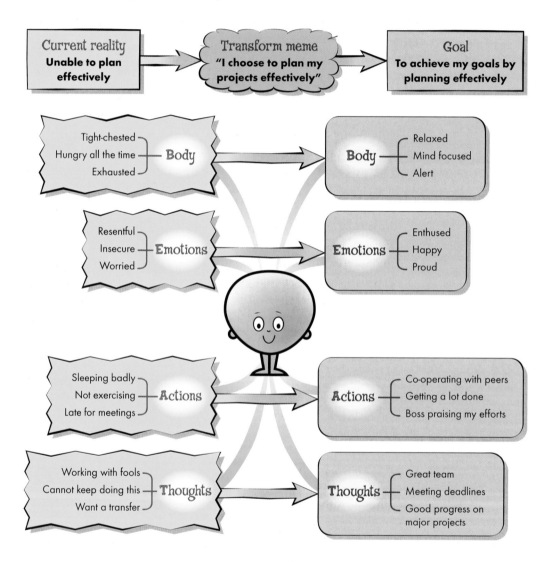

Mind Chi in action

After committing to your goal, create a plan of action to reach it. Planning takes place on two levels: in the 'big picture' organization and in your day-to-day plans. The more detailed your plan the greater your chances of success.

1   Involve your key people in the planning process. Communicating with everyone involved will ensure their buy-in to the process.

2   Schedule uninterrupted time to create or review your plans. Allow time to think of things that might be overlooked and allow for contingencies.

3   When considering the 'big picture', write or map your thoughts on a single sheet of paper so that everything you think of is captured in one place.

4   When developing a more detailed plan, list the action steps individually on small pieces of paper and then arrange the steps. Next write the whole plan out in sequential order or map it with mapping software that can help with project planning and integrated timelines.

5   An effective project map will propel your team towards success; it encourages co-operation and allows the flexibility to respond quickly to problems.

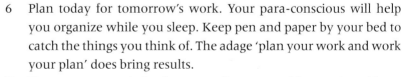

Make your goal a reality with Mind Chi Applied!

On a daily basis:

6   Plan today for tomorrow's work. Your para-conscious will help you organize while you sleep. Keep pen and paper by your bed to catch the things you think of. The adage 'plan your work and work your plan' does bring results.

7   Keep an open mind when you discover problems, as problems often show you a better way forward if you allow for some creative thinking (Creativity, page 156).

8   Reward yourself (and the team) as you achieve markers along the way and especially when the whole project is completed.

3 Setting priorities

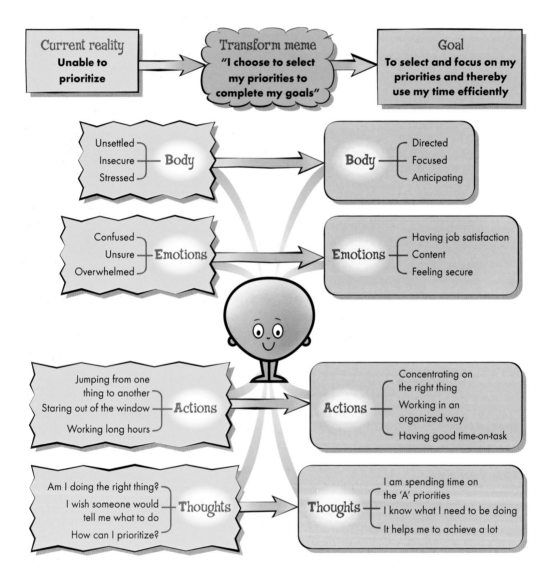

Mind Chi in action

Do you find it difficult to set priorities? Here are some suggestions:

1   Write each activity that is pending on a sticky note. Then sort them. You will find there is a natural grouping or that some things must be done before others. (Check with other people who are involved in stages of the task.)

2   Now look at every activity and consider which things can be done quickly and in one go, and which will require several steps. Colour code them as 'quickies' and 'longies'. Put a 'Q' or 'L' on each activity (or use different coloured sticky notes).

3   Ask yourself which actions will help you to achieve your goals fastest, or what will move you ahead most. Mark them A, B or C priorities, bearing in mind the Pareto principle that 80 percent of your effectiveness comes from selecting the right 20 percent of activities.

4   Think about your personal energy rhythms. At what times of day are you at your smartest and best?

5   Schedule the 'A' items for your 'bright' spots and lump together the 'Quickies' to tackle while you are in a bit of an energy slump.

6   Now keep to your schedule! Don't be reactive, and watch out for time-stealers such as emails and the telephone. You don't have to answer them immediately (unless that is your job!). Make sure that you take enough time to do each task right, the first time. If not, where will you find the time to do it all over again?

Make your goal a reality with Mind Chi Applied!

Warning: If you don't set priorities, a chunk of ten years can fly by while you stay 'busy with the everyday content' just moving lots of stuff about with no achievements to show for it. If you can set your priorities and start to work on the really important things, even if for just a few minutes a day, you will be surprised at how many goals you can achieve.

4 Mastering time management

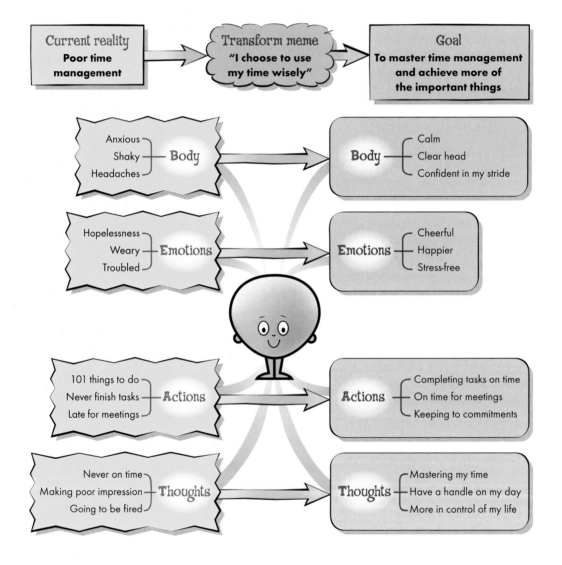

Mind Chi in action

Time is a magical quality. It seems you can stretch and shrink it; but everyone has a daily allotment of just 24 hours. How can you make the most of yours? How often do you experience being 'in the flow' – so engrossed in your task that time seems to disappear? Or are you constantly rushed, with that late 'flutter' inside you? For those who need new ways to manage yourself in time, here is your plan:

1   Map out all you think you have to do, ideally the day before you need to do it. Create a quick brain 'bloom' of all work and non-work related things that are floating about in your head (Bloom, page 76). Leave space for things that you may think of or be asked to do additionally.

2   Now look at your priorities in the light of any imposed restrictions on the day. Do you have some meetings already scheduled? Group complementary activities together (and set a time limit), and break up the long or not so interesting deeds with things you prefer to do (as mini-rewards).

3   Ask yourself what times of day you will be at your brightest and when you will not be so bright. You *could* use your brightest time to do your most difficult work, don't waste it on menial tasks. During your energy 'dip' focus on the things that energize you, such as talking to people, or do something that is fairly routine.

4   Prioritize ruthlessly. First consider the three 'D's. Ask yourself, what can you ditch, delegate (Delegating effectively, page 152) and what do you actually need to do? Highlight or cross through anything non-essential. Then prioritize the 'Do's. If a new 'urgent' comes in, assess what needs to fall off. You cannot do it all.

5   Make sure that you plan adequate time for the 'A' items. Just this one piece of advice can make a great positive difference. Arrange a block of time when you can give your full concentration to an 'A' item, set a timer and 'lose' yourself in the task.

6   Stop and ask, 'Am I making the best use of now? Answering this question will help make the most productive use of your time.

Make your goal a reality with Mind Chi Applied!

5   Conquering procrastination

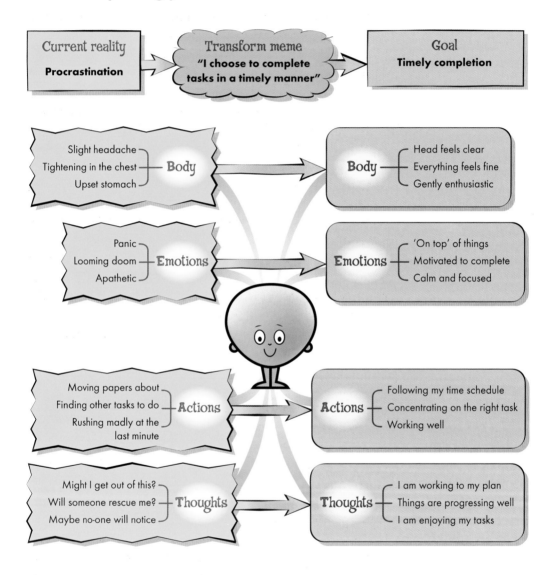

Mind Chi in action

Procrastination is a state of mind and a stressful habit. You know from experience that leaving things to the last moment means that you can never deliver your best work and there will be no time to deal with last minute problems (page 94).

1   If you know that you work better under pressure, create a make-believe deadline that falls several days before the real time due and plan to work 'frantically' to that!

2   If it is a big task, then break it down into bite-sized pieces. Set realistic timelines for each section and reward yourself for keeping to each date.

3   Use the term 'live-line' rather than 'deadline' – it will put you in the here and now.

4   Just start! Even if it is just a matter of taking some paper out, or opening a new file on your computer, do it. Build some fun into the task. Yes, fun! It will help to keep your motivation high and it is always easier to focus on something that is enjoyable.

5   Pick one thing that you usually leave until the last minute and commit to completing it to a suitable timetable.

6   Know that the phone will always ring and e-mail will always arrive, so TURN OFF your phone (or set it to mute); schedule times to check e-mails and build in time for interruptions.

Make your goal a reality with Mind Chi Applied!

7   Keep your eye on the clock. Remember that there is a limited length of time that you can invest in any one task.

8   Learn to let go by working on the 'good enough' principle, especially if you have perfectionist tendencies. Decide in advance what level of perfection is appropriate for the task.

9   If you are always late for appointments, set your watch 5–10 minutes fast. Realize that by being late (either in person or with a task) you are showing lack of respect for others. Someone will be inconvenienced by your poor manners. Concentrate on how it feels to be on time and not rushed and stressed. Revel in that feeling. (Procrastination worked example, page 94.)

6   Delegating effectively

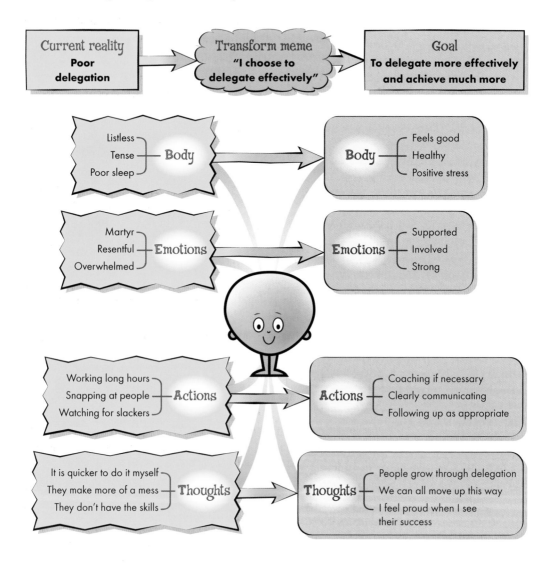

Mind Chi in action

Delegation is an art. As a delegator, you may worry about losing control over your task. Perhaps it feels too much trouble to teach someone else to do the work. You may be anxious that another person could do a better job than you, or conversely, no one could do the task as well – or as fast – as you can. For successful delegation here are some considerations:

1   You need to be sure that the 'delegatee' has the necessary skills. Discuss the task with her and solicit agreement that she will do it in an agreed way.

2   Be clear about the exact nature of the task that you are delegating: your expectations, limitations of the task, and delivery time.

3   Make sure that your communication was understood with an open question. ('Will you tell me what you are to do?' not 'Do you understand that?')

4   Initially, check in quite often, so you are sure they are starting off in the right direction. Decrease the frequency as you see their confidence build (and yours too!).

5   Compliment the completion of the steps of the task and reward the conclusion of the whole task.

6   If you see things going wrong, take action quickly by asking how they see the situation and what do they think they can do. (Do NOT rush to take it back, just help them to fix it.)

Make your goal a reality with Mind Chi Applied!

7   If they demonstrate 'selective ineptness' – another term for 'I don't want to do this', do not rise to their bait, but ask what tools or skills they need to be able to do the job.

8   Delegation does not mean abdication of responsibility, so keep in touch and remember that the task was a part of your job and you are still ultimately accountable.

9   Remember that if you give someone a task with certain responsibilities, he or she must also be given the appropriate authority to be able to carry them out. One must go with the other.

10 Management Skills

7   Increasing creativity

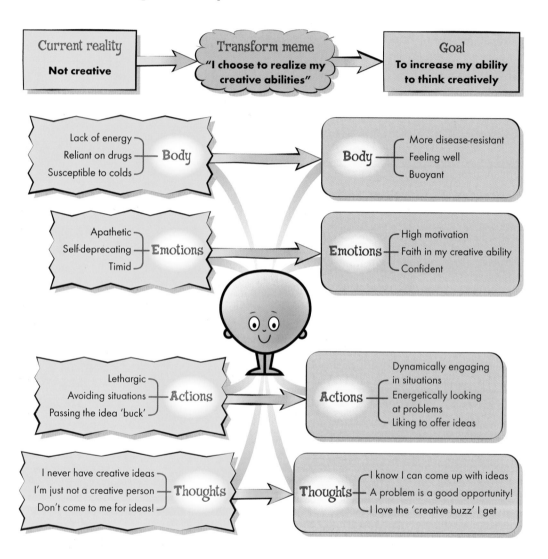

Current reality
Not creative

Transform meme
"I choose to realize my creative abilities"

Goal
To increase my ability to think creatively

Body
Lack of energy
Reliant on drugs
Susceptible to colds

Body
More disease-resistant
Feeling well
Buoyant

Emotions
Apathetic
Self-deprecating
Timid

Emotions
High motivation
Faith in my creative ability
Confident

Actions
Lethargic
Avoiding situations
Passing the idea 'buck'

Actions
Dynamically engaging in situations
Energetically looking at problems
Liking to offer ideas

Thoughts
I never have creative ideas
I'm just not a creative person
Don't come to me for ideas!

Thoughts
I know I can come up with ideas
A problem is a good opportunity!
I love the 'creative buzz' I get

Mind Chi in action

Ask yourself four questions:

1   *On a scale of 0–100, how creative do you believe yourself to be?* (0 = not at all creative; 100 = bristling with creativity). Write that number down, we will come back to it.

2   *Do you mentally limit what might be possible?* If a baby sees a pen, she explores it for its multi-sensory possibilities (its taste, shape, texture, sound). Adults think 'pen' and simply use it to write. Mostly that is appropriate behaviour, except when thinking creatively; then you want an open 'baby possibility' mind.

3   *What do you think the relationship is between the quantity and quality of ideas?* Most people assume that if the quantity of ideas goes up, the quality will go down. You search for an idea, assess and possibly reject it. This approach cauterizes creative thought by imposing evaluation too soon. The reality is that as quantity rises, quality increases *overall*. This means that while each separate idea may not have value, a part of one idea may connect with a part of another idea and *voilà*! – you have an exciting result!

4   *Where are you when you have your best ideas?* We find the answers vary: floating in the bath; taking a shower; falling asleep; in the garden; running; walking; sitting on a train (or on the toilet!). We have yet to have someone say 'At my desk!' Yet that is where the best ideas are needed.

Make your goal a reality with Mind Chi Applied!

To develop the crucial skill of 'creativity on demand':

- Believe you can come up with creative ideas! Increase your creativity score (Number 1 above) as it will influence how you respond.
- Check your creative limits. Challenge thoughts and beliefs that may influence and stifle your creativity.
- Capture creative thoughts wherever and whenever they appear – using pen and paper, phone, computer or a special 'Ideas' book.

8 Managing change

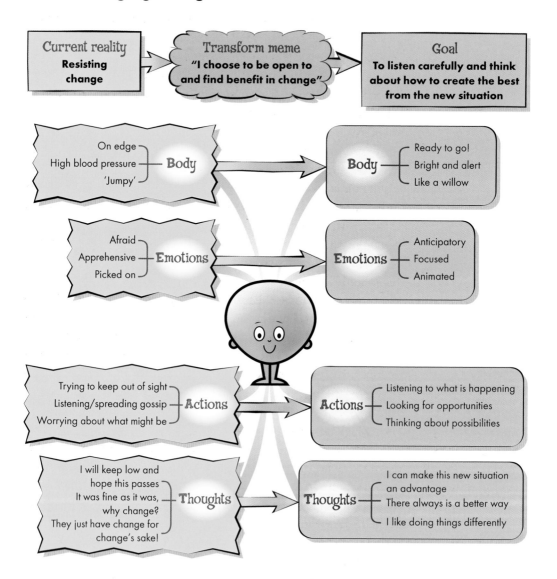

Current reality
Resisting change

Transform meme
"I choose to be open to and find benefit in change"

Goal
To listen carefully and think about how to create the best from the new situation

On edge
High blood pressure — **Body**
'Jumpy'

Body — Ready to go!
Bright and alert
Like a willow

Afraid
Apprehensive — **Emotions**
Picked on

Emotions — Anticipatory
Focused
Animated

Trying to keep out of sight
Listening/spreading gossip — **Actions**
Worrying about what might be

Actions — Listening to what is happening
Looking for opportunities
Thinking about possibilities

I will keep low and hope this passes
It was fine as it was, why change? — **Thoughts**
They just have change for change's sake!

Thoughts — I can make this new situation an advantage
There always is a better way
I like doing things differently

Mind Chi in action

Resisting change in your life may be difficult. Change is inevitable; it happens constantly. Can you look at change as energy? It is like water, constantly able to take different forms and yet always water. It may become ice or steam, yet the same molecular form remains. These steps will help you, so instead of feeling that change is being done to you, you will have control of your aspect of the change:

1   When change first hits you are likely to have some wobbly moments. Think of those wobbly toys with a weighted, round base. Even when pushed about, they always come back to a central resting place. You are like one of those toys. You have an emotional place of equilibrium and can naturally return to it.

2   Once you face the change and start to take the bit between your teeth, you will work out what to do, and where you can lead your part of the change. You are starting to take the reins.

3   When you have sussed out what is happening, you might be able to see advantages in the change. Explore the full potential of your situation and then see if you can gently start to make your mark.

4   Stop, think and question. Give yourself time to analyse situations thoroughly. Are others involved? Before you become concerned, obtain the pertinent information. This will allow you to make informed choices.

5   Think about the consequences of dealing with a situation in various ways. Ask, 'What will you lose?' and 'What will you gain?' 'What affect will this choice have on your career?' And very importantly, 'Why is this being done?'

6   Prepare for change with continuous learning. Somewhere, someone has probably successfully dealt with the same situation. Even circumstances that seem most devastating carry within them the seed of a new beginning and benefit.

7   Be clear about your own values. Your principles will guide your actions.

Make your goal a reality with Mind Chi Applied!

9 Running effective meetings

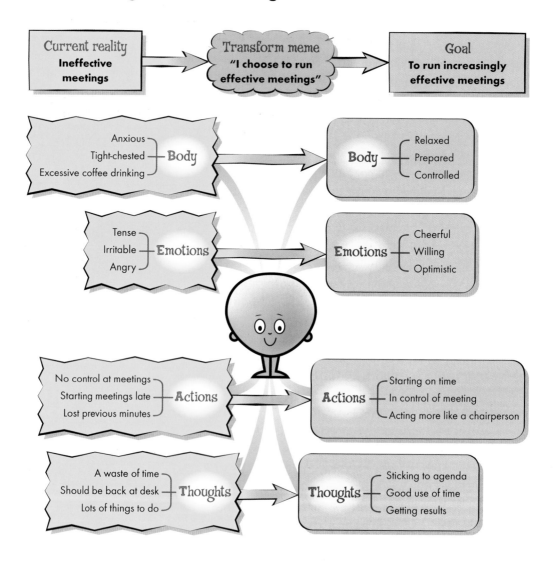

Current reality
Ineffective meetings

Transform meme
"I choose to run effective meetings"

Goal
To run increasingly effective meetings

Anxious
Tight-chested
Excessive coffee drinking
— Body

Body —
Relaxed
Prepared
Controlled

Tense
Irritable
Angry
— Emotions

Emotions —
Cheerful
Willing
Optimistic

No control at meetings
Starting meetings late
Lost previous minutes
— Actions

Actions —
Starting on time
In control of meeting
Acting more like a chairperson

A waste of time
Should be back at desk
Lots of things to do
— Thoughts

Thoughts —
Sticking to agenda
Good use of time
Getting results

Mind Chi in action

Poorly managed meetings can be time-stealers, causing attendees to become disengaged. Sitting through a boring, off-course meeting can drain you for the rest of the day, whereas participating in a purposeful one will move you, your team and your projects forwards. To help you to organize meetings in advance and keep them on track, here are four important ideas to order your thoughts, encourage active listening and make meetings more worthwhile:

1   Set your outcomes in advance. Make your meeting stay on course by asking yourself: Why are you meeting? What needs to be done before, afterwards and by whom? If you are managing the meeting, plan to have it completed within 50 minutes. It can be done!

2   In longer meetings, take a break after 45 to 50 minutes. Your brain can only focus for this long before wandering into a day-dream state and you will lose interest and focus (Memory, page 234). A meeting that presses on for longer will become less productive and more tiring. The break can be as short as five minutes (do not let people return to their desks!) and then you can continue. If your meeting goes into a second hour have water and a light snack available; this will keep up the energy level of the group. After the break, make a quick recap of where you were and what has yet to be achieved.

Make your goal a reality with Mind Chi Applied!

3   Listen purpose-FULLY. This is one of the most important skills you need in life. Take down key points. People speak in real time and once those words are spoken they are gone (Listening actively, page 185). Use 'mapping' (Maps page 73) to help you focus on what is being said. If anything is ambiguous, ask for clarification.

4   Listening and mapping will provide a tight summary of the discussion. Use the map to create minutes and an action plan to agree who needs to do what, by when. This assists accountability. Bring your maps to the next meeting to enhance your recall of what was previously covered and to ascertain that people have done what they should!

10   Constructing positive teams

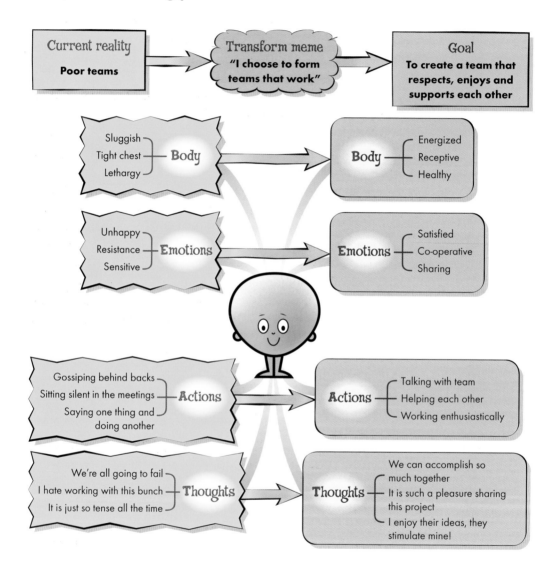

Mind Chi in action

When a team works well together it is magic and worth the effort to make that happen; when a team goes bad, every person on the team will suffer. Here are a few considerations, especially as you start a new team:

1   Every team needs a clear goal that tells them why they are together, what they are to achieve and by when.

2   Everyone on the team needs a role. Make sure each person understands their responsibilities, to avoid MIS-understanding and duplication of effort.

3   A well-balanced team will (or should) comprise of different skills and people types. Typically there will be a visionary – the one who sees the big picture and steers in that direction; the administrator, who will keep minutes and records; the analyser – who will anticipate possible problems – and hopefully their solutions; the synergiser – who tends to bring everyone together and encourages contributions from all; and the action-er – the one who just wants to get started and plods on through anything – just make sure it is in the right direction!

4   If the project is a long-term one, ensure there are plenty of short-term goals to be achieved and celebrated along the way. Make sure that credit is shared. Speak of team success. Introduce a project management process so you can track progress and identify problems in advance.

> Make your goal a reality with Mind Chi Applied!

5   When a group is working closely on a project, it is easy for MIS-understanding to occur. Every now and then, create a 'Bloom' map (Bloom, page 76) to ensure that everyone is still on the same page. (This is especially important when working in virtual teams or with freelancers.)

6   Tell your members 'We are all on the same team', should certain persons need reminding.

7   If the team is unduly negative or unproductive, then close it down and start again – there is no point in it.

11 Coaching skills

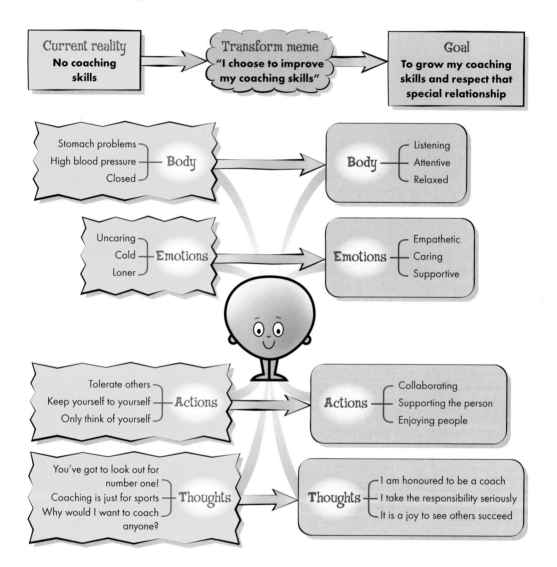

Mind Chi in action

Coaching in business is a relatively new concept and has become very popular. It is different from both counselling and mentoring in that counselling focuses on personal problems and feelings and may delve into the past for insight, while mentoring is usually undertaken by a senior person who takes juniors 'under their wing' and gives advice. A business coach is more like a coach in sport: the coach doesn't hit the ball or swim the pool, but harnesses the athlete's training to maximize his ability.

1 Coaching is a collaborative process, in which the role of coach and 'coachee' are clearly defined. The coach is responsible for keeping the conversation focused on a clearly defined goal, facilitating the other person's thinking, keeping track of progress and delivering constructive feedback; the coachee is responsible for generating ideas and options, taking action to achieve the goal, and reporting back on their own progress.

2 Coaching is a 'goal-focused conversation'. The coachee sets themselves a goal (even if it stems from a problem) that meets all the SMART criteria: Specific, Measurable, Achievable, Realistic and Timed. The coach moves as quickly as possible to help the 'coachee' look at the possible solutions and how they can be achieved.

Make your goal a reality with Mind Chi Applied!

3 A coach needs to listen more than talk. A coach is NOT there to give advice, but to assist the coachee to discover his or her own solutions. The coach needs to observe, and reflect back, body language, facial expressions, words and tone.

4 Observational feedback is crucial. Do not make judgemental statements as they are not specific enough. Ask questions such as, 'What was the response?' 'What else could have happened?' Empathize or 'feel' what the other is going through, and ask questions that help personal discovery.

5 Follow through and evaluate. Was the goal met? What did the coachee learn from the experience? What will happen next? Celebrate the actions taken and the completed success.

11 Sales

12   Prospecting

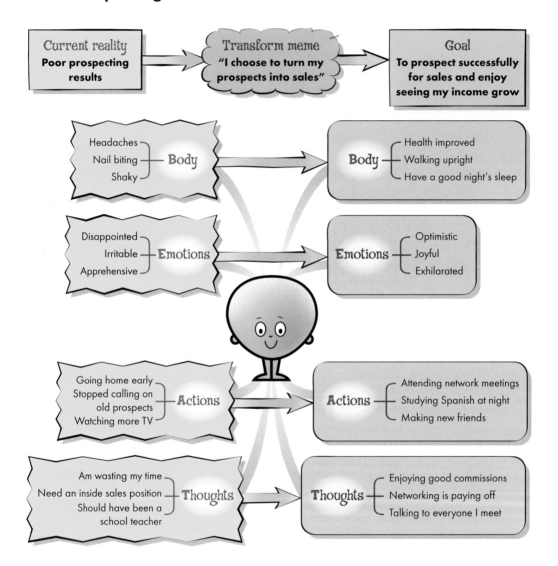

Mind Chi in action

Here are some tips you might consider:

1   Telephone prospecting is the most productive way to build up your sales volume; there is minimum up-front expense and you can do this from any location.

2   Have a highly targeted prospecting list. If necessary buy one with 400–500 names. Always ask satisfied customers for prospective names so that you can keep building your list.

3   Call all the names on your list every four to eight weeks (unless they ask you to stop!). Move the conversation along. If appropriate, ask for an appointment. If the prospect says 'No' or 'I am not interested', thank them for their time and move on. Your time is money too and you must move on to other calls.

4   Schedule your prospecting sessions for two to fourhours daily, with a 10 minute break hourly.

5   Record yourself so you can study the conversation after the call. Did you sound genuine and interesting? How did you respond to objections? What would you do differently next time? This is your best learning tool for improving your prospecting skills.

6   For you to be a successful salesperson keep accurate records. You will be able to review and learn from these. They will save you time from making repeated mistakes as well as reminding you what works best for you.

7   Prospecting really is a 'numbers game'. The most important numbers are your 'Dials per Hour' and the ratio of prospecting 'Offers to Dials'. As you improve your skills you conversion rate of calls to appointments will improve.

8   Ask for three minutes of their time. Most prospective clients would be intrigued. Then have a 2:50 minute snappy presentation ready. After that, the client will either want more information, or not; so your speedy approach will save both of you time!

Make your goal a reality with Mind Chi Applied!

13 Coping with rejection

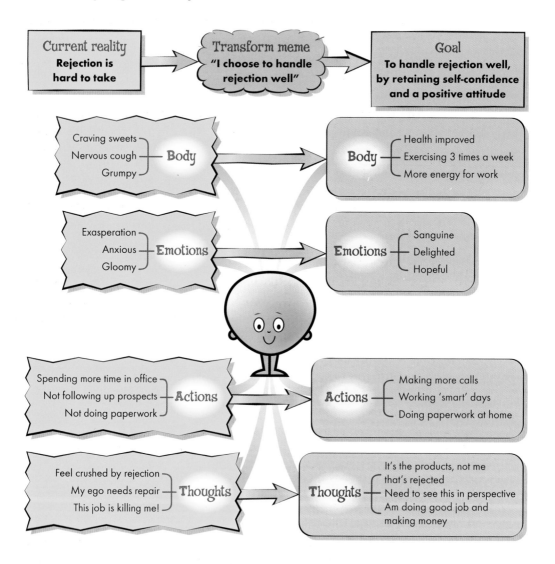

Mind Chi in action

Why is 'No' so hard to take? It is probably the major reason why people quit selling after a few weeks of starting a sales career. Many salespeople take 'No' as a personal rejection and it negatively affects their self-esteem.

There are many reasons why a prospect won't buy or won't even see you, it could be: the price factor, the timing, or that they are satisfied with their present supplier. But even when you know this is the reason, it is far too easy to take rejection on an emotional basis.

The higher your self-esteem the easier it is to be resilient in the face of rejection. Here are some tips on handling rejection in sales:

1   Find the real objection. Ask your prospect: 'When you say "no", is there anything I have not covered?' Then wait for the other person's response. It often leads to uncovering the real objection.
2   Don't take a 'no' personally. Remember, it probably is the product, service or timing that is being rejected, not you.
3   Start a conversation, be friendly and expect the best. If you should receive a 'no', then turn the situation around and ask for a referral. Ask, 'Do you know of someone who might use our product or service?'
4   Be creative and use different styles of approach. Find ones that work best for you and with which you feel comfortable. Be true to yourself and your desire to fulfill your client's need with your product or service.
5   Keeps notes on all your sales calls regardless of the outcome. You are building up a wealth of contacts and knowledge which you can review and continue to learn from. How have you handled rejection? What coping strategies you can use in the future? Are there certain responses that push your buttons?
6   Don't take yourself too seriously. Lighten up and have fun!

Make your goal a reality with Mind Chi Applied!

14 Closing sales

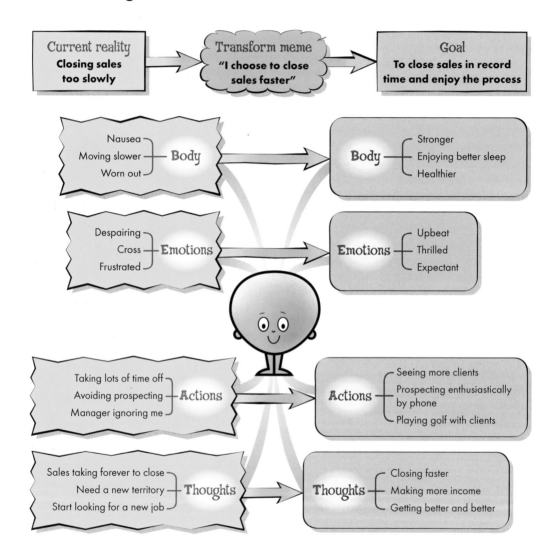

Current reality
Closing sales too slowly

Transform meme
"I choose to close sales faster"

Goal
To close sales in record time and enjoy the process

Body
Nausea
Moving slower
Worn out

Body
Stronger
Enjoying better sleep
Healthier

Emotions
Despairing
Cross
Frustrated

Emotions
Upbeat
Thrilled
Expectant

Actions
Taking lots of time off
Avoiding prospecting
Manager ignoring me

Actions
Seeing more clients
Prospecting enthusiastically by phone
Playing golf with clients

Thoughts
Sales taking forever to close
Need a new territory
Start looking for a new job

Thoughts
Closing faster
Making more income
Getting better and better

Mind Chi in action

Here are some tips to help you close a sale (faster!):

1   Remember that your potential customers have a preferred way of communicating. Are they more visual, auditory or kinaesthetic (physical)? Provide information in the manner that is most likely to catch their attention. If you are not sure, then cover all three styles. As well as the 'big picture' overview to details or vice versa.

2   In the last four feet, the literal or figurative distance between you and your customer, every moment counts. Have you ever walked away from buying something you really wanted because of a negative interaction with the sales person (or process, if you're online)? Treat possible customers as you would like to be treated.

3   Keep in touch regularly. Buyers can change; new decision-makers appear. They may bring other suppliers with them. This is particularly important when you are selling to a committee.

4   Keep informed through the news and industry magazines which affect your prospective client. Stay on your buyers 'front page' by sending article or links of interest on your products or services.

5   Keep abreast of your competitors. Is your prospect happy with your competitors' products and/or services? If not, why not? Is this an opening for you?

6   Keep the sale moving forwards. It is your responsibility to keep the contact. What do you have to do next? Supply samples, testimonials, or some research? Check out specifications? Always have something to take back to your prospective client and ask for the order in a clear and straightforward way.

7   Be creative. Think up new ways to gain your client's attention and sell your product or service. Have fun with this. Be (appropriately) outstanding – you will be remembered.

Make your goal a reality with Mind Chi Applied!

15 Beating the competition

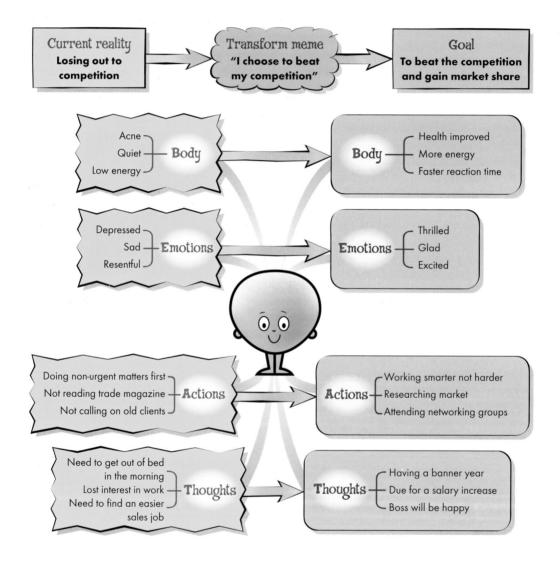

Mind Chi in action

Today there is increased competition between similar companies. You need to use your creative brain to find new and exciting ways to meet the rapidly changing needs of your customers as well as keeping watch for that window of opportunity. Many companies have had to morph as their original product or service is no longer needed. Of course this means there is a new set of needs, so the ability to respond quickly to re-invent your company will keep you ahead of the competition. Here are some ideas:

1   Remember the basics, such as: know your competitors, meet them at trade shows and keep spreadsheets of their facts and figures compared to your own. Do your homework; there is no substitute for having all the relevant information to make the best decisions you can. The web is a potent tool here.

2   Look for the windows of opportunity among the (possible) 'bad' news. For example a current economic downturn has meant that people want old items repaired – so repair shops are opening.

3   Have a 'blank sheet of paper' meeting annually: pretend that nothing of your company/business/department exists, and then assess what would be necessary to create it in the current market.

4   Use your 'gut feel' or intuition. You may feel you need to make a decision that isn't obviously on the radar; it could be worth a few well-calculated 'risks' for the potential payoff.

5   Learn from the best. Study successful models or ask your best clients for advice and then incorporate the appropriate strategies.

Make your goal a reality with Mind Chi Applied!

12 Communication

16   Giving feedback

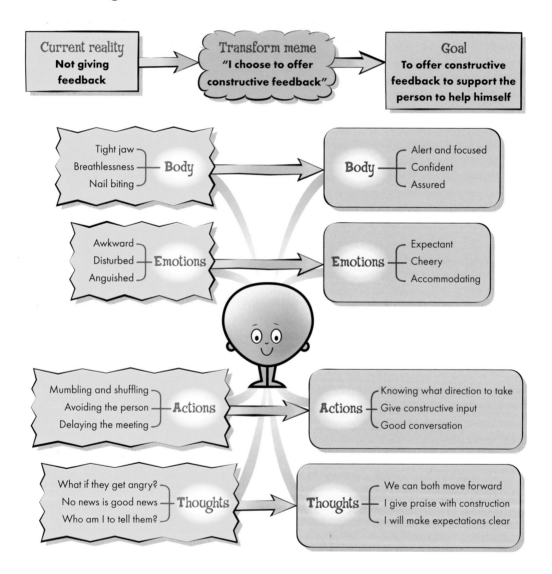

Mind Chi in action

Giving feedback when it is 'good news' is rarely a problem, but delivering negative feedback is more challenging. Negative feedback tends to raise the recipient's defenses and they may feel 'punished'. Here are some points to consider when giving feedback to make it as positive and constructive as possible for both of you:

1   Agree with the recipient their preferred time to receive feedback, a time when they are more likely to be open to discussion.
2   Choose an environment where you can share information privately and in comfort.
3   Carefully prepare your feedback; have the necessary documentation and specific examples ready.
4   Listen actively, by asking for clarification, and paraphrasing key points to make certain you heard and understood correctly (Listening actively, page 185).
5   Work with them to attain solutions that they feel are doable, or assist them to achieve the necessary skills.
6   Couch what you have to say in a positive, objective, constructive, realistic and future-oriented manner.
7   Look at the situation from their perspective; attempt to understand why they perform as they do.
8   Remember that it is human nature to give more weight to negative feedback. You might say four positive things and one negative thing, yet the one they remember will be the negative comment. Therefore, present your negatives in positive outcomes as much as possible; start and end your conversation with something positive (Memory, page 271).

Make your goal a reality with Mind Chi Applied!

17 Accepting criticism

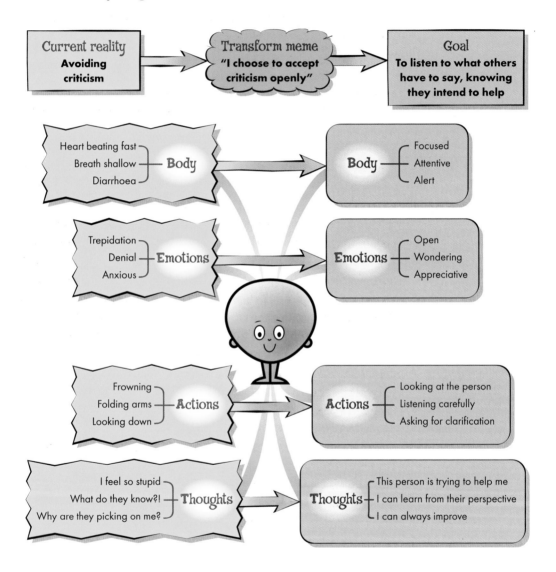

Mind Chi in action

Think of criticism as constructive, in whatever form it takes, as it tells you something about yourself as well as the person giving the criticism. The person who is giving it is in some way showing you their truth or enlightening you to the effects of some behaviour of yours. It is not necessarily a matter of 'fault'. Once you understand this, you can both move forward. Here are some pointers to help you have a broader view on receiving and accepting criticism:

1   Take the comments at face value. This is their opinion and they are sharing it with you. You do not need to respond, or change; just understand that is how they feel. It is their truth.

2   Make sure that you understand why the person is giving their views to you. If appropriate, ask for some clarification. This helps you to stay neutral and open to what they say. If they are making broad judgemental statements ask for more specific behaviours – 'You are a slob' is not helpful. 'Your work space is so untidy that I'm embarrassed to invite clients into the office. I feel it makes us appear unprofessional', clarifies a specific problem (Listening actively, page 185).

3   Ask what they would suggest you do. It might be that they do have a good suggestion.

4   Ask for some time to think before you respond or react. Calmly consider what they have said and what merit you give it.

5   Focus on facts, not feelings. We can all improve, heighten our sensitivities and enhance ourselves.

6   Remember that accepting the criticism does not mean that you must act on it. Deliberate on the issue and the person's motives, then decide if you want to modify your behaviour.

7   The change must be your choice, not pushed onto you.

Make your goal a reality with Mind Chi Applied!

18   Negotiating successfully

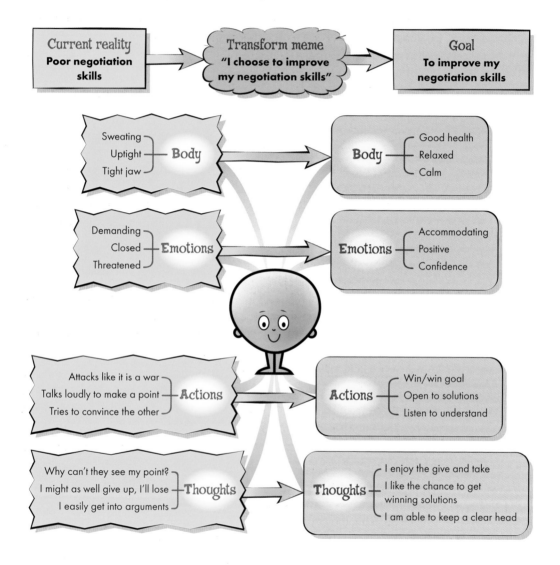

Mind Chi in action

Negotiating is a skill that you use every day – not just in formal negotiations but in conversations, in teamwork, with work colleagues, and especially at home! To negotiate requires finding out what someone else wants, expressing what you want and shaping an amicable agreement. Here are some steps to success for formal or informal negotiations:

1 Know what you (or the company you represent) want and decide in advance what your terms and compromises might be. Do your homework about the other person/company; find their hot spots and concerns. If possible, know their communication style: are they mainly visual, auditory or kinaesthetic (physical); do they tend to look at the big picture first, focus on the detail or vice versa? Mirror their preferred style.

2 Find a neutral and welcoming place to hold the meeting. Be sure that you both know what is about to be achieved and obtain agreement as to the goal/direction. Focus on keeping your body relaxed and your mind open for ways to work together.

3 Have confidence that you can always find a creative solution that improves the situation (Creativity, page 156).

4 Use mapping to identify the core issues (Maps, page 73). It can be useful for each of you to first map out the current problems from your relative perspectives, and then map out the possible outcomes and establish where compromise and mutual ground exists.

5 After the 'maps' have been completed, take a short break and discuss them one by one. You may be amazed that there is a misunderstanding or a flexibility that could easily be corrected or utilized to result in a solution.

6 The map externalizes the problem and becomes something that both sides are looking to solve. It is not a question of, 'I'm right and you are wrong'. In this environment creative solutions can be found that are likely to be an improvement over existing situations.

Make your goal a reality with Mind Chi Applied!

19 Understanding MIS-understanding

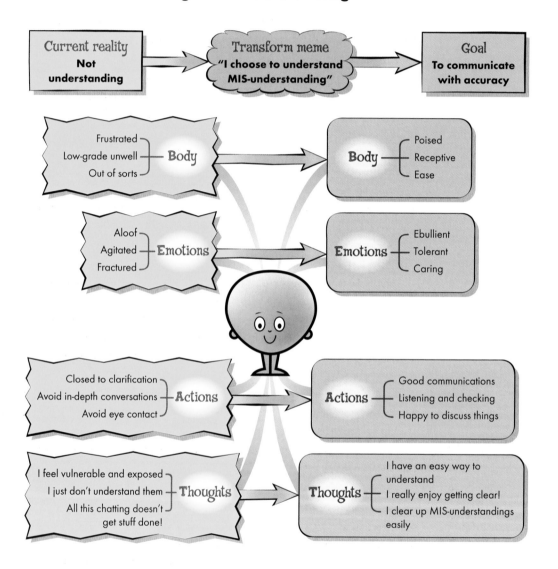

Mind Chi in action

Much of our language is based on abstract interpretation. Meaning is built on the definition of each word, the interpretation of that definition and the relevance of the word in your life to date. When it becomes clear that communication is not working there is MIS-understanding. It may occur during an important negotiation (Negotiating, page 181) or when you make assumptions about people you know or have known for a long time. MIS-understanding wastes time and energy and undermines working relationships. You can use 'bloom' maps to usefully unravel MIS-understanding (Bloom, page 76):

1   If you feel there might be a benefit to clarifying an aspect of a conversation, suggest that you each do a 'bloom' map on the topic or word that is causing the rift (Bloom, page 76).

2   Decide upon the word or topic to be placed in the middle of the page. Do quick, separate 'bloom' maps around that word or topic. Do not share or show at this time.

3   When you have finished (in a couple of minutes), share your words, one person at a time. Observe the words you agree upon, where there is a slight difference of opinion or where you are far apart. Discuss any that you are unsure about. Remember this is not about who is 'right' or 'wrong', you are both working to understand what each other's connections are (Support example, page 190).

Make your goal a reality with Mind Chi Applied!

One of the gifts of this process is that it 'de-personalizes' the situation, so you can talk about even sensitive issues and come up with an agreement and understanding. It is a very simple activity and yet the results are profound. Use it whenever you feel that communication is not as clear as you wish. It is a constructive way to learn about your associates' thoughts and the reasons for their responses. It builds work and personal relationships. An example of a 'bloom' map on the topic of support can be found at the end of this chapter.

20 Listening actively

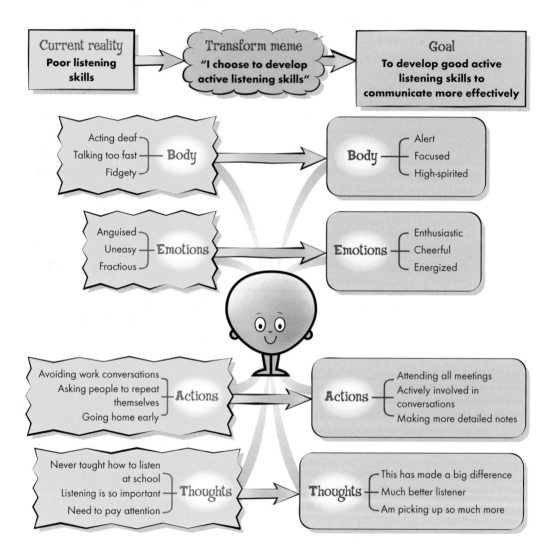

Mind Chi in action

Listening fully in conversation is the greatest gift one person can give another and it requires skill. Unfortunately, few of us have been taught how to listen actively. Part of the challenge is that listening happens in real time with no hard copy to check afterwards (unless recorded!):

1   Keep your attention focused on the person who is talking, not on your response or any other distractions. Watch his or her face. People who feel listened to will enjoy the communication more.

2   Observe facial expressions, tone of voice and stance. If the spoken words are projecting a message that conflicts with the body language (e.g. enthusiastic words but dull tone and crossed arms), enquire about it in your response.

3   Reflect back what has been said to be sure that you have understood. Use your own words. This does not imply that you agree, only that you are sure of the meaning.

4   If the speaker is being emotional it is important to listen objectively. This might be a good time for a bloom map to clarify abstract, emotionally explosive words.

5   After you have really heard what has been said, then it is your turn to speak. If you need time to consider, you may wish to ask for thinking time before responding.

6   Identify the key points that are being made. Map or note them to help your memory. This helps when you recap the key points. It also lets you leave your emotions out of the discussion while you are listening. Ask for clarification when you are unclear.

7   You may feel you do not have time to listen; however, think of it as a long-term investment as it builds your understanding and relationships and may help to avoid wasted time because of misunderstandings.

Make your goal a reality with Mind Chi Applied!

21   Presenting effectively

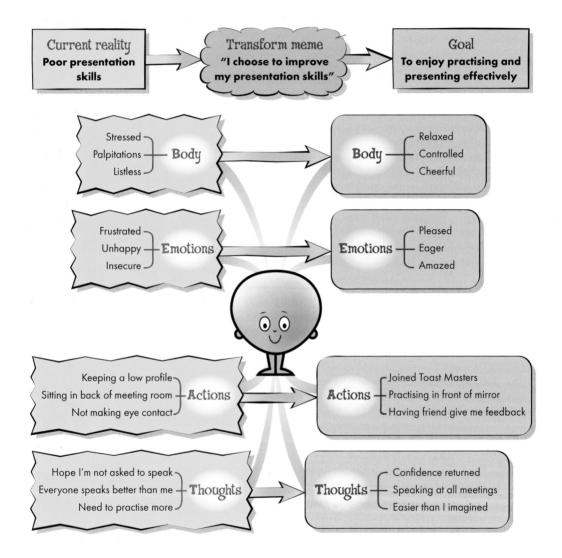

Mind Chi in action

Being able to present well is an important business skill. How can you improve? Two words: practice and feedback. Whenever possible practice in front of a live audience. When practising, ask an associate to sit in the back of the room and note the following:

1   Do you speak to the whole room, or do you tend to speak only to the left or right side (or worse still, to the one person who nods at you)? Do you make eye contact with the audience or do you tend to look down at your feet or up at the ceiling?

2   Assess your body language. Do you stand upright with your body balanced? Are you fidgeting? What are you doing with your hands? Record your presentation so you can notice both your words and actions. (Playback in fast forward shows repetitive mannerisms!)

3   How many times do you use 'hmm', 'err', or 'you know'? Irritating habits may distract your audience from what you are saying.

4   Are you being yourself? It's important to act naturally and not try to be someone you are not.

Useful tips to enhance your style:

Make your goal a reality with Mind Chi Applied!

1   Create a one page handout that summarizes your main points. Include your name and/or contact information on the handout.

2   Don't use notes, they trap you into reading them and you will lose eye contact with your audience. Instead use a map or a page of key points that you can glance at.

3   Use the power of FLORIA (Memory, page 274). Ensure that the First and Last parts of your presentation introduce and summarize the most important points. Include something Outstanding in the middle to wake people up and Repeat your key points in an Interesting way (and by providing a handout). Create Associations to help your audience remember what you are telling them. You will be a hit!

An example of a 'bloom' map on the topic of support

13 Job Smarts

Overview

22   Reinventing yourself

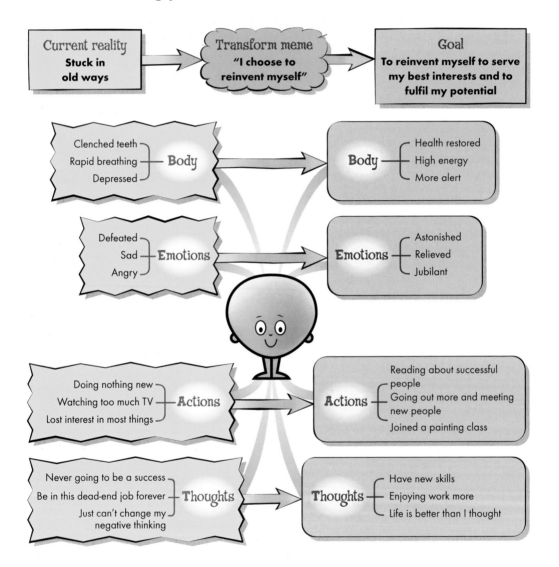

Mind Chi in action

When at work, you are paid for your expertise, performance and the unique 'you' factor, so the more expert knowledge you have, the more value you are to a company. When it comes to reinventing yourself, we recommend utilizing the 'expert strategy'.

1   Pick a topic that interests you, any area in which you would like to be an expert and which you think will be a hot ticket for your future business career.

2   Build your knowledge. Identify, read and map summarize as many books and articles each week as you can manage (Speedy-reading, page 212).

3   Review the information frequently to optimize your recall (Memory, page 278). After several months you will have enough information to be an expert in your selected field. (If you absorb one book a week, a year will see you well towards your 'expert-ship'!)

4   Now you need to market your new expertise. Begin by speaking about your topic at work, local clubs or voluntary organizations. This will give you practice in developing your public speaking skills and let prospective companies know that you are available for hire. Consider writing short articles on your topic, these can be published in the company newsletter, submitted to trade journals, blogs and given out at your talks. Join and participate in the appropriate social networks, forums and discussion groups. This will establish you as an 'expert' and is another way to get work.

5   Decide what companies and job classifications could use this information. A short search on the Internet will reveal the names and addresses of your target population. Contact them with your résumé and published articles. Before you know, you will have become an expert and reinvented yourself in a new work arena.

Make your goal a reality with Mind Chi Applied!

23 Upgrading for job security

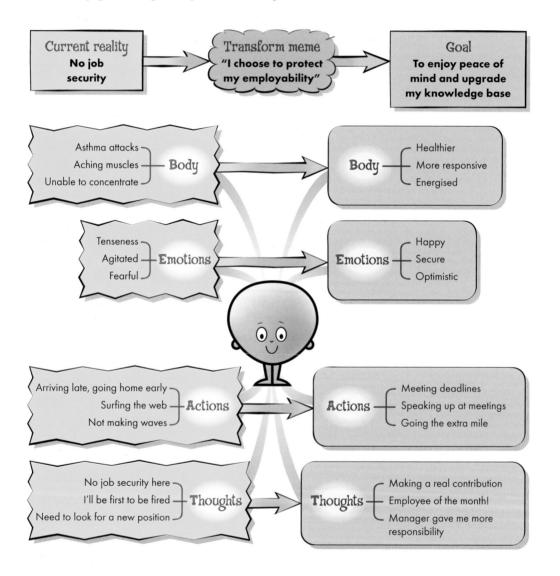

Mind Chi in action

How can you ensure that you remain employable and employed? Start by understanding that change will be a constant factor throughout your life and the best way to ensure employment is to constantly upgrade yourself. You do this with the three upgrading 'I' skills:

1   Info-management. This requires reading, comprehending, note taking and memory skills. You need to be comfortable reading between 800 and 1000 words per minute with about 75 percent comprehension. Use mapping processes to take and make notes as maps also naturally improve your memory. Self-knowledge about your natural memory rhythms and being able to distinguish between what you need to remember and what you need to find out are all necessary and effective tools (Handling information, page 210). Keep current – new information is breaking daily. Make certain you are on top of all the latest news regarding your area of expertise.

2   Innovation. You may need to develop your creativity and innovative thinking, be assured that you do have the capability (Creativity, page 156). Creativity is needed more than ever. Fresh ideas for new jobs, different ways of manufacturing and marketing goods or services will keep you ahead of the competition. Innovation tends to build your motivation as you mentally challenge yourself and come up with the goods. The pay-offs for time invested in developing your creativity are well worthwhile.

3   Interpersonal. Life is about relationships. Start by knowing yourself. Having good relationships with others is much easier when you focus your attention fully on them. This requires that you have a good self-concept and do not feel the need to reflect everything back to yourself in conversation.

Make your goal a reality with Mind Chi Applied!

Be aware that even if you stay in the same job, your job will not remain the same. Upgrading yourself lets you keep up with anything that the world may throw at you.

24 Preparing for job interviews

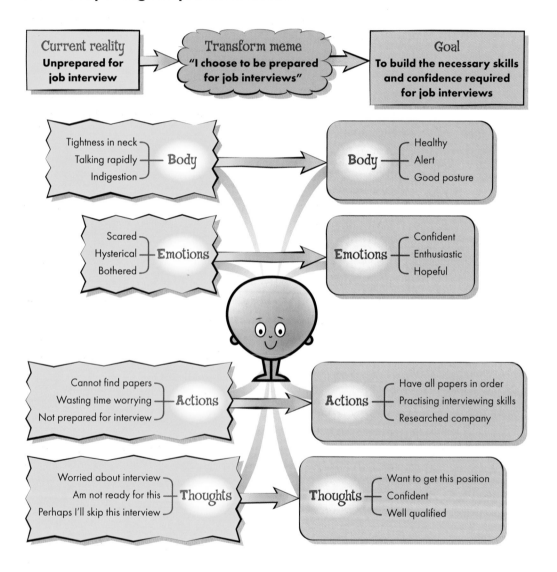

Current reality
Unprepared for job interview

Transform meme
"I choose to be prepared for job interviews"

Goal
To build the necessary skills and confidence required for job interviews

Tightness in neck
Talking rapidly — **Body**
Indigestion

Body —
Healthy
Alert
Good posture

Scared
Hysterical — **Emotions**
Bothered

Emotions —
Confident
Enthusiastic
Hopeful

Cannot find papers
Wasting time worrying — **Actions**
Not prepared for interview

Actions —
Have all papers in order
Practising interviewing skills
Researched company

Worried about interview
Am not ready for this — **Thoughts**
Perhaps I'll skip this interview

Thoughts —
Want to get this position
Confident
Well qualified

Mind Chi in action

Preparation is the name of the game when you want to be a success in that next job interview.

1   Keep your résumé up to date by adding a course or new responsibility. Include community activities, volunteering and fund-raising too. All are skills that relate to your potential work performance.

2   Prospective employers have to read hundreds of résumés, which all look alike. Make yours stand out by being a little different (but remain professional). Be creative. Show samples of your work. Map a summary of your career to date.

3   Practise your interviewing skills with an associate. It helps to video these mock interviews so you can see and hear how you are presenting yourself.

4   Prepare answers to typical interviewing questions: 'Tell me a little about yourself?' 'What do you consider your major strengths and weaknesses?' 'What attracted you to apply for this position and our company?' 'Why did you leave your last position?' 'What do you consider your outstanding achievements?' 'What have you been doing since your last job?' Spend time thinking through your answers, mapping them and practise delivering them. It is quite likely that an interviewer will put you on the spot to observe how you respond. Retain your sense of humour.

Make your goal a reality with Mind Chi Applied!

5   Do your homework. Research the organization, their products and services as well as their competitors and the market in general. Find out the appropriate dress code for that organization; better to 'overdress' for interview if in doubt.

6   Finally, remember that you are also interviewing them. Are they the right company for you? Do they have the right work atmosphere? Will you be able to advance your career as you wish? What are their ethics and standards? Why is this position vacant? Can you see the job description? What happened to your predecessors? Have some questions ready for them.

25 Networking skills

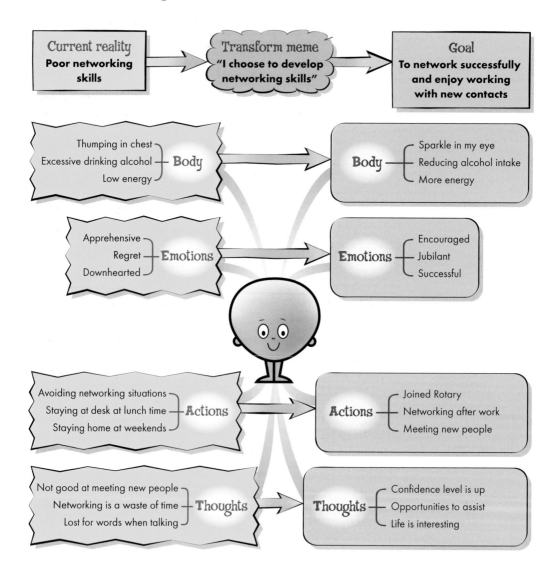

Mind Chi in action

Networking is an essential part of business today. Success is often dependent upon who you know – both in person and online. It is said that we live in a 'global village', that there is a social web that binds us all together and that there are only six degrees of separation between the person you are speaking to and someone you may wish to contact. The key is to know what questions to ask. Here are some steps to grow your network:

1   Find out what you can about the networking event in advance. Study the list of attendees beforehand and decide who you want to meet. Find out about them and their companies from the web.

2   Have your name tag on the right side of your clothing. Always carry your business cards, and a few pens. Supplying another networker with a pen is great way to make a contact (especially if the pen has your business details on it).

3   Study how to remember names and faces (see Recalling names, page 207). Have your 'opener' ready. Think in advance about how your skills and abilities might be of value to those you are meeting. Show genuine interest in the person to whom you are speaking.

Make your goal a reality with Mind Chi Applied!

4   If you said you would follow up after the event make certain you do so, otherwise you will lose credibility. Handwritten thank-you notes (or maps) make a memorable impression.

5   Use the power of social networking. Learn about Facebook, Twitter, LinkedIn, Plaxo and Blogging. These reach hundreds of millions every day!

6   Remember that any occasion, professional or social (supermarket; fitness club; laundromat or party), is a chance to network. Be ready!

26   Working well with my boss

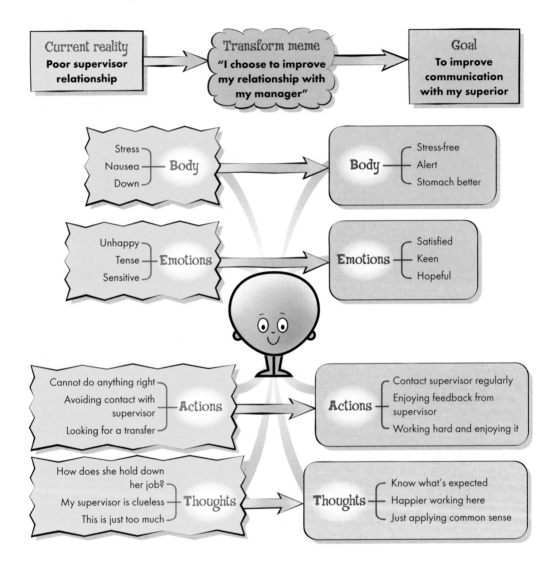

Mind Chi in action

What can you do if you have a boss, manager or superior who is a poor communicator and doesn't inspire confidence? Here are some tips:

1   Instead of avoiding talking to your manager, go out of your way to have a chat. Every contact helps in building bridges. Think through what you are going to say before you actually say it and look for common ground. Open conversation with something positive and keep the door to communication open.

2   Ask your superior to clarify her expectations. This is an important first step as often there is simply a lack of understanding. Matters can soon be resolved and harmony will ensue.

3   Communicate your position. Your boss is not a mind reader and you need to explain how his poor communication is affecting you. Be direct, focus on events and behaviours. Don't play tactical games, and don't personalize. Be yourself and be honest.

4   If you have ideas on how to improve the functioning of the team, share them with your superior. Even if they are not accepted, it shows you are thinking of ways the company can do better.

5   Be empathetic. If the poor communication is out of character, imagine what else might be going on for your manager. There could be health issues, or family problems or she may be under pressure from her boss. You can't change any of those things, but offer support and keep an upbeat and positive aspect about you.

6   If your boss is newly promoted and seems out of his depth, or keeps trying to do your job, he may be suffering from 'The Peter Principle', i.e. a person leaves a position where they were comfortable and successful, and joins an alien 'management' world with new rules. If no training was provided, he may be feeling very uncomfortable. Both the new boss and employee are 'stuck' in the situation. Ask what you can do to assist and support; you may help him over a difficult time.

Make your goal a reality with Mind Chi Applied!

27   Dealing with difficult people

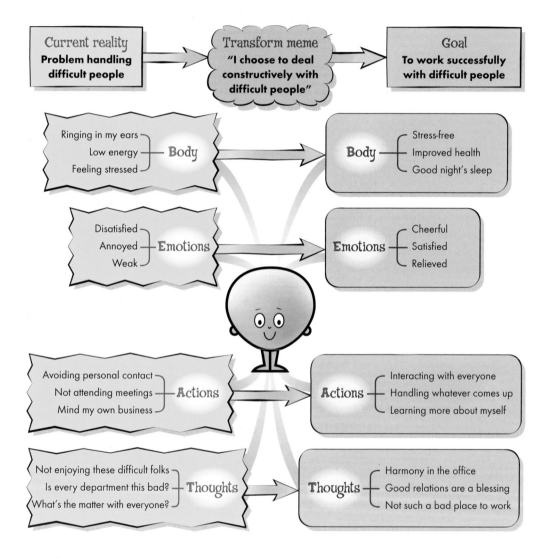

Mind Chi in action

What makes a person difficult? Is it one who does not see eye to eye with you or other members of your team, your boss, a supplier or client? One who appears to be uninterested in their work? Or is it someone who is either unassertive, or unnecessarily aggressive? There are numerous reasons why people appear difficult. Here are five key points to consider:

1   Show understanding and make an effort to know the person in question. One reason you go to work is for social contact and support. Have lunch, build trust and rapport. Talk in a non-threatening way. Always focus on the behaviours and not the person. i.e. 'Bert, are you having trouble with …?' as opposed to 'Bert, are you stupid or something?'

2   Don't be condescending. Keep to the facts and look for ways to resolve the issue. 'Jane, any headway with the key account? What appears to be the problem and what can we do about it?'

3   If the person is your co-worker, ask if inadvertently you have offended him? It is so much better for all involved to have a positive work environment. Is there some way that you can both work towards that?

4   Always think through what you are going to say before you start the conversation and open with a positive. It is important not to damage self-esteem (Growing self-esteem, page 250).

5   Finally, keep the conversation constructive. Don't get dragged into a negative spiral which leads nowhere. Help the person come up with some positive solutions.

> Make your goal a reality with Mind Chi Applied!

Be tactful, thoughtful and professional, it will enable a positive outcome for all. Always consider that the individual may be facing personal issues with health or relationships, which they are attempting to keep out of work.

14 Training

Overview

28   Reversing poor memory

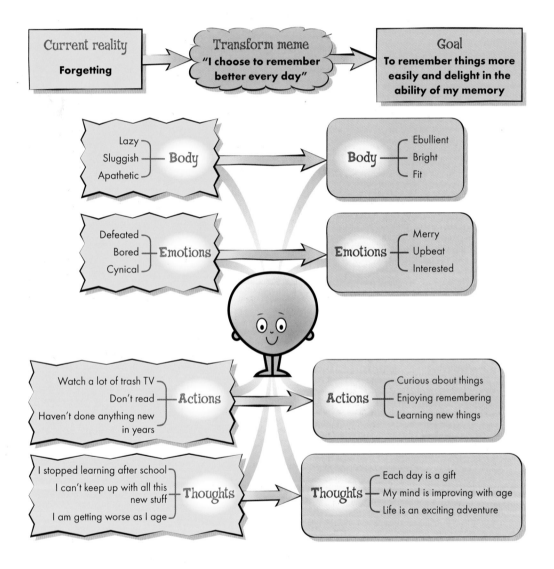

Mind Chi in action

Amazingly, you store away every piece of information/experience/sense/ thought that you have ever had. It is just that you cannot always recall it as required! To magically convert your 'forgettery' into a superb memory (Memory, page 276) here are some brain-friendly aids:

1   You naturally remember 'firsts'. So your first kiss, car or job is easily recalled. You naturally remember 'lasts': for example, your most recent cup of coffee or conversation. However, the longer that middle period, the easier it is to forget things. The answer? Create lots of new firsts and lasts by taking frequent breaks.

2   Create 'outstanding' moments and link them to what you are try-ing to remember, this will increase the efficiency of your natural memory.

3   If you want to remember something long term, then all you have to do is to use 'spaced repetition': review it one hour after the learning is over, then one day, one week later and then one month and finally one quarter and by now it is associated with other knowledge and firmly in your head!

4   Consciously raise your 'interest quotient' by imagining how good it will feel when your task is completed, or the horror of the disaster if it is not done! Finally, the natural brain function of association assists in retention – the more conscious associations you create – and recall – by reviewing your association chain, the more you naturally remember.

Make your goal a reality with Mind Chi Applied!

5   Be aware that everything you do, say and think draws upon memory and that 99 percent of the time your memory is incredibly efficient. Yet you tend to focus on the few occasions when you can't readily recall a detail: 'I've lost the car keys.' 'I've forgotten what I came upstairs for!' – often this is because your attention and interest were elsewhere. Such small incidents make you think you are losing your mind. Begin a memory appreciation day and recognize and thank your magnificent memory for all it does do!

29   Recalling names and faces

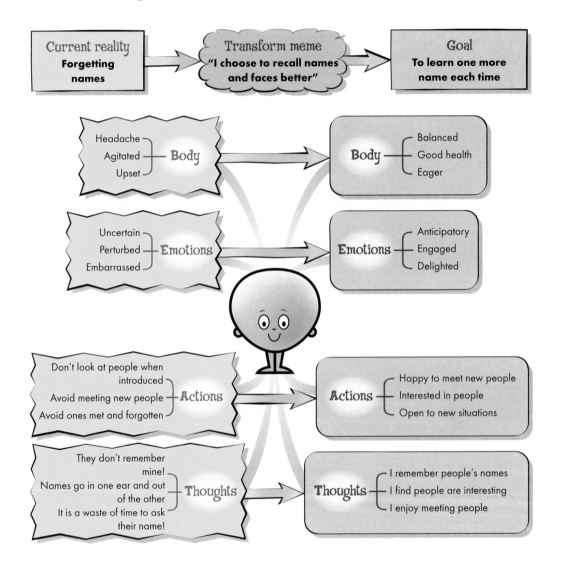

| Current reality
Forgetting names | → | Transform meme
"I choose to recall names and faces better" | → | Goal
To learn one more name each time |

Body — Headache, Agitated, Upset → **Body** — Balanced, Good health, Eager

Emotions — Uncertain, Perturbed, Embarrassed → **Emotions** — Anticipatory, Engaged, Delighted

Actions — Don't look at people when introduced, Avoid meeting new people, Avoid ones met and forgotten → **Actions** — Happy to meet new people, Interested in people, Open to new situations

Thoughts — They don't remember mine!, Names go in one ear and out of the other, It is a waste of time to ask their name! → **Thoughts** — I remember people's names, I find people are interesting, I enjoy meeting people

Mind Chi in action

When you meet people in business, whether colleagues or clients, do you find it hard to recall their names and faces? From now on, encourage yourself to learn by using the acronym FACES: (F = focus; A = attitude; C = check; E = exaggerate; S = slowly).

1 **F = Focus**. Currently, because you 'know' that you will forget, you don't fully focus on the person who is being introduced. Nor do you want to stare; so you look away and lose real contact. From now on, look at each person with interest; do they make eye contact? Listen to the tone of the voice, is there a dialect? When you shake hands, feel the hand, is it calloused or smooth? Is the shake firm or limp?

2 **A = Attitude**. Choose to be open and interested: 'I am meeting a new person with amazing stories to tell' (everyone has amazing stories).

3 **C = Check**. Names are often said quickly or mumbled. Check, by asking, 'I didn't quite hear that, your name is …?' or 'I haven't heard that name before, would you spell it for me?' Getting business cards is a comfort in a business meeting. The oriental culture of receiving them with two hands and reading and commenting on them is valuable because it allows you time to check and register the details in your mind. Placing the cards in the same order as the seating can also assist you.

Make your goal a reality with Mind Chi Applied!

4 **E = Exaggerate**. Just a bit of fun here. Does the person have any feature that can be exaggerated? Or an absurd connection with a part of their name or occupation? (Be a bit careful here!)

5 **S = Slowly**. Be gentle with yourself. Repeat the name in conversation (though not too often!) and certainly as you say goodbye. You will recall the first and the last person you meet, the ones in the middle will more easily be forgotten, unless there is (or you make) something outstanding about them. Remember one more name each time you attend a meeting and enjoy the process.

30 Handling information overload

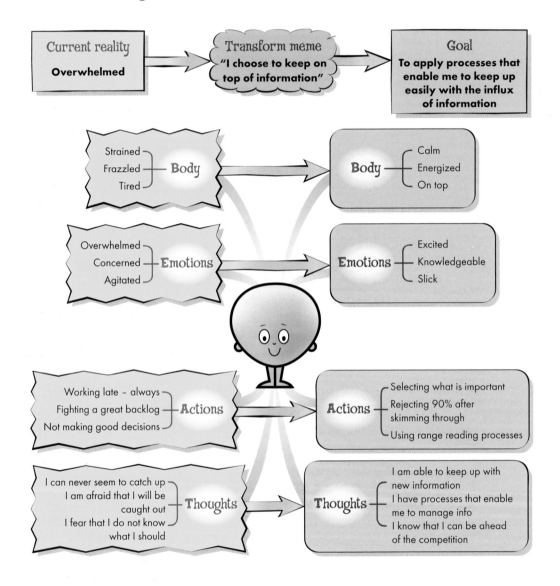

Mind Chi in action

Information Overload (IO) has been shown to decrease overall effectiveness. New information is coming at you daily, so fast that it is hard to know when to stop and act. This new form of paralysis is rather like 'yips' in golf, where the golfer is momentarily paralysed and unable to putt. The constant stress resulting from IO eats away at your health and happiness. You are seldom able to complete a task without being interrupted; this impairs your ability to think deeply about it and get good closure.

Here are three important information management skills, not commonly taught, that are crucial for being able to keep up in this information age:

1   Speedy-reading is a valuable tool. In a single day of training in this skill, business people can progress from an average reading speed of 250 words per minute to twice and up to four times as fast, still maintaining about 75 percent comprehension. It is a tremendous aid to workflow. Learning how your eye/brain actually takes in information enables you to develop a range of reading speeds and comprehension levels, appropriate to your tasks. (Speedy reading, page 212.)

Make your goal a reality with Mind Chi Applied!

2   Learning how to map the information is a powerful process that enables you to manage all the facts you need (Mapping, page 73). Look at 'mapping' software to see which suits your needs. An electronic map can be the ideal tool for managing vast quantities of information from one source. Reports, spreadsheets, meeting notes and letters can all be hyperlinked to a central map. A live web-map is a dynamic way to allow instant global cooperation and input from colleagues.

3   Developing the skill of disregarding anything that you don't need, that you already know, or that contains repetitions or faulty logic is also immensely useful. You will discover that there is only a small amount left!

31 Speedy-reading

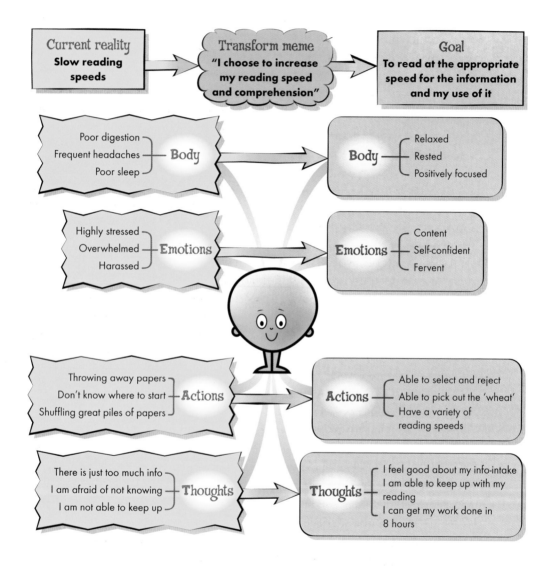

Current reality
Slow reading speeds

Transform meme
"I choose to increase my reading speed and comprehension"

Goal
To read at the appropriate speed for the information and my use of it

Body
- Poor digestion
- Frequent headaches
- Poor sleep

Body
- Relaxed
- Rested
- Positively focused

Emotions
- Highly stressed
- Overwhelmed
- Harassed

Emotions
- Content
- Self-confident
- Fervent

Actions
- Throwing away papers
- Don't know where to start
- Shuffling great piles of papers

Actions
- Able to select and reject
- Able to pick out the 'wheat'
- Have a variety of reading speeds

Thoughts
- There is just too much info
- I am afraid of not knowing
- I am not able to keep up

Thoughts
- I feel good about my info-intake
- I am able to keep up with my reading
- I can get my work done in 8 hours

Mind Chi in action

Your mind is able to take in information much faster than the very slow way we have been taught. You can easily listen and understand at 600–800 words per minute. When you read music you take in nine plus vertical lines of notes and several horizontal bars forward in one visual 'gulp' and think it quite natural – so why not with reading? (Speedy-reading, page 212.) Unlike the 'reading skills' you were taught at school, this new skill, called 'info-intake' aids business reading and has new 'rules':

1   First read through your material once, fast, to get an overview and understand the framework. Set your mind to look for new or specific details (these will stand out, in the way you would see your name easily). This is a small percentage of the total text. You can then:
   a)   decide if the material is worth a second look;
   b)   know where to find what you want; and
   c)   know where to recall relevant details from within the frame.
2   NEVER read slowly and carefully from the start, it offers the lowest level of efficiency. If the document warrants more than one reading, (such as a contract) then go through fast as many times as you need, to add the level of detail you require. It is easier to understand material at speed – and the multiple times through improves your memory.

Make your goal a reality with Mind Chi Applied!

3   Always use a guide. Your finger or pen works best. The guide 'pulls' the eye along, greatly assisting the ease and accuracy of the eye movement. You can run the guide under (or over) the line of text. This pulls your eye forward and stops 'back-skipping'. You only need to run over the middle section of the paragraph as with your 'focused vision' you can see 3–5 cms (an inch or so) either side. Begin by speeding up the movement of the guide under each line.
4   Other factors that will assist your speedy-reading are: to make sure the light is good and you are sitting in a comfortable, ergonomically safe way; read in short bursts with frequent breaks.

32   Reading from the screen

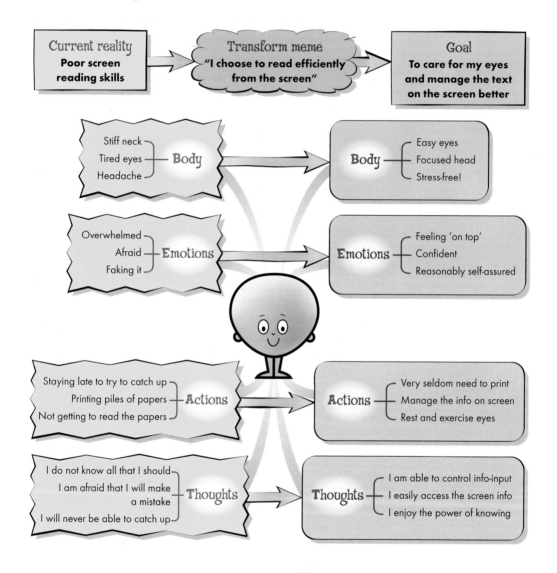

Mind Chi in action

Screen reading requires a new style of reading skill. Here are several things you can do with your screen to make reading easier:

1   Sit at arm's length from the computer screen; sit upright – head up, back straight and arms at 90 degrees to your desk.

2   Tip the angle of the screen back and lower the screen to eye height or a little lower. It is crucial to use a guide: use a finger or your curser; this will enable your eyes to track efficiently.

3   With a few clicks you can make text much easier to read. 'Select All' from Edit function and:
   a)   Change the size of the font to 12 or 14 point;
   b)   Change the font to Arial;
   c)   Make the column width approximately eight words;
   d)   Change the colour of the font; and
   e)   Change the background colour (Black on white is a poor contrast, experiment with what is best for you).

4   Care for your eyes: change eye range by looking far away and close-up as a break; remember to blink frequently; the flicker of the screen means that we tend NOT to blink, this is very bad for your eyes and tires them; use artificial 'tears'.

5   Exercise your eyes by closing them when you can (e.g. when taking a phone call) and either rest them closed or look at the eight points on an imaginary compass. Hold each position for at least five seconds and really feel the stretch.

6   Eye rests are necessary at least every hour. 'Palming' is done by rubbing your palms together to make them warm, then cup your hands and place them over the bony part around your eyes (remove glasses). Close your eyes and think of beautiful black things (a black cat's fur, black velvet etc.). Rest your elbows on your desk and stay like this for just a minute, slowly remove your hands and blink a few times. Your eyes feel as good as new!

Make your goal a reality with Mind Chi Applied!

33 Taming emails

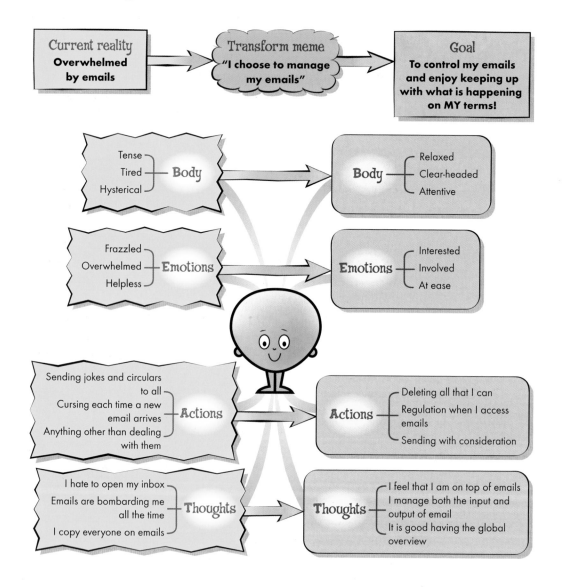

Mind Chi in action

Being online is the biggest addiction of the 21st century. Are you affected? By responding instantly each time the 'new mail' notification bleeps, you are lowering your intelligence as well as decreasing your competence and raising your constantly negative stress level. Recent research has shown that we cannot multitask with any degree of efficiency if activities are in the same 'band width'. So doing emails and talking on the phone does not work! What to do?

1   Decide how many times a day you need to take in a fresh batch of emails. A suggestion (this is generous) is early morning; before lunch and about 4pm, as a maximum! Turn the notification bleeper OFF.

2   Flag the five percent that actually require any action from you: easily identified by the name or the subject. Delete (or put in a 'wait and see' file) all the ones you think you can live without. Empty your 'wait and see' files as appropriate.

3   Either *skim* over the content of an email to see if there is anything you need, or *scan* for specific names/info – this literally sets your radar to let it leap out at you. Deal in one batch with the responses (as much as you can). Before copying people in on a return email, ask yourself, 'Do they really need to know?'

4   Endeavour not to print emails (wastes valuable trees); you only throw them away after! Stop sending and receiving jokes and circulars (you will never get rich nor will your wish come true that way!). If it is really urgent, the person will phone you!

5   Use your subject line to show the focus or outcome required. There are three categories of business emails: providing or requesting information or action.

6   Make your emails user-friendly with colour, keywords and phrases, variety of type, **bold,** highlights and underlines. Use the KISS principle (Keep It Short and Simple).

Make your goal a reality with Mind Chi Applied!

34 Writing reports and letters

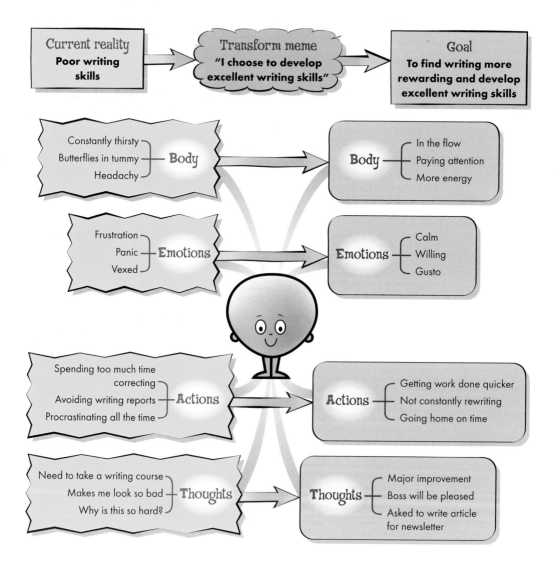

Mind Chi in action

It is important to know what style of communication is appropriate in different business situations. For example, when sending texts and emails, the use of abbreviations and a direct communication style are quite acceptable. However, when writing letters or reports, a more formal style is required. The written word is still a powerful and necessary tool of communication and all successful business people know how to use language to their advantage. A level of 'judgement' occurs if it is not up to standard. Poor grammar or spelling may lead to the unfair assessment that, 'This person couldn't even string a sentence together!' Inappropriate style will probably not land you the job or sell your product. Understand the basics:

1   There are two main considerations in writing: the purpose of writing and your audience.
2   Start by creating an outline or a mini-map of what you want to say, on paper or computer, to help you clarify your thinking.
3   After your outline or mini-map, write a draft. Then take a break as you will return with 'fresh eyes' and can see areas that may need updating (Memory, page 271).
4   Read for logic, then do any reorganization – and watch out for poor grammar and spelling mistakes. Use your spell-checker; and if it's an important document have someone else proofread it for you.
5   Be aware that these days, being too formal can be offputting to the new generation of business people. Remain professional, but modify your style of presentation or expression depending on your audience.
6   As there is already too much to read, remember the three most important words in good writing: cut, cut, cut.

Make your goal a reality with Mind Chi Applied!

35   Learning to learn

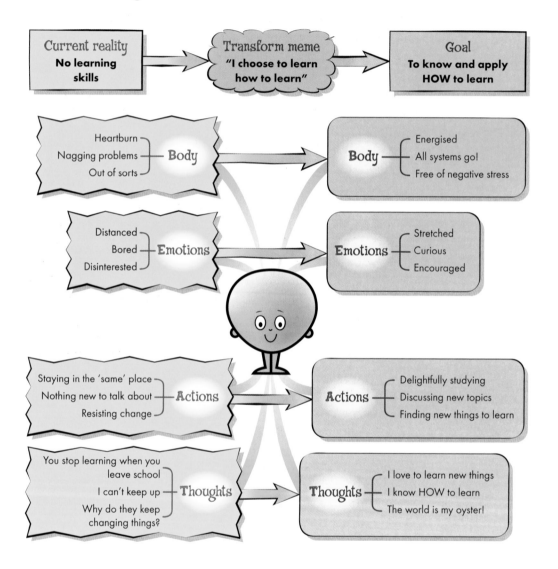

Current reality
No learning skills

Transform meme
"I choose to learn how to learn"

Goal
To know and apply HOW to learn

Heartburn
Nagging problems — **Body**
Out of sorts

Body — Energised
All systems go!
Free of negative stress

Distanced
Bored — **Emotions**
Disinterested

Emotions — Stretched
Curious
Encouraged

Staying in the 'same' place
Nothing new to talk about — **Actions**
Resisting change

Actions — Delightfully studying
Discussing new topics
Finding new things to learn

You stop learning when you leave school
I can't keep up — **Thoughts**
Why do they keep changing things?

Thoughts — I love to learn new things
I know HOW to learn
The world is my oyster!

Mind Chi in action

In spite of years of schooling, few of us ever learnt how to learn. However, with some basic training everyone can take in new information, effectively and enjoyably, throughout their lives. Learning is what your mind was designed for. Your brain is an adaptable learning machine. Its plasticity provides built-in adaptability. Here is MIMA – an acronym for the key skills needed to live and flourish in our information age:

1   Mapping – take and make notes that are compatible with the way your brain actually works (Mapping, page 73). Maps make the whole process of learning and managing information enjoyable and effective. Additional advantages are that your memory is automatically improved and your ability to think clearly is enhanced.

2   Info-intake (Speedy-reading, page 212) – to be able to select the information you need and reject the repeated/known/untrue or unnecessary. Having an info-intake speed of approximately 1000wpm will mean that you are through the stack of research in a reasonable time!

3   Memory techniques – allow the easy storage and retrieval of information. Use FLORIA (First, Last, Outstanding, Interest/imagination, and Association) to improve retention. Just a few simple techniques like the journey video or your favourite room, when added to the information about the spaced repetition (one hour/day/week/month and quarter) makes any information very sticky! (Memory, page 271.)

4   Attitude – the secret to eternal youth is to remain curious, interested and full of wonder and gratitude. All of these are lovely ways to feel anyway and will also fuel the desire to keep learning, playing, exploring and living to the full.

Make your goal a reality with Mind Chi Applied!

15 Health

36   Multi-tasking

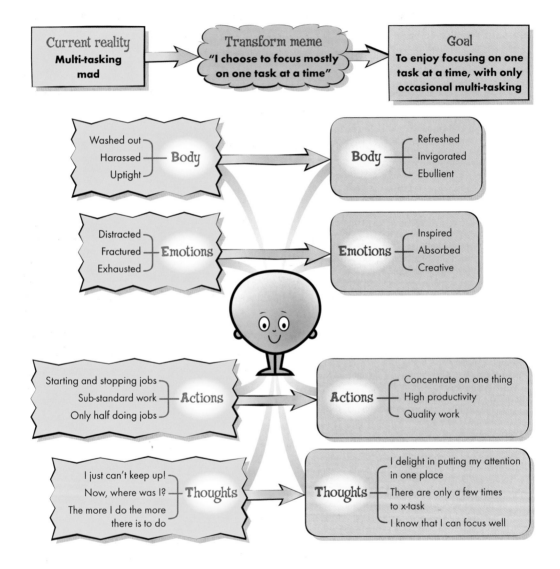

Current reality
Multi-tasking mad

Transform meme
"I choose to focus mostly on one task at a time"

Goal
To enjoy focusing on one task at a time, with only occasional multi-tasking

Washed out
Harassed — **Body**
Uptight

Body — Refreshed
Invigorated
Ebullient

Distracted
Fractured — **Emotions**
Exhausted

Emotions — Inspired
Absorbed
Creative

Starting and stopping jobs
Sub-standard work — **Actions**
Only half doing jobs

Actions — Concentrate on one thing
High productivity
Quality work

I just can't keep up!
Now, where was I?
The more I do the more there is to do — **Thoughts**

Thoughts — I delight in putting my attention in one place
There are only a few times to x-task
I know that I can focus well

Mind Chi in action

'I am a multi-tasker' is the badge proudly worn by many today. The other side of the badge may say 'Most things I do are sub-standard', but you don't show that side of the badge, even if you know it to be true. Under pressure in today's workplace, where more seems to need to be done than ever before, many have adopted the multi-tasking habit – but it seldom works.

There are times when multi-tasking is essential, such as when preparing a meal, but doing emails while using the phone just does not work. The negative sides to multi-tasking are:

1   Heightened stress. An occasional blast of multi-tasking can be quite exhilarating, but keeping it up day after day has a detrimental effect on your overall health. Problems that occur include: errors in your work, feeling spaced out, being constantly irritable, being easily distracted and even suffering burnout. If that is not enough to put you off, add social isolation where you text or send an email rather than talk to a person! This causes you to lose the spontaneity of interpersonal relationships. If you are at a computer for two or more hours a day, you can expect to develop neck and back problems. When you are keeping tabs on everything and focusing on none, the net result is ineffectiveness and no time to focus and think deeply about anything.

Make your goal a reality with Mind Chi Applied!

2   Ego-connection! Research has shown that many link their personal value to their connectivity. Do you measure your importance by the number of emails, 'tweets', phone calls or messages you receive?

How can you break the multi-tasking addiction? Take a 12–15 minute power nap (Taking mini-breaks, page 234); vary mental assignments; group tasks together and vary the pace and complexity; take control of the quantity and quality of your work; gain some self-awareness; do one task at a time; consider some form of meditation.

37   Converting anger

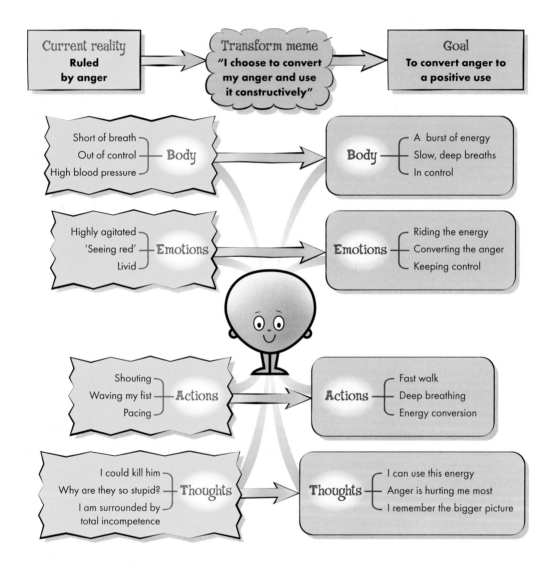

Mind Chi in action

Anger is just energy. You create it and can defuse it with your response. There is a tendency to point the finger, saying 'You made me angry!' That is not correct; you made yourself angry. The first thing to know is that anger is the tip of the iceberg. Ask yourself the real reason for your outburst. 'I am angry because …?' Think of the last few times you felt angry. Did you feel embarrassed, or afraid? Were you feeling unworthy? Had you made a mistake? Were you feeling doubt, worry, or under threat? The list goes on. Here are some ideas to assist you to convert your anger energy:

1   When you feel an outburst on the horizon, walk away and assess the reason for your emotion. Then judge the appropriate response.

2   Communicate with those with whom you are angry. Say, 'I am feeling very angry because I am under a lot of pressure.' Instead of escalating a shouting match, look at how you can work together to fix the situation.

3   Since anger is such a burst of energy, see if there is something useful you can do with it. Take some exercise. Clean out a drawer – yes, just tip the contents on the floor and sort it out! Walk fast to a far office to deliver some papers.

4   Any sudden physical changes will also do the trick: looking up will interrupt the negative patterns; stand up and stretch while letting out an audible sigh; exaggerate and change your facial expressions; walk over to a window where there is sunlight; do ten jumping jacks; do a ridiculous dance.

5   Remember that the energy of anger can be redirected for a positive use. Anger hurts you most! All forms of meditation, breathing and relaxation exercises are good as a way to re-establish a calm interior. Find ones that suit your personality.

6   Also find a way to laugh; if you can just gain perspective, the 'anger scene' is often quite amusing! If not, then keep some funny DVDs or things you know tickle your sense of humour.

Make your goal a reality with Mind Chi Applied!

38 Controlling depression

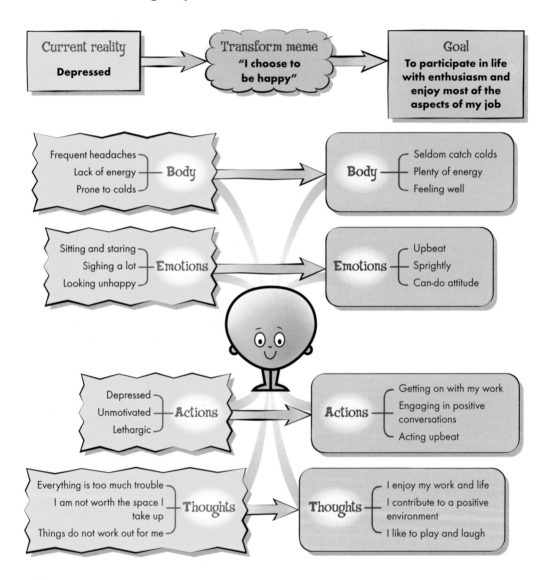

Mind Chi in action

Depression can almost be 'caught' if that is the predominant mood around you. It can be brought on by the winter weather or an upset in your life. You may also become more susceptible to whatever bug, virus or cold that is going round. Everything becomes an effort and you may envy people who seem to have energy. You need to start an upward positive spiral, where your thinking and behaviour create the endorphins that encourage more positive thinking and behaviour. Here are some ideas:

1   Make a list or map of things you like to do and that you know pick up your spirits. What people do you know who help you to feel 'up'? As soon as you start to feel yourself slipping into a slump, go to your map and put an appropriate one into action.

2   If you have experienced a loss in your life, then do not try to push the emotions away. It is a part of life to experience them. So be gentle with yourself. Start to balance appropriate sadness or regret with allowing a little joy back in to help you lift your spirits. The past is set – and most importantly, it has passed. So consider that you do not want to keep bringing it back to life in the 'now'.

3   When depressed, it is easy to say that the whole day (month/year/decade/life) was awful. So one skill is to look for the moments of contentment that occur during the day: the cup of tea that is just the right temperature and colour, or a smile from a child.

4   Other assists are: exercise, even a short walk, or beam some sunshine on you – either a full spectrum light, especially if you suffer from SAD (Seasonal Affective Disorder) or take a quick break away, if you are able. Of course, get enough sleep and eat a good, healthy and balanced diet, too.

5   If you are in severe depression then you may need a short medical intervention. However, make sure that your doctor assists you in coming off any medication quickly, and strengthen your change with a positive therapy, like CBT (Cognitive Behavioural Therapy).

Make your goal a reality with Mind Chi Applied!

39   Forgiving

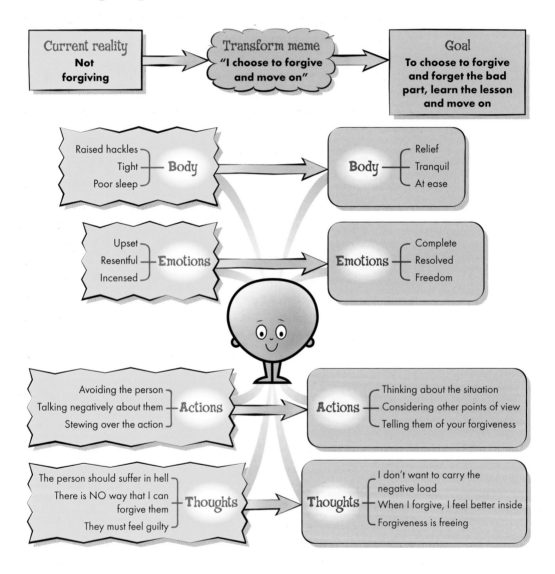

Mind Chi in action

The choice to forgive lies within and it is a powerful liberator from whomever or whatever perpetrated your anger or distress. Being bitter and unforgiving keeps you linked in to the situation. Take control of your responsibility, choose to forgive, and reclaim your own state of well-being. If you do not forgive, what happens? You slowly eat up your insides with the sour feelings. You may lose a business, family member or friend as a result. You feel that the world is not fair and you have the short end of the stick. Some things to consider:

1   Let us say you caused an accident and hurt someone. Whatever the situation, you did not set out to create that outcome. It was an accident. Yes, you may have been careless, but who among us has not? Is there anything that you can do to assist the situation? If there is, then do it. Can you pass the lesson on to others? Do what you can and release yourself from the pain of non-forgiveness.

2   If something was 'done' to you, consider taking some level of responsibility. This can be a bitter pill to swallow; however, it prevents you from adopting a 'victim' mode.

3   Even the worst situations can allow new and better doors to open. So allow new opportunities to present themselves.

4   Sometimes you can forgive in one go, just wipe the slate clean and say, 'I don't need to carry this any more'. Sometimes you might need to do it in stages, to desensitize yourself to the situation. Whichever you do, start the task of forgiveness as soon as possible, before it impacts on your health and lasting happiness. In some cases it will be appropriate to begin reconciliation with the other party; they may well be suffering too.

5   There are many benefits in learning to forgive: improving health, relationships, and having clearer thinking. Instead of focusing on your wounded feelings and thereby giving away your power, learn to look for the love, beauty and kindness around you. Forgiveness is linked to increasing personal power and contentment.

Make your goal a reality with Mind Chi Applied!

40   Calming stress

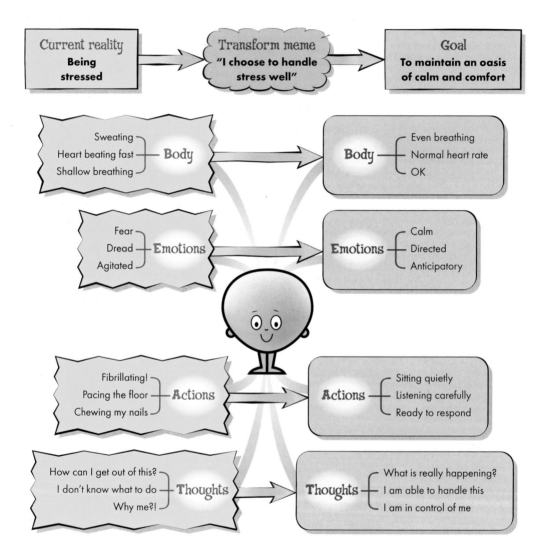

Current reality	Transform meme	Goal
Being stressed	**"I choose to handle stress well"**	**To maintain an oasis of calm and comfort**

Body
- Sweating
- Heart beating fast
- Shallow breathing

Body
- Even breathing
- Normal heart rate
- OK

Emotions
- Fear
- Dread
- Agitated

Emotions
- Calm
- Directed
- Anticipatory

Actions
- Fibrillating!
- Pacing the floor
- Chewing my nails

Actions
- Sitting quietly
- Listening carefully
- Ready to respond

Thoughts
- How can I get out of this?
- I don't know what to do
- Why me?!

Thoughts
- What is really happening?
- I am able to handle this
- I am in control of me

Mind Chi in action

As soon as you feel stressed, your body responds as though a wildebeest is chasing you. This is very useful if a wildebeest *is* chasing you but unfortunately your body does not know how to differentiate between fantasy and reality and so prepares you for 'fight or flight' (Stress, page 299). So, what to do? Your breathing and autonomic nervous system are closely related. As soon as you perceive a stress situation, your breath, adrenalin, cortisol and blood pressure all react accordingly. Fortunately, if you know how to control your breathing, you can make your nervous system perceive calm. Here are some suggestions:

1   Distinguish between those things that you can do something about and the ones you can't. The daily news headlines can be a real negative stressor, but you can do little to affect any aspect, so only have one helping a day – that is more than enough!

2   As soon as you think you are in a stressful situation, start to take long slow breaths. This starts to calm all the natural responses and lets you be in control. Learn to keep your body tranquil regardless of what might be happening around you.

3   Put aside time to play – have fun and relaxation on your agenda. Add it to your diary as it is one of your most important tasks (not necessarily during work hours, although you must have breaks during the day if you are to be a good worker). Also make sure you have good (approx six hours) sleep a night.

4   Enrol in classes on how to relax; do exercise and meditation; start music or dancing classes; tend a garden; help an elderly neighbour; take up a new hobby – give yourself a life outside work.

5   If you do not take action to reduce your negative stress, you are heading straight towards constant fatigue, burnout and serious sickness. Performing your Mind Chi routine will bring back control and serenity in your life.

Make your goal a reality with Mind Chi Applied!

41 Taking mini-breaks

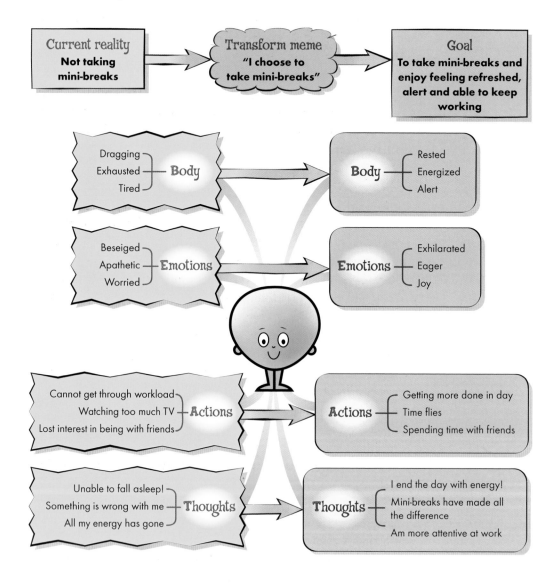

Mind Chi in action

Study the lives of outstanding people and you will note that many took mini-breaks during the day – Sir Winston Churchill being one notable example. Taking small, periodic breaks allows you to have a mini-mental escape from the constant strains of work; it is also an opportunity to reduce built-up physical tension. Every 45–60 minutes your body needs to move and stretch. Regular mini-breaks mean that you can get through even a very busy day, and still feel alert and focused as well as being productive.

Some more ideas:

1   If possible, take a 15 minute mini-break after lunch; this is a naturally low time for the body and a short rest has maximum therapeutic value. Progressive companies understand the value of this and some have recreation rooms available for their staff.

2   Even in a busy office you can close your eyes and take a mini-break. Or put a beautiful picture on your wall or screen-saver of a place you would like to visit and let yourself stare at it, close your eyes and experience it at a multi-sensory level.

> Make your goal a reality with Mind Chi Applied!

3   Take some complete Mind Chi breaths, a few minutes of sitting up straight or tilting back, but keep your spine straight, so your lungs can take in the maximum amount of air.

4   If seated at your desk, do some stretching exercises. Stretches can be performed throughout the day, to keep your body flexible, happy and healthy. Hold stretches for 15–30 seconds and perform them one to three times, depending on the amount of time you have. Hold the stretch in a position in which you can feel the muscles comfortably stretched.

5   Take a 10–15 minute mini-break from what you are working on and do something completely different. Even doing work of a different tempo and type can provide your mini-break.

42 Transitioning

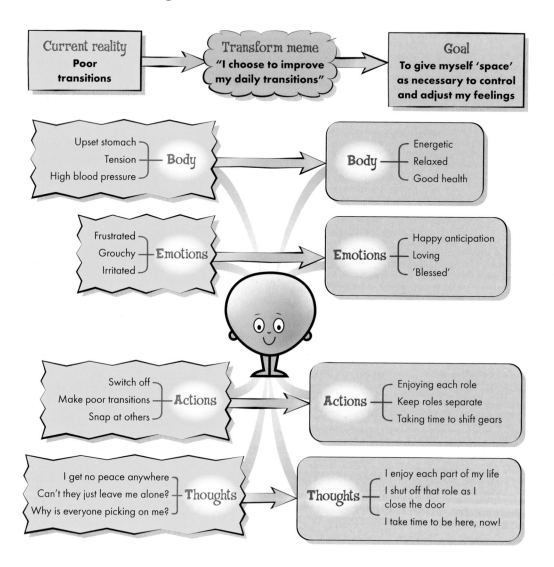

Mind Chi in action

A transition is any shift from one environment or role to another: leaving home to go to work; leaving a meeting to return to your office; leaving the office to go home etc. Most of the time you shift from one role to another seamlessly – partner to boss; negotiator to manager; manager back to partner or parent. However, sometimes it goes wrong: commonly after work – the going home part. The day did not go as you wanted and the traffic is awful. When you open your front door, feeling tired and angry, you snap at your partner, shout at the children and bad feelings escalate until everyone is upset. You need to create a transition for everyone's benefit:

1   A transition is a space that you create for yourself, where you conduct an attitude adjustment: for example, perhaps you were in a nasty meeting and leave feeling upset. Before you return to your desk, walk around the building or have a glass of water or take a comfort break and take stock.

2   Do your Mind Chi BEAT check (Aware, page 58). What is your Body doing? (Fast, shallow breathing? Heart racing? Sweating? Chest feeling tight?) How about your Emotions? (Angry? Frustrated? Disappointed?) What were your Actions? (Did you frown? Did you snap? Did you slam a door?) And finally your Thoughts? ('I have just wasted two hours!') OK, that is where you are – you now know you need to choose to make some adjustments to your BEAT.

3   Stop and do your Mind Chi breath. This will untangle the state you put yourself in so you can consider 'What would I choose to have instead?' Slow down your actions and do nothing for a minute.

4   Change your thinking, 'What does it look like from their point of view?' 'What have I not explained well enough?' 'Can I achieve my goals via another route?'

Make your goal a reality with Mind Chi Applied!

Your transition is now complete. You may still need to discuss the situation, which is best done in the memory 'dip' (Memory, page 274), but you won't be tempted to spread your discontent any further.

43   Stabilizing work–life balance

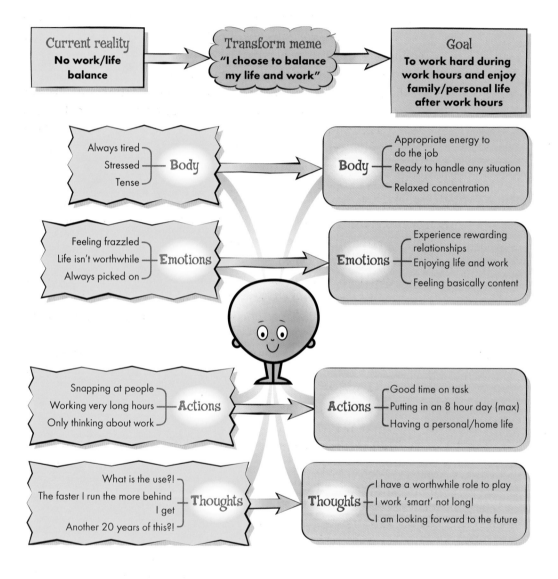

Current reality
No work/life balance

Transform meme
"I choose to balance my life and work"

Goal
To work hard during work hours and enjoy family/personal life after work hours

Always tired
Stressed
Tense
Body

Body
Appropriate energy to do the job
Ready to handle any situation
Relaxed concentration

Feeling frazzled
Life isn't worthwhile
Always picked on
Emotions

Emotions
Experience rewarding relationships
Enjoying life and work
Feeling basically content

Snapping at people
Working very long hours
Only thinking about work
Actions

Actions
Good time on task
Putting in an 8 hour day (max)
Having a personal/home life

What is the use?!
The faster I run the more behind I get
Another 20 years of this?!
Thoughts

Thoughts
I have a worthwhile role to play
I work 'smart' not long!
I am looking forward to the future

Mind Chi in action

A useful time to take stock of your work–life balance is when you have a birthday (especially when it is the birthday with a 'zero' in it!). Where has the year (decade) gone? What do you have to show for it? It is so easy to allow the everyday content – the stuff you do to maintain life – to fill every moment (those emails, phone calls, meetings etc.). To keep work–life balance you need a context: your purpose or goal for your life. This gives purpose and makes you create a plan of action. Work hard and then balance your life with home and a complete change of pace. Keep both your wheels round and balanced!

1   Make two circles. One is your twenty-four hour day as a pie chart, divided into the time you take for your main activities (sleep; travel; work; personal; family and friends; hobbies and activities). The second circle is for the people and things that are most important to you. Allot a section of the pie for each to show their relative importance. Now compare your pies! How much time are you spending on the people and things that are the most important to you?

2   A 'bloom' map is a very good way to find out if others close to you perceive balance in your life (Bloom, page 76). A man did this exercise with his four-year-old son to see what he felt about his daddy. They started the game. 'Away' was the first word his son associated with him … 'work' was next followed by 'money' and finally 'cross'. 'Anything else?' asked the dad, hopefully, 'nope' was the reply. When he asked his wife about the conversation, she said 'Well, he wakes up and asks for his daddy, I say you are away. "Where?", he wants to know, so I tell him, you are at work. 'Why?' is the next question and I reply, 'To make money so we can live in this nice house and have toys and holidays … and if he plays up before he goes to bed you get a little cross.' Needless to say, this made a big impression on the father and he quickly changed his time priorities. He was so glad that it happened then and not ten years later.

Make your goal a reality with Mind Chi Applied!

16 Self-concept

44   Developing leadership skills

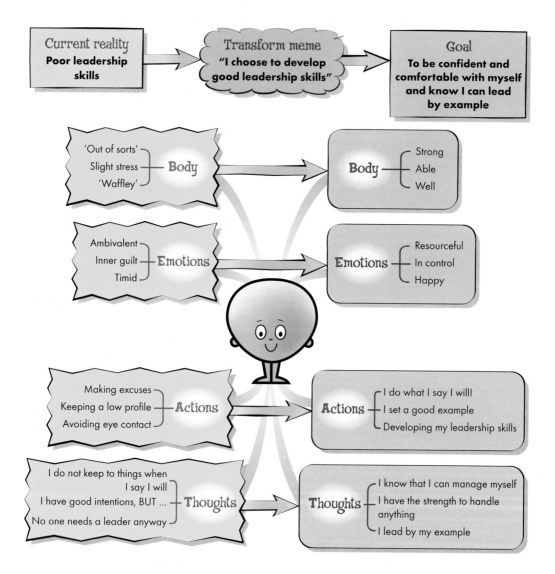

Current reality
Poor leadership skills

Transform meme
"I choose to develop good leadership skills"

Goal
To be confident and comfortable with myself and know I can lead by example

Body
'Out of sorts'
Slight stress
'Waffley'

Body
Strong
Able
Well

Emotions
Ambivalent
Inner guilt
Timid

Emotions
Resourceful
In control
Happy

Actions
Making excuses
Keeping a low profile
Avoiding eye contact

Actions
I do what I say I will!
I set a good example
Developing my leadership skills

Thoughts
I do not keep to things when I say I will
I have good intentions, BUT ...
No one needs a leader anyway

Thoughts
I know that I can manage myself
I have the strength to handle anything
I lead by my example

Mind Chi in action

Here is a brief story that shows the building of self leadership. A person started and ran a business for twenty years before being forced into liquidation. At the same time her professional and personal partner left. Further, her sole remaining family member, whom she had been looking after, died. Add to this scene a birthday with a zero in it and a desire to celebrate it by taking on a physical challenge. The only thing over which she had control was herself. Life will always throw difficulties at you, so trust that you can rely on your 'inner core of steel' to be able to handle them and move on. Here are a few extra considerations to develop self leadership:

1   Do things with discretion – put your ego away! Do for the sake of doing and do it to the best of your ability, rather than expecting a certain response.
2   Live in wonder! Experience new things, welcome new ideas, keep each day fresh (even if you are doing the 'same' thing), it is now a new day and so all things are different.
3   Live with high levels of honesty and integrity. Your values allow you to look yourself in the mirror and know that you have done your best. Have faith in yourself and your abilities.
4   Champion change and remain a life-long learner. Be on the lookout for new ways and ideas; encourage the same environment in the workplace and live it yourself. Release your natural humour.
5   Join the 'I shall not complain' club. Fix what you can and concentrate on other (good) things.

Make your goal a reality with Mind Chi Applied!

When it comes to leading others, a study at Harvard University revealed that the one quality that shows most leadership potential is that of 'persistence'. Also, have and share a detailed vision (with plans) of how your desired futures will be. Be totally committed – then others can follow with a 'learn from your mistakes' philosophy.

45   Building motivation

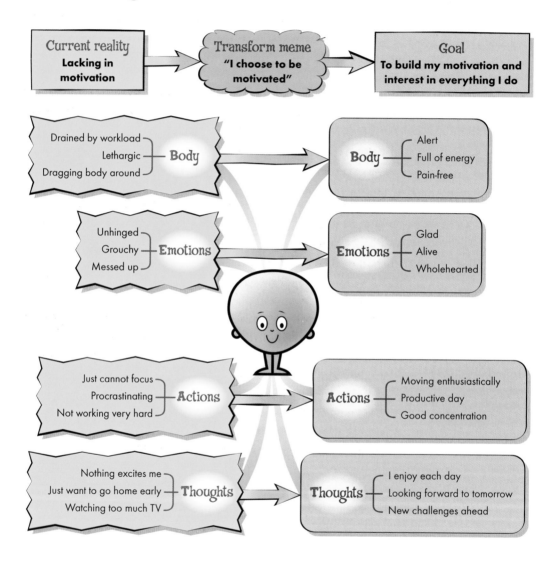

Mind Chi in action

Motivation is your reason for wanting to do something. Together with its partners – willpower and volition – motivation will help you to 'make a difference'. Here are some extra thoughts:

1   Motivation is uplifting and creates a positive state of mind. It is the opposite of boredom. On a 'boredom to motivated' continuum, where do you place yourself?
2   Do the work you love and love the work you do. When you enjoy yourself at work, it doesn't feel like work at all. (Getting paid is a bonus!)
3   Set yourself 'live' lines (more motivating that 'dead' lines!) Set up a series of mini-action steps, building up to your desired result. (Setting priorities, page 146).
4   Recognize your achievements. Make a point to reward yourself for reaching a goal. Even a small reward recognizes and marks your advance.
5   If you are responsible for others, think about what they need. By understanding this you will be able to help people keep themselves happy and productive. Research shows that the best extrinsic motivator is personal recognition. Between the carrot and the stick, the carrot has better results.
6   Be creative – think inside and outside of the box! Come up with ideas of how to do things in fresh ways. Look for joy in the small everyday instances. Remember your gratitude.

Make your goal a reality with Mind Chi Applied!

46 Staying positive

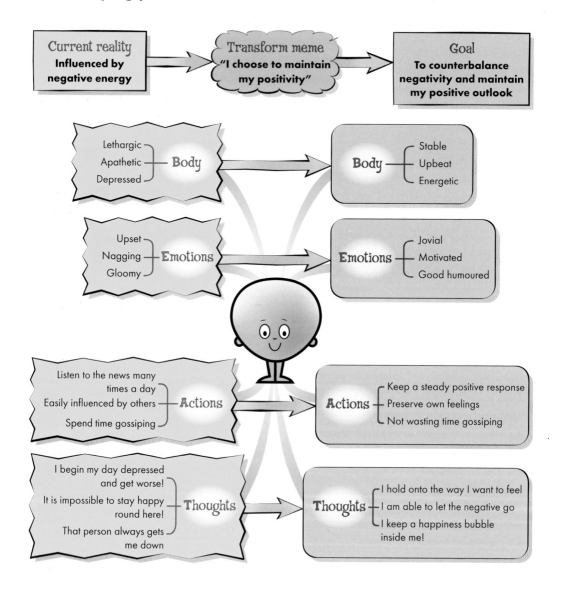

Mind Chi in action

When working in a predominantly negative environment people often feel justified in complaining. This is catching, so it's important to take precautions to avoid infection and boost your immunity!

Here is a story for you. An experiment was conducted with two young boys. One had a room full of toys, the other a room full of manure. Both boys were left alone for a few hours. When the scientists returned, they heard wailing and crying from the room of the boy with the toys. Would the boy with the manure be even unhappier? Approaching his door they could hear scraping and whistling and found the boy busily digging away. 'What are you doing?' they asked. He replied, 'Well, with this much manure, there must be a donkey in here somewhere!' So, if you find yourself in a negative situation, just think … 'Where is my donkey?!' The lovely thing is: if you look, you will always find one!

1   Remember that you are always in control and can choose the emotion you want to experience.
2   If you are about to meet a negative person or situation then see yourself in a beautiful iridescent bubble of happiness that deflects any negativity. Don't directly challenge it – it may make matters worse!
3   Remain detached. If your work place is negative – stay focused on the facts and remain as positive as you can.
4   Build your positivity by being aware of the things that bring a little smile to the corners of your mouth. Every interaction is a chance to make small gestures that increase the positivity and joy quotient for others. Vanda puts a ☺ in her signature; this has caused so many positive comments and smiles over the years.
5   Remember that to have work is a blessing in itself! The more you become aware of positive joy, the more you will discover. The more you discover joy, the more you will share. The more you share and create the more others will also benefit. The more you know that you give, the more you receive back. It is a very good system.

Make your goal a reality with Mind Chi Applied!

47 Being prepared

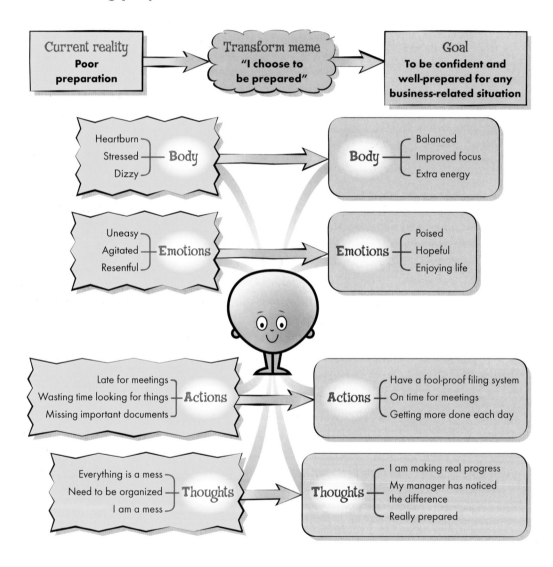

Mind Chi in action

Being prepared is a philosophy of life. The Scouts have a motto: 'Be prepared' and, within reason, that is a very good idea. After a perfect performance, a gymnast was about to fall on dismount, however, he was able to save himself and stood with arms up to finish. When he was asked, 'How long have you practised that incredible dismount?' He replied, 'For years!' Every hour of practice had enabled him to be prepared for that situation. It can be the same for you as well. All of your life and learning to date has been in preparation for whatever comes next. This is especially true in challenging times.

1   Do you tend to under-prepare or over-prepare for things? You need to find the happy balance. Allocate an appropriate amount of time to prepare in advance, based on the importance of your upcoming activity and the number of steps involved.

2   Preparation says you care. It shows respect, both for yourself and for others. It shows consideration and increases personal commitment from all parties.

3   Preparation is 80 percent of your success. It is professional and it bolsters your self-confidence to arrive at a meeting knowing you are well prepared for whatever is to follow. Review previous contacts, notes and maps. What do you know about the people/ company you are meeting with?

4   Create a checklist (or map) to work from, especially if you are repeating activities you have done before; it is easy to overlook something. This is why pilots always complete their flight-check before take-off.

5   Allow time for contingencies and pre-set your watch ten minutes fast to keep you on your toes.

> Make your goal a reality with Mind Chi Applied!

48 Growing self-esteem

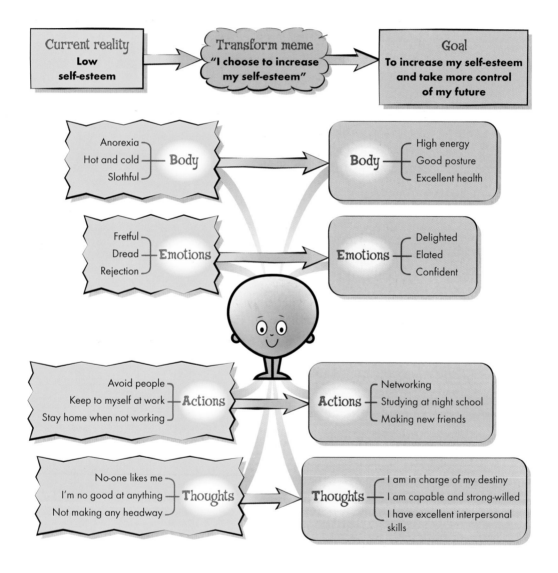

Mind Chi in action

What you think of yourself is the most important first step towards achieving business success. Lack of self-belief not only reflects a poor state of mind but will be reflected in your behaviour and be noticed by others. Here are some tips on improving self-esteem:

1 Build up your self-esteem. Take an inventory. Observe your basic beliefs and emotions. Rate them as positive, negative or neutral. Do you need to take any actions?

2 Celebrate your journey, as well as your destination. Learn to feel good about where you are now, in the present moment.

3 Be active. Take the initiative. Be decisive; make choices – don't let others decide what is best for you.

4 Treat each person you meet as if s/he is important. Train yourself to listen. Pay more attention to the other person than to yourself. Put yourself in the other person's shoes. Show you are caring. You will discover this will help your own self-esteem.

5 Focus on your strong points. Ask your friends what your strong points are – you may be quite delighted. If they mention your humility, this shows very positive self-esteem.

6 Smile! A simple smile improves your appearance. When you look at yourself in the mirror, smile at yourself. It changes the chemicals in your brain, and the immediate responses of those around you.

7 Do something that makes you feel good. Go for a walk, have a workout, soak in a bath or listen to music.

8 Be yourself. You are a unique, wonderful person, let that shine.

Make your goal a reality with Mind Chi Applied!

Remember: self-esteem means how you see yourself. It is all in your head. Ask your 'Chi' to keep reminding you how powerful you really are (Chi, page 31).

49 Creating a difference

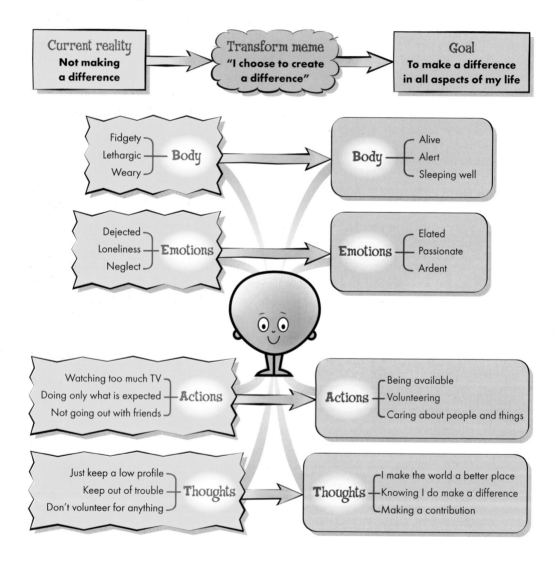

Mind Chi in action

'Two roads diverged in a wood, and I took the one less travelled, and that has made all the difference.' This famous quote by Robert Frost sums up the essence of making a difference. Throughout the centuries we have been inspired by stories of individuals who have made a difference, from Mother Theresa to Nelson Mandela. What do they have in common? It is perseverance, timing, taking advantage of opportunities, hard work, an overriding purpose and wanting to make a contribution to society.

1   How do you wish to 'make a difference'? What is going to be your contribution to society? Select something that you feel strongly about, something that gets you passionate! This can be a doing or a being. Do you want to be an excellent parent? Employee? Boss? Or create a happy and more productive department? Find something that you can throw yourself into. Be prepared to go the distance. Regardless of your field of endeavour, have the determination to keep going. This is usually a joy as 'making a difference' is most energizing.

2   Having a positive mental attitude helps. Use your leadership skills (Developing leadership, page 242) and motivation (Building motivation, page 244) to keep yourself on track.

3   Keep yourself in shape. Being mentally and physically well enables you to tackle whatever lies ahead.

4   Be involved, not a bystander. Involvement will provide you with the opportunities to make a difference.

5   Develop friendships along the way. Friends are your treasure, so value them accordingly. They support and nourish you in good and bad times.

Make your goal a reality with Mind Chi Applied!

50   Keeping commitments

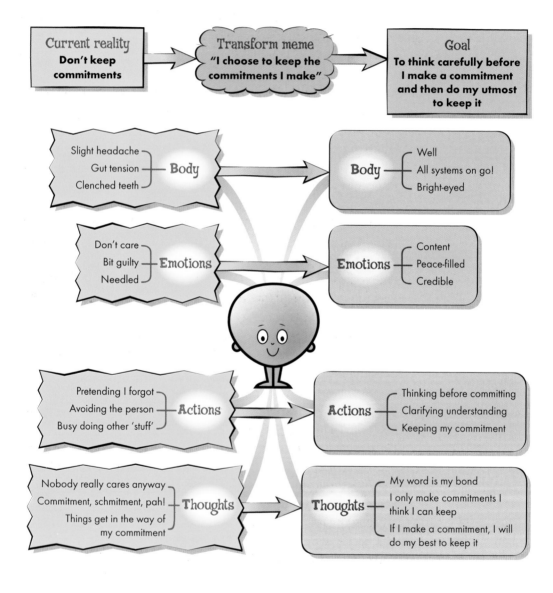

Current reality
Don't keep commitments

Transform meme
"I choose to keep the commitments I make"

Goal
To think carefully before I make a commitment and then do my utmost to keep it

Slight headache
Gut tension — **Body**
Clenched teeth

Body — Well
All systems on go!
Bright-eyed

Don't care
Bit guilty — **Emotions**
Needled

Emotions — Content
Peace-filled
Credible

Pretending I forgot
Avoiding the person — **Actions**
Busy doing other 'stuff'

Actions — Thinking before committing
Clarifying understanding
Keeping my commitment

Nobody really cares anyway
Commitment, schmitment, pah! — **Thoughts**
Things get in the way of my commitment

Thoughts — My word is my bond
I only make commitments I think I can keep
If I make a commitment, I will do my best to keep it

Mind Chi in action

A commitment can vary from being small to very big. Regardless of size, it is still a commitment. Your word is important and if you do choose to make a commitment, you should do your utmost to keep it. As commitments are mostly made to people who are close to you, it is even more important to keep them if you want to maintain the relationship. Some thoughts about commitments:

1   If someone tries to push you into a commitment, resist. Take your time to make sure that if you do say yes, you can deliver. It inconveniences others if you say yes and then back down.

2   If you initiate the commitment, check your enthusiasm for just a moment. It may be safer to not commit, but to say that if possible, this or that will happen. In that way, you do not raise expectations unnecessarily.

3   Make your word your bond. A commitment represents the core of you. So treat it with due respect and then others will respect that in you as well.

4   If you make a commitment that for some unforeseen reason you cannot keep, explain this to the other person(s) involved. Work out a new plan of action.

5   Consider your stance on difficult issues such as honesty, morals and values before you need to draw on them. Then, when you are under pressure, it becomes easier to know how to act.

6   If you do not keep your word, everything else you say may depreciate in value in the eyes of those around you. It is the old 'cry wolf' story, no one will believe you. This undermines the very heart of every relationship – especially with yourself! Better to under-promise and over-deliver than the other way around.

7   The satisfaction of keeping a commitment, both to yourself and others involved, is deeply gratifying.

Make your goal a reality with Mind Chi Applied!

Part 4

Mind Chi Plus

17 Mind Chi Vehicle

Overview

Your Mind Chi Vehicle
About Cognitive Behavioural Therapy (CBT)
About Structural Tension (ST)
About the 4-R Method
About natural memory enhancers
Put your mind in gear!

The brain is an intriguing subject and we have included here a heady mix of well-established scientific research, well reputed psychological processes, and applications that are 'new territory' to whet your interest. We will share with you incredible information about your mind, what actually goes on in your brain and why it is so important and exciting to see how you can be in control of your thoughts, yourself and your future.

We have worked hard to simplify information about many profound and complex brain processes. It is our ardent desire to make the theories accessible and useable. In so doing we hope that we have not diminished the full implications of the theories and findings.

In this section we summarize interesting facts and scientific information about the mind and how it works, and explain how they relate to the Mind Chi principles. Because of the limited space that a book can offer, the information we can share with you is only the tip of the iceberg, but further resources and references are included on page 323, and on our website (www.MindChi.com).

Mind Chi will work for you whether or not you read the research material, but we encourage you to dip in as the information is so exciting. We have tried to make it inviting reading – so come with us on the most magical of mystery tours of your mind!

Understanding how an abstract theory can have relevance in everyday life can be challenging. For example, when we ask people whether they are aware of Roger Sperry's research on the 'split brain' (the popularized right/left brain theory) from the late 1960s most people are aware of it. If we then ask whether anyone has changed habits, their approach to life or activities because of it … the majority look at us blankly and ask, 'What do you mean?'

Just in case you too are wondering, initially the polarized information was that the left was the 'logical and analytical' side and the right was the 'creative' side. People were then labelled as having either 'left' or 'right' brain dominance. How limiting – and untrue. We now know that all the functions in the left and right cortex support each other (through the corpus callosum in the centre of your head). In practical terms, this means that, to improve your memory for example, you need to blend logic with novelty, mix colour with order and include rhythm with repetition.

Your Mind Chi Vehicle

We know from our years of practising the Mind Chi processes and sharing them with others that the Mind Chi Program *will* work for you, because the techniques that underpin the process incorporate 'what to do' into a powerful 'how to do it'. The concept works with the mind to increase its effectiveness *exponentially*. This is why we are very excited about its potential.

At the heart of Mind Chi are four theories of personal development that have been rigorously tested and used to help many hundreds of thousands of people around the world to either overcome severe problems or achieve lifetime goals. They are:

1   Cognitive Behavioural Therapy (CBT) and Rational Living Therapy
2   Structural Tension (ST)
3   The 4-R method
4   Natural memory enhancement

> Your Mind Chi Vehicle has a carefully crafted and 'full spec' engine to take your mind on a journey of change with style, speed and grace!

All of these therapies are woven into the Mind Chi Program. Combined they have become your 'Mind Chi Vehicle' that will carry you forwards and make it possible for you to regain control over yourself and progress to where you have always wanted to be. This will enable you to make the life changes you want with the greatest of ease.

Further, once you have mastered Mind Chi, you can apply the process to anything you want to do for the rest of your life.

Now, put your foot on the accelerator of your mind and enjoy journeying through the following pages in your Mind Chi Vehicle – safe in the knowledge that the engine is fast, smooth and highly efficient. Fasten your safety belt, please!

About Cognitive Behavioural Therapy (CBT)

We begin with a brief history of CBT, as many people have worked on its development and evolution. The initial wellspring of inspiration came from 'rational therapy' developed by Albert Ellis in the 1950s; it then moved on to incorporate the work of Aaron Beck, who concentrated on studying the cognitive aspects of behaviour in the 1960s; and further to the 1970s, when Arnold Lazarus blended both the cognitive and behavioural aspects and added the importance of the awareness of physical feelings (as distinct from emotional states). He called it 'multimodal therapy'. Most recently, Dr Aldo Pucci has integrated the previous elements to create Rational Living Therapy – devised as a systematic approach to help people make themselves better.

CBT stands for Cognitive Behavioural Therapy. And what does *that* mean? From The Royal College of Psychologists comes this definition:

> *'CBT can help you to change how you think (cognitive) and what you do (behaviour). These changes can help you to feel better. Unlike some of the other talking treatments, it focuses on the "here and now" problems and difficulties. Instead of focusing on the causes of your distress or symptoms in the past, it looks for ways to improve your state of mind now.'*

CBT can help you to make any change you want by breaking it down into small steps. This makes it easier to see how your behaviour and actions are connected and how they affect your mental energy. First there is the event, the 'stressor' or habit you wish to change or put in place; then your thoughts, emotions, physical feelings and actions culminate in your response. Any of these four areas can affect the others. How you *think* about a situation can affect how you *feel* physically and emotionally. It can also alter what you do about it. This 'vicious circle' can become a negative and destructive habit so easily: an event can trigger a response in any of the four parts which in turn can exacerbate a downward cycle.

CBT helps you to analyse the separate parts of the behavioural responses clearly so you can change them – and in so doing modify the way you feel and act. CBT aims to help you to a point where you can 'do it yourself' and work out your own ways of tackling future problems. CBT is the therapy of choice for most cases of behavioural disorders.

CBT in action: your Mind Chi BEAT

To assist you with putting Mind Chi into your life as a positively addictive habit – that requires little conscious thought, yet empowers your every day – we have introduced some of the Mind Chi activities in an amended CBT format.

The 'now' stage of your Mind Chi routine is the area most closely associated with the practice of CBT.

Step 5: Be aware (page 58) and Step 6: Choose (page 60) introduce you to the role and impact of your Body, Emotions, Actions and Thoughts on your current reality and your future goals via your Mind Chi BEAT. You will ask yourself:

- What were/are/will be – your **B**ody's physical responses?
- What were/are/will be – your **E**motional responses?
- What were/are/will be – your **A**ctions?
- What were/are/will be – your **T**houghts?

Repeating these questions each day will gradually increase and strengthen your overall awareness (and thereby control) of your feelings and behaviour and their repercussions on your progress towards your goals.

With practice you will develop your mindful *awareness* and be better able to bring your *attention* into the 'now': the present moment. Increased awareness of your present Mind Chi BEAT enables you to *choose* how to direct your energy and motivation towards your future goals. This is very powerful.

Further, your 'Chi' will assist your willpower to make the choice that you actually want to make (rather than the easy 'default' that otherwise may occur).

We ask you to do the Mind Chi BEAT 'check and choose' once every day because it is easy and useful in a variety of contexts. You may find that you start to apply it naturally during the day. Once the Mind Chi BEAT becomes an automatic check, you will find that you use it when you feel tense or stressed: 'Is your neck tight?' 'Are your emotions distraught?' 'Are you acting in haste?' 'Is your thinking muddled?' Just check your Mind Chi BEAT. As soon as you develop awareness of the source of the tension, you can choose to change that aspect of the BEAT.

The even better news is that if you improve in one area, you are likely to experience improvement in other parts of your life as well. Let's say that you decide to concentrate on relaxing your neck: your emotional outlook will brighten because you have taken action; you will probably slow down a bit and start to think more clearly.

The 'vicious' circle that we mentioned before (page 41) can become a 'virtuous' spiral – to be the opposite of vicious circles to assist you to make the changes you do want and achieve your goals. So awareness can lead to one choice after another and begin a virtuous upward spiral (page 264). Nice!

March to the BEAT of your choosing

About Structural Tension (ST)

In the 1970s there was a great leap forward in our understanding of how the brain functions and the associated processes we need to help us to learn and to live better. One of the many guiding lights in the field was Robert Fritz with his concept of 'structural tension'.

The term 'structure' in structural tension means 'a complete or whole thing'; for example: a car, a building, a business, or a human body. A structure is an entity that is undivided, complete and total. Your life is a structure and, like all structures, it will behave and work in certain ways in line with that structure.

Fritz says that people have two basic structural patterns: *advancing* and *oscillating*.

Advancing is a structural pattern in which the success you have achieved becomes the platform for future success. The platform allows you to build momentum over time, and the sum total of your life experiences leads you forward. (For example: learning to drive one step at a time via a series of lessons and practising weekly to build on previous knowledge.)

Oscillating refers to a structural pattern in which the success you have created is neutralized, because each step forward is followed by a step backward. Within this kind of structure, success cannot last in the long term. (For example: having a one day 'crash course' in learning to drive and then not practising for several months.)

It is possible to change from an oscillating to an advancing structural pattern, but the change requires you to become more directly involved in your own life-building process: you create more of what you truly want, and you broaden the quality of your life experience.

Fritz calls the relationship between a future goal or vision and current reality Structural Tension. The idea is based on a principle of nature: 'tension seeks resolution'. During the creative process, your focus is split between where you are currently and what you want to achieve. In order to reach your goal, it is necessary to create a detailed, incremental plan of actions and steps to move you forward.

Fritz identifies three steps to resolve Structural Tension:

1 Define (create) the vision/goal.
2 Generate Structural Tension by defining current reality.
3 Resolve the tension by creating a path of least resistance via actions and steps between your current reality and your vision/goal.

It is necessary to keep assessing your current reality, to observe carefully where you are now and with your flexible focus, see where that puts you in relation to your desired goal. This means that you maintain the structural tension and therefore seek ways to resolve this tension and attain your goal.

Structural Tension in action: The Mind Chi Plan and your 'Chi'

Within the Mind Chi Program, the principle of structural tension is incorporate within the Mind Chi Plan. Each plan enables you to assess your current reality in a specific area that you wish to change and then create the goal/vision of how you would rather have your life.

We have provided 50 Strategies for Success to choose from. Each is a Mind Chi Plan in a format that reflects Fritz's theory of structural tension. You can select any of them, or create your own from the blank DIY Mind Chi Plan. The contrast between your 'current reality' and your desired future 'goal' will enable you to prevent oscillation and catapult you into action.

Use structural tension to reinforce your Mind Chi goal or vision. Whenever you have a moment to daydream, we suggest that you re-run the short 'film' of your vision of how you would like your life to turn out. Use your Mind Chi BEAT to experience your life 'as though' you are living it now to make the process more rigorous (page 265). As you strengthen the force of your thoughts and goal actions, you will reinforce your platform of success in line with Fritz's theories and build up momentum for positive change.

Make your plans a reality by crafting your Mind Chi in action steps and applying Mind Chi to your chosen Mind Chi Plan for a minimum of 28 consecutive days. Your Mind Chi Plan will reinforce your positive Mind Chi Meme and assist you to resolve the structural tension between where you are (current reality) and the changes you need to make to achieve your goal (future reality).

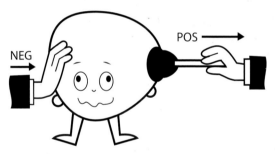

NEG

POS

Experience the negative 'push' and the positive 'pull'

'Chi' your Mind Chi mentor (page 31), will help to reinforce the advancing of your line of progress by ensuring that any negative voices ('You are always late!' 'You know you'll mess it up') are replaced by your new positive Mind Chi Meme ('I am reliable', 'I deliver excellent work on time'). Negative self-talk is a major factor in preventing progress – so make sure the voice of your 'Chi' remains positive at all times. If a negative thought slips in to your head, make yourself repeat your positive alternative four to ten times. Write your Mind Chi Memes on small cards and keep them in your wallet or purse so you can read them frequently. Get your 'Chi' working on your behalf, not against you.

About the 4-R method

Over the past 20 years, Dr Jeffrey Schwartz has worked with patients who have Obsessive-Compulsive Disorder (OCD) and has undertaken to assist them to change their behaviours. His research is particularly interesting because he is working to train the brain to overcome behaviour brought about by chemical imbalance. The results are highly significant to Mind Chi as they show how the mind can control your brain's chemistry and circuitry. You really *do* have the power to transform yourself.

Dr Schwartz's process of retraining is in four parts. Each step is important, as each influences and increases the synergy of the next. The four parts, in relation to OCD are:

1　RE-LABEL. Recognize that intrusive obsessive thoughts and urges are the result of OCD: there is a brain malfunction. Learn to recognize and re-label an OCD thought and to know that it is not relaying an accurate message. This is achieved by becoming mindfully aware of OCD urges as they first rise up. This stage recognizes *what* is happening.

2　RE-ATTRIBUTE. Realize that the intensity and intrusiveness of the thought or urge is caused by OCD; it is related to a biochemical imbalance in the brain. The key phrase here is 'It is not me, it is the OCD'; as such it is possible to choose NOT to react to the thoughts. (This is *not* the same as saying, 'I behaved badly because that is my personality and it's not my fault!') This stage recognizes *why* it is happening.

3　RE-FOCUS. Work around OCD thoughts by re-focusing attention away from the obsessive thought and onto something else. For at least a few minutes, *choose an alternative behaviour*. This stage is vitally important for building new neural pathways. This is the stage *when* change occurs.

4   RE-VALUE. Do not take the OCD thought at face value. It is not significant in itself. This realization develops understanding of your brain. Re-valuing will place faith in *your* ability, with patience and perseverance, to respond and gain control. This is *how* you re-prioritize.

Schwartz says:

'By understanding this process by which we empower ourselves to fight OCD and by clearly appreciating the control one gains by training the mind to overcome compulsive or automatic responses to intrusive thoughts or feelings, we gain a deepening insight into how to take back our lives. Changing our brain chemistry is a happy consequence of this life-affirming action.*

True freedom lies along this path of a clarified perception of genuine self-interest.'

The 4-R method in action: Mind Chi Basic, Mind Chi Applied and your 'Chi'

Why is the 4-R method so important to Mind Chi? Because if the technique can help overcome the severity of OCD, then those dealing with relatively minor obsessions, habits and traits can have confidence in the realization that they will definitely succeed. We have included the essence of this information at a subtle level in your Mind Chi Basic and Mind Chi Applied programs.

Your 'Chi', your Mind Chi mentor, will also heighten your awareness and assist you to think in positive ways. Put your Mind Chi Meme into action by remaining mindfully aware of how you speak to yourself. Replace each negative thought you have with a positive thought, and repeat it four to ten times. With this mindful awareness, you *re-label* your old thoughts and turn them into new ones. Your 'Chi' (as your brainy observer) can be trained to listen for voices that need changing.

During your daily Mind Chi Basic (and Applied) routine, pay increased attention during Stages 3 and 4 as you review and rewind your past 24 hours (pages 52 and 54) and observe whether your actions and reactions were unhelpful or a help in progressing towards your goal. Over the 28 days you are likely to find that even though old unhelpful habits may continue to recur, you will gradually, with increasing awareness, catch and change your responses to create new and positive habits. You can *re-attribute* the reasons for your old unhelpful thoughts and actions and craft them consciously into new and helpful ones.

Mind Chi allows you to *re-focus*. Re-focusing lies at the heart of the Mind Chi process and stands on the shoulders of re-labelling and re-attributing to enable you to redirect attention to your thoughts and actions. Re-focusing occurs during Stages 5 and 6 of Mind Chi Basic/Applied, in the 'now' (current reality) phase of your daily routine. If you can 'catch' your thoughts and intentions when they initially bubble up, you will become more aware of them and can choose whether or not to act on them. Once again, the Mind Chi BEAT provides an excellent way to focus for a minute and consciously change one or more of your responses. The inner voice of your 'Chi' will help you to catch your thoughts at the earliest 'bubble' stage and this will enable you to redirect them in the most productive way possible.

Experience the joy of being in control of your 'self'.

The final function of your Mind Chi Basic and Applied, during Stages 7 and 8, is to evaluate your plan and be grateful for the progress you have made to date. This action provides you with the opportunity to *re-value* your goal, your thoughts and your actions. Concentrate on your chosen goal, visualize it as your new priority, and be filled with gratitude at all that is and will be happening. This is a useful way to reinforce the impact of your entire Mind Chi Program.

About natural memory enhancers

As a child you experienced the wonders of your memory working naturally for you. Without knowing you employed all the factors that we will now examine, and you learned with ease and joy. Natural memory enhancers are innate skills that are built in to your brain. They allow you to become first 'consciously competent' and then as 'unconsciously competent' as you were in your childhood. A memory that works for you and brings you the greatest satisfaction is one that uses the most efficient memory techniques.

Firsts and lasts

You will naturally remember things that occur as 'firsts' and 'lasts' more easily than those things that occur in between. So, your first kiss and your most recent kiss your first job interview and your most recent job interview can be recalled more readily than the kisses or interviews you had in between (unless something occurred that was so outstanding that it sticks in your memory … read on). Between your memorable 'firsts' and 'lasts' stretches the big dip of familiarity and sameness. And the longer the dip continues, the bigger your 'forgettery' phase will be. In order to increase your ability to remember events, you need to create more firsts and lasts. These can be made in the form of breaks. Taking a break every 45–60 minutes when studying (or working on a large project) will allow your brain to consider and integrate the details of your work more readily.

Bluma Zeigarnik (1900–1988) discovered that when you interrupt yourself in the middle of study (or any reading/writing/computing task) you improve your attention to (and thereby memory of) what you have been reading. She noticed that breaks give your brain a chance to file things away and make better sense of them, providing more firsts and lasts.

A phenomenon called 'the reminiscence effect' also has a part to play. Reminiscence is the opposite of forgetting as it refers to the rise in your ability to recall information about five to ten minutes after you have stopped learning about it. (This is especially true if you are interested in the topic.) So, during your break, your brain is still working on the task in hand and the brain's memory enhancers tie the facts and the memory together.

The 'first and last' principle impacts on conversations too. You will be remembered more by how you start and end a conversation, rather than what you say or do in between (see pages 274–5). This is why offering a cheery greeting to people in the morning starts the day so well, and why closing a conversation with a positive comment or summary lends a constructive tone to the discussion that is naturally remembered.

Outstanding moments

But how can you best tackle the big dip of 'forgettery' that sits between 'firsts' and 'lasts'? Hedwig Von Restorff (1906–1962) is the man to assist with the big dip. He observed that things which are 'outstanding' are most easily remembered (i.e. things that stand out from the mass). So, you might choose to do something different in the middle of your presentation to create an 'outstanding' moment and to wake people up and regain their attention. (However, it does need to be appropriate and linked to your topic!)

Outstanding moments are also an effective way to distinguish one year from another. Think back through your life. You will be able to remember your age in relation to an event, a song or a holiday that anchors you to a place and time. (Looking forwards, why not plan to do one thing that is new and different each year, so it becomes the theme/ feature of that year?)

Repetition

This is an important and again natural aspect of assisting your memory to work. As a child you loved to hear the same stories over and over or repeatedly sang songs that 'taught' you your alphabet. As an adult whose hobby is golf, you will practise your swing at the driving range, over and over again. Unfortunately, when you think of repetition in learning, you may have more negative memories, such as the dry hours of repeating times tables at school. So when you wish to repeat something, set yourself the challenge of making the repetition as much fun as you can and you will reap the rewards.

Interest

Of course, the more interested you are in the subject, the easier it is to remember! You know this and do it naturally, but there are also ways in which you can 'artificially' raise your interest quotient. Doing so will increase the efficiency of your memory. Employ your imagination to fuel your interest and your memory will automatically improve as you use the strength of your visual abilities, to 'see' things in your head.

Associations

Sir Francis Galton (1822–1911) was a half-cousin of Charles Darwin and the founder of psychometrics. He was the first to document the power of association to assist your memory. Your memory works by associating everything you see, hear, feel, touch, smell and sense with a previous experience based on similar associations. Associations are your prompt to recall information (hence the smell of fresh coffee may transport you back to your favourite student café, or a nostalgic song might remind you of a moment in childhood). Associations are the natural way for your brain to link and connect all you have ever known with any new information. The stronger the (multi-sensory) associations you can make in your mind the better will be your ability to accurately recall the events.

The power of FLORIA

'FLORIA' summarizes this powerhouse of effective memory enhancers (and as an acronym is also a memory technique).

First	You remember the 'first' of things – your first kiss; first job; first car …
Last	You remember your most recent partner; job; and cup of coffee …
Outstanding	You remember outstanding events, people and feelings …
Repeated	You do need to repeat in fun ways, things to remember.
Interest	Increase your interest and engage your imagination.
Association	You use your senses to link and connect information.

These all help you to remember (putting in) in such a way as to make recall (taking out) easier.

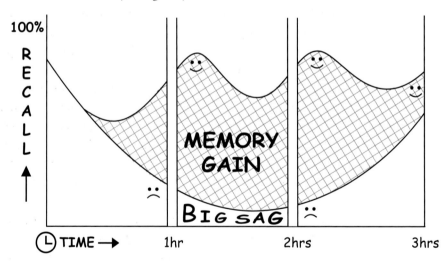

In the diagram above, the vertical axis is your ability to recall and the horizontal axis is time passing. Research has shown that you begin with about 80% recall of a topic, the longer you study (here, up to three hours is shown) the greater the dip in your ability to recall – you may understand what you are studying, but that is not the same as remembering. By taking a break every 45–60 minutes you increase dramatically your ability to recall. When you add the 'reminiscence effect' which occurs after a break, it heightens your ability to recall (without you doing anything) so you see the significant increase shown by the hashed section above.

Natural Memory Enhancers in action: Mind Chi Basic and Mind Chi Applied

The FLORIA technique is fundamental to your Mind Chi Basic, Applied or developing your Mind Chi Plan:

F   **F**irst, let your mind briefly experience the achievement of your goals by thinking of yourself as having already succeeded.

L   The **L**ast thing you did, when completing your Mind Chi Basic and Mind Chi Applied was to enjoy a minute of gratitude for all you have and will accomplish. Remind yourself of that sense of joy.

O   What stood out as your **O**utstanding moment? We leave your sense of play (and what you can get away with) to create new outstanding moments.

R   **R**epeating the Mind Chi Basic and the Mind Chi Applied every day for 28 days will embed your new habit, power up your self-control and strengthen new and positive neural pathways.

I   Your **I**nterest reminds you why you are inspired by your choice of goal and reminds you WIIFM (what's in it for me?). In the context of Mind Chi, it strengthens your self-belief and your willpower. This is the reason for your commitment.

A   The mighty muscle of **A**ssociation flexes itself by creating memory links between the eight steps of Mind Chi and your Mind Chi Plan, especially when using Mind Chi Applied to direct your desired goal or outcome. You can strengthen these associations by increasing your use of sensory memory triggers such as squeezing your fist when you hold on to the successes you have recalled in Step 4.

Putting FLORIA to work for you just eases your natural ability to recall and increases your delight in the fact that you *do* have a mind that can and is still working for you. Remember that the entire plasticity of your brain is there to assist you to learn and experience new things. This is what you are 'designed' to do. FLORIA enables your brain to develop flexibility of thought and positive determination at the highest level.

Trouncing your 'forgettery'

Do you feel that you are better at forgetting than remembering? Would you say that your memory is deteriorating? Do you harbour quiet fears that you may be showing early signs of dementia? Let us first reassure you that in many cases poor memory results from false ideas about how your memory works.

The first step towards remembering more is to shift the way you think about your memory. Remember: everything that you do or say or think, emanates from your memory. Today you woke up, got dressed, made and ate breakfast (well, hopefully you did, as a healthy breakfast sets you up for a successful day!), and travelled to your place of work where you greeted people and started your day. Every nano-piece of that activity was driven by your memory. We take it for granted, because most of the time it works so perfectly.

Next, think back to childhood when you believe your memory was 'perfect'? Was it really?

Are you sure?

If you were able to check you would probably find that you were forgetting the most important things, and often, 'I can't find my sports kit/lunch/homework/violin/project/money/shoes!' is a common cry from most children. The BIG difference is that you weren't troubled by your 'forgettery' in childhood, whereas you are now. Today you focus on your forgetfulness and talk about what you have forgotten; you trade forgetting stories with your associates instead of the more accurate conversation which would go, 'Guess what? I remembered to wake up, dress and find my way here today, I've read the newspaper, answered emails and spoken on the phone, isn't my memory fabulous?!' It becomes less than 'perfect' when your attention is on other things.

The art of forgettery

OK, so you forgot to attend an appointment! And why was that? Because you:

1   Did not input the information in such a manner as to easily recall it.
2   Are stressed. Your memory functions at its lowest level when all of your systems are geared for 'fight or flight'. It is very likely that you, like the majority of business people we have dealt with over the past few years, are in a constant state of negative stress arousal and your ability to return to 'normal' has been lost: your breathing is shallow, there are increased levels of the stress hormones, cortisol and adrenalin in your bloodstream, you may have raised blood pressure, and blood tends to be pumping more to your extremities (your feet and hands) rather than your head. Over an extended period, this state becomes unhealthy and means that your cerebral functioning is impaired.
3   Have fallen prey to the most insidious trap of all: by focusing your attention on your forgettery, you are exacerbating that negative situation.

Your body will end up in a permanently stressed state and your memory will become impaired when you:

1   Do not care for your body and brain. Your body requires healthy food, regular exercise, sufficient oxygen and proper breaks.
2   Are not sleeping as you wish. Sleep is necessary for your brain to sort out your day. When you are asleep, your memory files the things to be remembered, your brain clears unwanted information and it links together and connects old and new information (which is why you often wake up with the answer to a problem).
3   Experience side-effects from medicines, like beta blockers and anti-cholinergic drugs – which can diminish short-term memory.

Your body and brain are the engine room and power source for all you think, say, do and feel. Neglecting them is like owning the most precious diamond and displaying it covered in dust.

Improving memory over time

Can you prevent 'forgettery' over time? Enter Professor C.A. Mace (1894–1971) to assist you with 'spaced repetition'. He discovered that there are certain times after learning when your ability to recall the information seems to 'drop off'. However, if you are able to review the data just before those 'drop off' points you will keep the memory fresh. Further, it only takes five (maximum six) of these reviews to embed the memory, as the information integrates with your other knowledge and becomes a part of your long term memory (LTM).

Specifically, in order to capture information permanently in your long-term memory, you need to review the information at memory 'drop off' points, in other words, repeat at spaced intervals. What does that mean you need to do?

- As you are reading or studying (and want to remember) stop about every 40–55 minutes and note down the key points that you want to keep. (A map is a very effective way of doing this.) At the end of the day, look over the information carefully.
- Now put the information away in a file (scan or save) until the following day (or keep adding to the map/notes if it is a big subject). Put a reminder on your diary system to look at it again.
- Open your document the next day and spend a few minutes looking over the key points. Save it again for the next review in one week.
- After one-week review, file/save it for one month.

Now you have converted that plasticity to 'rigidity', meaning that you have made your new Mind Chi habit permanent.

Bravo!

- At the one month review, see how much you can remember or recreate before you take out your document. Then check the original to see what is missing, concentrating on those missing bits. Put it away again for three months (one quarter of the year).
- At the one quarter review, you will probably find that you have incorporated the information into other areas of thought and action and it is becoming a natural piece of available data, like your phone number. If you feel it might be beneficial, have one last review in a half a year.

Yes, that is it! Simple and highly effective. You have now made your new Mind Chi Strategy a permanent part of your life. Just let all your natural memory rhythms keep working for you.

If we apply Professor Mace's findings to the 'forgettery curve' – it looks like this!

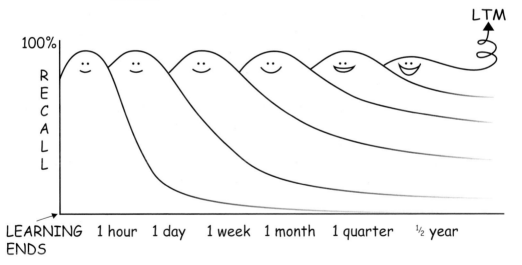

This is the way to create a permanent memory. (In this diagram the vertical axis is your ability to recall and the horizontal axis is time passing.) Research has shown specific times to review. These have an exponentially positive effect. Five or six reviews place information in your long term memory.

Put your mind in gear!

The Mind Chi Vehicle will transport you towards regaining your self-control and an overall better quality of life. You can direct it towards any specific area you choose. What drives the Mind Chi Vehicle? Well, to continue the metaphor:

- the Mind Chi BEAT (based on CBT) is the air intake,
- the Mind Chi Basic (based on OCD) is the fuel intake,
- the Mind Chi Plan (based on ST) is the combustion, and
- the Mind Chi in Action (based on Memory) is the exhaust!

All highly carbon-efficient and environmentally friendly of course!

From our extensive research and years of learning, experimenting and observing, we have crafted a deluxe, super turbo-charged Mind Chi Vehicle that has street credibility and will transform your life by taking you anywhere you want to go. And it is all yours! Slip right into the driving seat and enjoy the 'new car' aroma. All the bells and whistles are bright and shiny; it beseeches you to drive it away. Remember to program your 'Chi' as your highly reliable 'satellite navigation' system!

We hope you feel energized about getting started on your Mind Chi journey. We certainly feel this way about the privilege of sharing it with you. Yes! We have unbridled enthusiasm and we look forward to your catching it too.

Your Mind Chi Vehicle will let you roar into action!

18 Mind Chi Assistance

Overview

Types of thinking

For those who like to understand the background to what they are embarking upon, here, for your review, are some concepts that will help to put your new Mind Chi ways into context. Both authors have found these ideas to be useful and hope that they may serve you well too.

The voice inside your head that we have called your 'Chi' (page 31) chatters away in response to anything and everything that happens to you. By now you will know that you can intercede when that chatter is not in your best interest. Alerting your 'Chi' to the types of thinking you do and do not want will help you achieve a more positive future outcome.

Types of thinking

1 Rational thinking

Achieving goals requires the ability to think in a clear and systematic way. Under stress and strain it is easy to succumb to negative thoughts and to allow your emotions to hijack your reactions. If you find that this happens to you, here is a series of questions that you can ask, which will return you to rational mode:

Do your thoughts and reactions tend to be based on facts or feelings?

In our global electronic age where myths and misconceptions abound and can be catapulted round the world in minutes, it is always worth checking the source of the information you are reacting to. Where did the information come from? Was it from a reliable source? Can you focus solely on the facts and separate your emotions, suppositions or perceptions? Sort your facts from your feelings in a mini-map (page 77): a superb way to collect them for reflection while considering your response.

Does your thinking help you to achieve your goals?

Consider whether your thoughts are constructive. Do they take you closer to where you want to go? If the answer is 'no', then you need to adjust your thinking. Ask yourself whether you are fully committed to your goals; consider with whom you need to see or speak, to help you achieve your goals.

Does your thinking help you to feel positive?

This is a good time to check your Mind Chi BEAT (page 39) to see how you are feeling and what you want to change. What emotions, thoughts and actions need to be adjusted to help you to become more positive? Remember that you are the one in charge of your responses. If you don't like the way you feel at present, focus on what you do want and use your Mind Chi routine to create steps to achieve your goal in future.

2   *Reflexive thinking*

Many of your thoughts and responses occur automatically; they are a learned reflex that may have developed over years. Reflexive thinking is frequently irrational: someone 'presses your buttons' and you react before you have given any consideration to your response – and often you regret that response. Unfortunately, those closest to us – the ones who know us best – are the most likely to 'press' those buttons and suffer the consequences. You may feel as if you can do nothing about this kind of automatic response – but with practice you can change your thinking. The secret is to catch yourself before you respond.

If this is an area where you wish to improve, then bring your attention to the very first trigger your brain receives. Exercise your free will (think of it as your 'free won't' in this case) and distract yourself: walk away, close your eyes, and hum a favourite tune – anything to give yourself the space to think before you react. Be aware of when and with whom those incidences occur. If appropriate, ask others to work with you to help you to change. Extend the length of the gap before you respond each time, until you reach a point where the 'reflex' has lost its power and you have regained yours.

3   *First you had the thought*

Rarely will you do or say anything without thinking about doing it first; otherwise you would be a puppet with someone else pulling your strings. Although it may feel as if that is the case occasionally, be assured that your thoughts and your choices are always your own. It may be easier to point the finger and say, 'It was his fault' or, 'She made me do it!' However, the truth is that you are the source of every response that you have.

Square your shoulders and repeat, 'I am the only one responsible for my actions and emotions'. Liberate yourself by saying, 'Yes, I am in control'.

Feeling out of control of your own life and thoughts is highly stressful; it results in feelings of hopelessness and helplessness. Taking *total* responsibility for *all* your thoughts and actions is greatly to your advantage.

Encourage your 'Chi' to take action to make you aware of your thoughts at a conscious level (page 31). If necessary take a minute to think while you bring to your focused attention the choice of action or response you want to make. Say, 'I choose to be responsible for my thoughts, emotions and deeds' and release the power of that freedom.

FIRST
THE THOUGHT

4   Thoughts you 'should' not have

'Don't *should* on yourself!' How much time and energy do you spend each day thinking that you *should* do, feel or think this or that? Bring your awareness (your 'Chi') to these thoughts when they bubble up so that you can decide whether they are useful to you or not. If you think that your 'should' is valid, then schedule a time to do it and commit to completing it. Many 'shoulds', when looked at rationally, are found to be *ir*rational or caught up with feelings of guilt or duty. Make up your mind what you are going to do – and then plan it and do it.

The same applies to the 'have tos' that you impose on your life. If your day seems to start with a stream of guilt and regret, fix yourself a hot drink, close your eyes and do your Mind Chi BEAT check (page 58). Imagine the day as a blank sheet of paper. You are free to decide *what* you will do and *when* you will do it. You may end up *choosing* to do what you previously felt that you *had to* do! If so, the shift in perception will have a very positive effect on your motivation for the task. For example, you may think that you don't want to work on that report. Upon reflection, you may decide that completing it (possibly early) will feel fabulous – with the added benefit that your team will be very impressed. You decide that you want to experience those outcomes, and so you plan accordingly.

5   *Thinking your emotions*

You are responsible not only for your thoughts, but also – yes, you guessed it – for your emotions. All your experiences and responses to date are stored in your memory. When your emotions are aroused your mind will trigger previous memories associated with similar feelings and you will tend to react based on those. If your emotional response to an event is trouble-free for you and others, then all is well. However, if your experience has negative associations, then you are free to change your response in future and choose another emotion from the range available to you.

You may think, 'But, I wasn't angry before, so and so *made me* furious!' In reality, another person in the same situation might have responded without anger. We are each free to choose how we behave towards one another.

Focusing on your 'Chi' will heighten your awareness and activate your attention to changing your thoughts and emotions in any situation. Once you have focused your attention you will realize that you do have a choice – several in fact! For example, you can choose whether or not to respond to a provocation, and if you do decide to respond, what type of response it will be.

Trying this out can be fun! You can explore using different emotions in different situations and see what kind of responses you receive back.

You might say to yourself, 'I am experiencing a mixture of emotions here. Hold on, I will select the one I choose to share.'

Realizing that you do have emotional choice allows you to choose to change other unhelpful emotional responses such as nervousness or shyness.

Once you have achieved greater emotional awareness and started to choose your reactions, you will no longer feel like anyone's puppet. You will discover that you are in command of your own mind and knowing that will feel very good.

6 Flexible focus – or 'panhandler' thinking

In America, the term 'panhandler' is used for a street person who begs for food or money. We use this term as a metaphor to challenge the way you think. In order to change entrenched thinking patterns, it is necessary to develop the skill of 'flexible focus': being able to switch your thinking from one perspective to another. Enter the panhandler! When you observe a panhandler on the street corner, what is your reaction? Do you feel sympathy for him? Do you think he is poor or bankrupt? Do you see him as being different from you?

Now change your perspective and switch to the panhandler's point of view. He may surprise you with his thinking, which might be truly entrepreneurial. He may be focusing on the flexibility and freedom of his working day; he may see himself as a businessman and consider himself to be rich as a result of the offerings from passers-by; he may enjoy the repartee that he has with people.

His possible thoughts are illustrated in the manga-style cartoon following. The lesson here is that the panhandler despite his appearance and occupation is channelling his Mind Chi to positive outcomes; whereas those of us who judge the situation may be making assumptions about the situation from traditional thinking habits.

Panhandler thinking

19 Mind Chi Beliefs

Overview

Identifying beliefs
Discover your true beliefs
Challenge limiting beliefs
Conni's art lesson
Discover what you really want

Underlying your Mind Chi BEAT (Body, Emotions, Actions and Thoughts) are your beliefs and your core values, which are an essential part of who you are. They drive your thought processes and the emotions that impact on the way you feel and, ultimately, impact on your choices of action. The model below shows how your thinking system works:

- *Beliefs and values*: Your beliefs and value systems are generated from influences around you from childhood, through adulthood, and throughout your lifetime.
- *Thoughts*: Those beliefs and values influence your thoughts about life and how you interact with yourself, others and the world at large.
- *Emotions*: Beliefs, values and thoughts drive your emotions. For example, if you are thinking negative thoughts you may feel anxious; if you are thinking positive thoughts you are more likely to feel calm.

- *Body*: Your emotions and thoughts have a direct effect on your body. If you are feeling anxious then you will trigger the 'fight or flight' stress response; if you are feeling joyous then you will feel energetic and alive.
- *Actions*: All the previous steps influence your choice of action: what you choose to do in life and how you decide to behave.

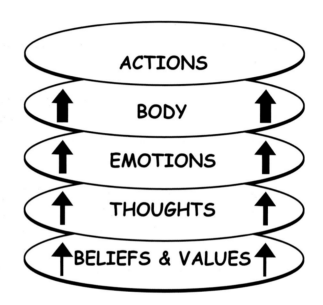

Identifying beliefs

Beliefs are ways of thinking and behaving that are literally 'soaked up' during the course of a lifetime from your parents, family, teachers, friends, employer, colleagues and role models. Their influence (positive or negative) will reinforce your chosen set of values and the social and moral guidelines that shape everything you do. You may have been influenced by your parents' religious beliefs; maybe you were told to suppress your emotions ('big boys don't cry'); or you may have entered a profession because others told you that you would be secure there for life.

Going against the tide of acceptance is never going to be the easy option. Adopting beliefs and values that gain approval and maintain the status quo is always the safest path. It is natural to be a social creature or to seek approval of your superiors and peers. The strong need to bond with others and be a team player tends to over-ride the wish to challenge the beliefs and values of others.

Every day in every workplace you can hear the sound of self-limiting beliefs, carried on the basis of hearsay and assumptions: 'That won't work, we tried it before.' 'We don't have the time or resources.' 'They'll never buy it.' 'You can't; it's too late.' These common beliefs sabotage new ideas, close doors to creativity, and prevent new approaches from being tested. This is where the 'panhandler thinking' is needed (page 286). Flexible focus enables you to see another point of view and challenge when appropriate.

It takes maturity and self-confidence to challenge the accepted order of things and ask a simple 'Why?': 'Why are we doing it this way?' 'Why won't it work?' 'Why have we never tried before?' 'Why don't we make the time?' Your Mind Chi practice will encourage you to ask 'Why?' on a regular basis – to become a change-maker and trailblazer, rather than a follower.

Your beliefs are stored in both your para-conscious and conscious mind (you may act with or without being aware of their origin). The habits resulting from your belief system affect the way you think, learn, behave and communicate, yet you can be totally unaware of these silent forces at work. Beliefs are so pervasive that it can be difficult to notice when they start to trigger your responses automatically.

Next time you have a limiting belief, ask yourself 'How do I know this is true?' and note your answers. Keep repeating this question 'How do I know this is true?' until you are satisfied that you have uncovered the truth. It is a revealing exercise.

Discover your true beliefs

1   *Journaling*

By writing down your thoughts you can uncover beliefs that have remained hidden while sabotaging your achievements. To journal successfully, write down not only how your current day went or what you plan for tomorrow but also ask, 'Why did I choose to do that?' and follow up with 'Why do I feel that way?' In this way you will explore your true motivations more deeply.

2   *Self-analysis*

By self-analysis, we mean noticing carefully what you feel when certain things happen. Your Mind Chi BEAT (page 39) is designed to assist you in this. Using your Mind Chi BEAT while journaling is a good idea, but it is far more effective to use it when you are actually living the experience. If you are stressed and about to eat the chocolate cake, stop and ask yourself:

1   What Body sensations am I experiencing now?
2   What Emotions am I feeling now?
3   What Actions am I doing now?
4   What Thoughts am I having now?

Practice using these questions through your day so that you learn to focus your attention by living in the present and noticing your responses. You will become gradually in tune with your Mind Chi BEAT and use 'Chi' you Mind Chi mentor to adapt your inner voice accordingly.

3 *Observing and questioning others*

Discussing your beliefs with others can be very revealing. Whether others' beliefs differ from or are similar to your own there will be many things you can learn from one another. For example, if you hear someone say that, 'I used to be terrified of public speaking, but not anymore', ask how he or she changed this limiting belief. The response could be, 'I started with small steps. First I spoke at home in front of a mirror, then with a few associates present, next at full business meeting. Finally I accepted an invitation to give a ten-minute talk at a Rotary club about our next fund-raiser.' Not only might you then change your belief that you could never speak in public, you may also take heart from the evidence that big changes can result from taking small steps towards the desired behaviour. Your Mind Chi Plans are your path to changing your beliefs and creating a new reality.

Challenge limiting beliefs

Consider for a moment the limiting belief 'I cannot draw'; a common belief held by many. If you believe that you are no artist then ask yourself 'How do I know this is true?' Perhaps a teacher told you you couldn't draw and you have been carrying that thought around in your head ever since!

Conni Gordon's patented '4-step Art Method' has been taught to over 16 million people worldwide and earned her a place in the Guinness Book of World Records as the 'World's Most Prolific Art Teacher.' Once you have completed her art class you can change your limiting belief from 'I can't draw' to 'I can draw.' Think of other limiting beliefs that that are currently holding you back in the workplace. What steps can you take to update those?

Conni's art lesson

Follow Conni's art lesson below to create an instant landscape. Read all the the instructions and follow the guided example before putting your pencil to paper.

1 OUTLINE IT   Follow box 1

In the blank box provided, place a dot in the centre of the box.
Half way below the dot, add a waterline across.
Curve uneven hills in between.
Then slant the bottom landline.

2 UNDERTONE IT Follow box 2

Scribble uneven distant bushes across waterline
keeping them below hilltops.
Vary their heights. Next, draw light disconnected horizontal
waterlines as shown.
Then darken bottom land area unevenly. Contrast the light,
medium and dark areas.
Then darken the landline down to the bottom. Easy!

3 OVERSHAPE IT   Follow box 3

Start the fun details! Freely draw a top of tree
(a fat, upside down, shallow 'u' shape).
Curve a 'Y' shaped tree trunk down to land
and right of centre dot, as shown.
Don't copy exactly. Give it your rhythm!

4 DETAIL IT   Follow box 4

Finish picture your own way. Darken the trunk.
Darken some leaf groups, letting sky show between them.
Add thinner 'V' or 'Y' shaped branches.
Curve bottom weeds. Sign, date and enjoy!

Wow – you did it!

Your masterpiece here

Conni's art lesson demonstrates that the most complex activities can be reduced to a series of small steps and learned in an orderly progression. Your Mind Chi in action incorporates a series of steps en route to achieving your goal. It's these many, many small steps that you take every day that add up to successful outcomes.

It is very likely that you will experience the 'awkwardness gap' (page 107) as you develop your new artistic abilities, or any other creative or developmental pursuit. The very important lesson is to use ADOCTA (page 99) and keep going. Success is assured!

Discover what you really want

Beliefs colour and shape your thoughts and result in emotions and actions that are the keys to your success in life. Beliefs represent a set of filters through which you see yourself and the world around you, they shape your perspective and prejudices and the decisions that you make. You develop them to help you gain a sense of control and to manage the many situations you face daily. Some will serve you better than others. Some of your perceptions will be more objective or rational than others. It's time to review and update your belief systems.

Here are some guidelines to help you to start to discover what you really want:

1   Ask yourself 'What do I really want?' Then write down your answer in the present tense as though it is already accomplished.
2   Be specific. Ask yourself, 'Will you recognize it when you have it?'
3   Do not let your feelings and/or emotions dictate your choices. After all you are setting a new thought pattern and you don't want to revert to unhelpful and entrenched ways of thinking no matter how enticing they may be.

4   Choose what *you* want and not what someone else wants for you. How many people are in professions and occupations they are unhappy with because they felt coerced, or feel a duty to follow that path?

5   Do not condition your choices by adding a qualifier such as 'if' – they are procrastinators that encourage false wants. How often have you heard, 'If I receive the promotion we will be able to afford …'?

6   State the desired result (what you want) clearly and separately from the process (how to obtain it). Do not let yourself fall into the trap of merging the two. For example: 'I want to earn £70,000 by this time next year' is a result, but it doesn't mention how you will earn the £70,000. However, 'I will learn a foreign language in the next year (process) which will help me earn more (result)' spells out both the plan of action you intend to take to attain the end result. The two (process and result) are very different and you need to make the distinction clear in your mind.

7   Do not let prior investments (of time, learning, connections etc.) dictate what you want in your future. For example, 'I spent the last ten years working in a corporation and now I have to choose between staying at the company with a promotion, or doing what *I really want*, starting my own business.'

8   Finally, do not limit your 'wants' only to what you currently think is possible. There are countless case studies of business people who have made successes of their lives by not limiting their thinking. One example of this is Fred Smith, the founder and president of Federal Express, which generates over $22 billion in annual revenue. Fred Smith has run the company for over thirty years and is one of the richest men in America. In 1971, a few years after he started the company, it collapsed. He was advised that his idea was an impossible dream. That did not stop him from starting again with his idea and making Federal Express the global success it is today.

20 It is all in your Mind Chi

The final chapter of Mind Chi looks at four significant aspects that are frequently referred to in your Mind Chi Program: stress, your senses, your imagination and the creation of your Mind Chi Meme. Understanding the might of these influences will add to the increased control and positive direction of your life.

About stress and strain

The term 'stress' has its roots in engineering. It is a term that relates to the weight placed on timbers and load-bearing walls. When building, you have to be sure that they can take the strain. Stress is 'the load applied' and strain shows 'the level of deforming'. Steel, for example, has a degree of elasticity, so it can absorb an element of stress. However, as the stress continues, the strain starts to deform the metal and the stress starts to show. If the stress is extreme, the strain will make the metal unstable and it will reach breaking point. In some materials (like concrete and glass) the strength and strain points are the same. The toughness of a material is measured by the amount of energy that the material can absorb before it ruptures.

Another interesting aspect is the amount of resilience in a material: its ability to absorb energy when it is deformed by pressure, and then return to its original form when the stress is removed (or reduced). A glass container has very little resilience, so does not return to its original form, whereas a canvas sail has a great deal, and can return to form quite easily.

In your Mind Chi Program, these concepts offer an interesting metaphor for how you might respond to stressors in your life. The same stressor (financial hardship for example) when applied to different materials (people) with different degrees of toughness and resilience, in different situations, will have different levels of yield, elasticity and rupture. Notice that the stressor is always the same but the influencing factors are the ones that make the strain show to a greater or lesser degree. Hence one person's stressful situation is another person's positive challenge; it depends on personal character and individual circumstances. Financial hardship may be considered greater if there is more than one person depending on the source of finance, or if there are debts, a mortgage and so on.

How would you rate your material, elasticity, toughness and resilience? More importantly, what can you do to change any of this?

The authors have researched the effects of strain on people over many years, studying the small percentage of people who remain resilient and flexible in the face of enormous strain – and who manage to survive and even thrive when their stress levels are off the scale of the standard stress quotient (a way of measuring levels of stress).

In this image, the same 'big stress' is shown, 'Chi' on the left is able to manage the strain because he uses the Mind Chi Program, 'Chi' on the right is showing the strain. The stressor is the same, only the individual response makes the difference of whether the strain is controlled or not.

Mind Chi is the latest incarnation of all that the authors have learned over many years. It incorporates an effective range of tools to combat negative stressors, to build elasticity, toughness and resilience and to prevent you from breaking under pressure, as that is no fun!

About senses

All information is processed through your senses, and what you hear, see and touch provides the greatest input. You will have a preference on how to save information to your memory. How can you decide which is the best way for you?

Think back to the last time you bought something that needed to be assembled. You arrived home, opened the box and found the various components needed for construction, written instructions, and a telephone number to call for help.

How you answered the questions are reveals:

1 Did you read the instructions then assemble the item?
   You used a *visual* approach.
2 Did you need to call the telephone number and ask for help?
   You used an *auditory* approach.
3 Did you ignore all the directions and assemble it?
   You used a *kinaesthetic* approach.

You will use each of these approaches in different situations and sometimes a combination of all three. This is why we suggest various different methods to train your memory such as: writing your Mind Chi Meme from your Mind Chi Plan on a small card, repeating your new thought over and over again (or singing it!), or by tuning into your intuition and learning the complete experience by sensing it at gut level.

Your senses act as your antennae for interaction with the world; through them you perceive what is happening about you. The philosopher, Aristotle, was the first to suggest that you have five senses: sight, smell, taste, touch and hearing. More recently another six have been identified. They are: nociception (pain), equilibrioception (balance), proprioception and kinaesthesia (joint motion and acceleration), sense of time, thermoception (temperature differences), and in some a weak magnetoception (direction). (Thank you, Wikipedia!)

We would like to be so bold as to add two more:

- Your sense of humour: to keep you in good stead, regardless of what you might have to handle in life.
- Your sixth sense: that feeling of intuition or gut level response is another form of 'Chi' – your inner voice. It is bringing your attention to a fast summary of all your experiences and learning that either says 'Go' or 'Don't go'. Making complex decisions is a mix of good research, logical thinking and listening to your inner voice, your 'Chi'.

A box of humour

About twenty years ago 'humour workshops' were the rage. They need to return! We always use natural humour in our seminars (and have sometimes been told to 'Keep it down; this is a serious workplace.' Oh dear!) Our offices have always been places where laughter can be heard and we know this means our employees are energized, hard working and happy.

How often do *you* laugh? It is said that children laugh many hundreds of times a day and adults less than twenty times. Laughter is superb medicine. It has been shown to bolster your immune system, improve your circulation – sending more oxygen to your body and brain, as well as providing your brain with a wash of positive chemicals; it is a great stress reducer and helps you to have a sense of hope. Pretty good stuff!

Here are some laughter nuggets:

1   Become aware, on a scale of 0–10, of how much laughter there is in your day. This is your 'laughter quotient'. Ask your 'Chi' to bring your awareness to potential laughter moments and enjoy them.
2   Select work associates and friends who have a sense of humour. A quick wit is connected with your intelligence, so interact and look for a laugh with all the people you may meet in your day.
3   Turn off the news, stop reading the papers, and revisit some of the great, funny shows and movies. Humour is very personal, but we love Charlie Chaplin, Tony Hancock, Victor Borge and Peter Sellers as perennial laughter inducers.
4   Listen to others laugh: as with a yawn, you will find it is almost impossible not to join in. As we are writing this it is Red Nose Day, raising money for Comic Relief in the UK, and we have a nose that laughs when you hit it. We have hit it frequently!
5   Observe all the funny things around you, including your good self! We often provide ourselves with an opportunity for mirth and hope that you discover that you can also 'mirth' yourself. Sharing a laugh with a colleague and/or partner adds a very special quality to that relationship. A good tip is never to take yourself too seriously.

About imagination

Imagination and visualization offer the means to see an experience as though it were happening, with the power of your mind. Many people doubt the power of their imagination and tell us that they can see only blackness when they look inside their heads; yet if asked what they see when reading a gripping mystery, and whether they experience seeing the images or feeling the excitement of the story, they will reply in the affirmative. When recalling where they left something, do they mentally retrace their steps? The reply is 'yes', again – though they are not sure how they actually got the information. Even those people who are blind from birth have the capacity to see inside their head. It is a very powerful activity.

In the context of Mind Chi we use the word 'imagination' to mean the experience of being able to conjure up a future experience as though you are enjoying a series of activities (or to relive something from the past).

The same process of projection is used when you are worried about something: you play in your head a thought-stream of this or that happening and going wrong in some way. Doing this habitually is to use the potent act of imagination/visualization against yourself; it is an invasive, demeaning activity. Imagining negative thoughts robs you of the energy to take positive action. Mind Chi is about turning this around and using imagination and visualization to improve your performance and well-being.

In the early 1980s, a classic study in the US demonstrated the benefits of visualization (or guided imagery) on performance improvement. The study examined the use of visualization in three groups of high school basketball players: the ones that used both the physical practice and the visualization techniques performed the best. Not only did their physical skills improve but also their intrinsic motivational level as well.

To make imaging most effective Korn and Johnson in their book *Sport and Business* suggest the following:

- Be committed – daily practice is needed to obtain results.
- Appreciate the role of conscious and para-conscious thought – in order to switch on the para-conscious, use focused attention, use all your senses, increase your interest on your goal for maximum effectiveness.

Now, in the 2000s, we are able to show that neural activity is affected by the ability to visualize. New connections are forged and ones not used are left to diminish; just as an unused path becomes overgrown if it is neglected. Visualizing or imagining the results strengthens the neural pathways just as if you had actually performed the activity. In your Mind Chi Program you use the potential of your 'imagination' to be able to influence and direct your outcomes.

Science has now shown that there are at least six Autonomic Nervous System (ANS) responses that react in the same way regardless of whether you *think* about performing a function or you actually *do* it. (They are: heart rate, digestion, respiration rate, salivation, perspiration and diameter of the pupils.) This is a crucial observation; your brain frequently makes no difference between your internal 'reality' (thinking/imagining) and the outside 'reality'. This assumption is at the core of the Mind Chi process.

Your mind responds the same way to 'imagined' or 'real'.

If you are not sure that is true, please think about a lemon. Weigh it in your hand, feel the skin's texture and smell the lemon aroma. Roll it in your hands to release some of the zest. See its lovely yellow colour. Now poke your thumb through the skin and suck some of the lemon juice. Mmm, lovely! Is your mouth salivating? And yet there is no REAL lemon in your hands!

Further, and most significantly, you will heighten your conscious awareness of those moments arising when you are able to make a choice thanks to the use of your 'Chi'. Your powers to change your mind will take on much more value to you and become an act that you will make with consideration, knowing that you actually can do it! In fact, as explained above about your imagination, in a way, from your minds point of view, 'just' thinking about it has already made it a reality! As the first step in change is so often the hardest, to think that you *have already done it* helps you to continue to move forward easily!

About the Mind Chi Meme

A new idea! A fresh way to think. A positive mind 'virus'. A catchy good habit.

All of these and much more is Mind Chi. One reason that memes are so important is that the memes you have already 'programd' in your mind will affect your future as a self-fulfilling prophecy. This is why we have spent so much time showing you how to create the programs that will give you the future that you desire.

The meme is a double-edged sword, a bit like the old computer saying 'Garbage in, garbage out!' If you fill your mind with some of the memes that bombard you daily: television, advertising, internet, all media, music, fashion – even conversations with colleagues have the possibility to give you the latest meme. Memes en masse become a virus. All you have to do to become resistant is to ask your 'Chi' to cast a 'meme screen' and just filter out the useless, demeaning, senseless and time-wasting ones. Two recent meme virus examples are 'swine flu' and fake computer viruses (where well-meaning friends warn you of a non-existent computer virus – to check, go to www. http://snopes. com). The 'bad' memes get to you through your very basic urges – the four 'f's': fury; fear; food and f … oops, reproduction!

Your good Mind Chi meme will probably have to do some battles over 'competitive plasticity'. You have some well-learned habits that have made neural highways and become 'rigid'. Given a situation, the default is to go off down the old highway. UN-learning or changing the rigidity is harder to do than to learn something new.

This is made even more difficult if they are in the same area (a second language is much easier to master as a child before a 'mother tongue' has become entrenched). A new language seeks a whole new place in the brain – which is why stroke victims who have lost the ability to speak English can sometimes speak their school-days French – so it is better to take a whole new approach and learn 'anew'!

Plastic **not** elastic!

Once your brain has changed, which it is by EVERY encounter and EVERY interaction, it NEVER returns to how it was! When you start to really realize the incredible nature of this scientific research – and this is about *you* – it is much easier to put up your meme screen and only allow the memes that will change your brain for the better.

How 'old' are you?

We know some teenagers who already exhibit 'old' memes and some ninety year young folk who will never catch the 'old' meme. What are the good qualities of childhood? Curiosity; enthusiasm; interest; laughter; involvement and fun to name a few. It is all in the meme attitude; one of the author's mothers was as fresh and enthusiastic, interested and easily delighted by even small things after 93 years on this planet. How old are you? If you are stuck in your ways, if you don't like change, if you resist all that is new, your brain has become rigid, you have 'old' memes. This is not an advantage to your overall well-being.

Mind Chi is your wake up call!

> Nature LOVES a vacuum – it rushes to fill it!

To update an 'old' meme, plan something different. Find a new friend; take up a hobby; eat something you haven't eaten before; take up a musical instrument; read different books; do mental quizzes; take up dancing; go somewhere you haven't gone; have a child teach you something and keep your plasticity alive and malleable and *you* young.

Hippocampal help

In the centre part of your brain – often referred to as the limbic system – live two seahorses! (Discovered by a British anatomist in the 18th century and given the Latin name for a seahorse – hippocampus – as they are seahorse shaped!) For many years it was erroneously thought that after we are born our brain cells just start dying off and so we have fewer and fewer as we age – a morbid thought. This is wrong in many ways – a fine example of a 'bad' meme – as the truth (as we now understand it) is that we have SO many cells and they interact with each other in even more ways, that our potential loss is the equivalent of going to the ocean and scooping up a thimble full of sea and expecting to notice a difference. More recently it has been discovered that the hippocampus DOES continue to make new cells and – even more wonderful and motivating – that continuing to learn encourages new cell growth AND prolongs their survival – doesn't that make you want to rush out and learn something?

Off and on switches

Different emotions that you may choose to express will have different effects upon your brain. Specifically, aggression and hostility are 'off' switches: they shut down brain activity – hence blame and guilt can hamper your reasoning. On the other hand, compassion, love, meditation and contentment are 'on' switches: they strengthen, stimulate and calm the mind. The end result is less stress in your body. For example,

The power of your mind can reshape your brain.

you cannot think of getting angry and making peace at the same time: you have to choose one 'switch' over the other.

The best 'on' switch of all is called BDNF (brain-derived neurotrophic factor). It plays a crucial role in reinforcing changes to the plasticity of your brain. Four wonderful things occur:

1   You may have heard the expression 'neurons that fire together, wire together'. This means that when the connections are consolidated they fire more reliably.
2   This speeds up the transmission of brain signals.
3   BDNF also lets you focus your attention (it is your 'Chi's' secret accomplice) and *keeps* it focused, which means that you remember more and more effectively.
4   Finally, after the learning experience is over, the BDNF strengthens key brain connections and then 'cleans up after the party'. This is the nirvana of effortless learning. How good is that? And you have it in abundance at the tips of your brain cells.

Our wish

It is the authors' ardent desire that Mind Chi will wake you up to your full potential and recognize what a miracle you are! Just as it would be such a waste to have the most beautiful castle ever constructed and to live in one small corner of the dungeon; so too we would like you to experience using your magnificent brain to its full capacity and living life to the full. Sadly we have experienced many people living their lives of precious promise at the lowest level possible. The aim of this book is to say 'Wake up! You are capable of so much more and the rewards of a life lived in such a way are treasures beyond words.'

Please go to www.MindChi.com for more information, help, resources – and to share your Mind Chi journey with us.

Be all you want to be – and make it Mind Chi-easy!

Mind Chi Glossary

Just as a legal contract has a preamble as to the terms used ... here is a nice, bite-sized introduction to the words and concepts that are an integral part of our everyday being and referred to frequently in *Mind Chi*.

Consciousness is an aspect of your mind generally regarded to comprise qualities such as subjectivity, self-awareness, sentience (capacity for sensation or feeling), sapience (having or showing great wisdom or sound judgment) and the ability to perceive the relationship between yourself and your environment.

Eudemonics (eudiamonia) is a structure that is designed to create happiness. The original Greek meaning was 'eu' for 'good' or 'well being' and 'diamon' for 'spirit' or 'minor deity'. Larger than happiness and even joy it was to mean 'human flourishing'. Yes!

Imagination is your innate ability and process to invent partial or complete personal realms in your mind from elements derived from your sensual perceptions of the world. Imagined images are seen with the 'mind's eye'. (Remember that your brain responds to them as if they were real!)

Meme was created from the word 'mimema' – this is Greek meaning 'something imitated'. 'The meme as a unit provides a convenient means of discussing "a piece of thought copied from person to person", regardless of whether that thought contains others inside it, or forms part of a larger meme. A meme could consist of a single word, or the entire speech in which that word first occurred. This forms an analogy to the idea of a gene as a single unit of self-replicating information found on the self-replicating chromosome.' (Thank you Wikipedia!) This is what gave Richard Dawkins the idea to create the word in 1976. It is our aim to offer you a 'good' meme that you can 'catch' and others can copy from you to make a Mind Chi 'virus'!

Memory is your ability to store, retain, and subsequently recall information. Even up to the early twentieth century, memory was put within cognitive psychology. Recently it has become part of a new branch of science called cognitive neuroscience, a marriage between cognitive psychology and neuroscience. Mental health is defined by Merriam-Webster as 'A state of emotional and psychological well-being in which an individual is able to use his or her cognitive and emotional capabilities, function in society, and meet the ordinary demands of everyday life.' One way to think about mental health is by looking at how effectively and successfully a person functions. Feeling capable and competent, being able to handle normal levels of stress, maintaining satisfying relationships, leading an independent life; and being able to bounce back or recover from difficult situations, are all signs of good mental health. This is what we are striving for with the directed use of your Mind Chi.

Para-conscious is just beside and around your immediate conscious, but not as inaccessible as an un-conscious or sub-conscious thought.

Positive psychology – mental wellness is based on the work of Abraham Maslow (1954); Carl Rogers and Erich Fromm have been brought into the modern thought spectrum by Martin Seligman (1998) who has spawned a plethora of interest in this subject. Positive is not diametrically opposed to negative, but is to allow a continuum (wherein we all travel). A 'Character, Strengths & Virtues' (CVS) handbook has been written (to balance the one on mental disorders) and includes six virtues viewed throughout history and across cultures as increasing happiness when practiced. They are:

1 **Wisdom and Knowledge:** creativity, curiosity, open-minded, love of learning, perspective
2 **Courage:** bravery, persistence, integrity, vitality
3 **Humanity:** love, kindness, social intelligence
4 **Justice:** global citizenship, fairness, leadership
5 **Temperance:** forgiveness and mercy, humility, prudence, self control, will power
6 **Transcendence:** appreciation of beauty and excellence, gratitude, hope, humour, spirituality

Psychotherapy is an interpersonal, relational intervention used by trained psychotherapists to aid clients in problems of living. Purposeful, theoretically based psychotherapy began in the nineteenth century with psychoanalysis. Psych means the 'soul, spirit or mind'; originally the Greek definition was breath, life, soul. However, the current interpretation is to do with mental DISorders.

Thinking involves the cerebral manipulation of information, as when you form concepts, engage in problem solving, reason and make decisions. Thinking is a higher cognitive function and the analysis of thinking processes is part of cognitive psychology such as CBT.

Volition/Willpower is your control, exercised by deliberate purpose over impulse, your self control. This is a purposeful desire of fixed intention, the energy of intention. This concept is one we shall explore further as recent research has actually shown where this rests in your brain and how you can use and build this attribute. It is like a muscle and needs a work out!

Bibliography

Adler, M. G., and Fagley, N. S., (2005) 'Appreciation: Individual differences in finding value and meaning as a unique predictor of subjective well-being', *Journal of Personality, 73*, pp.79–114

Amen, D.G. (2005) *Making a Good Brain Great*, Three Rivers, pp.4–6, 62–7

Baddeley, A. (2004) *Your Memory – a user's guide*, Firefly, pp.97–9, 253–61

Beattie, M. (1987) *Codependent No More*, Hazelden Foundation

Begley, S. (2007) *Train Your Mind Change Your Brain*, Ballantine, pp.26–48

Ben-Shahar, T. (2007) *Happier*, McGraw-Hill, pp.97–110

Braiker, H.B., (1989) 'The Power of Self-Talk', *Psychology Today*, December, pp. 23–7

Brodie, R (2009) *Virus of the Mind*, Hay House, pp. 1–18

Carroll, M. (2007) *The Mindful Leader*, Trumpeter, pp.115–25

Collins, S. F. (2003) *The Joy of Success: 10 essential skills for getting what you want*, William Morrow, pp.9–33

Dawkins, R. (1976) 'The Selfish Gene', *The Oxford Biologist*. He first coined the word 'meme'.

Damasio, A.R. (2007) 'How the Brain Creates the Mind', *Best of Scientific American*, Dana, pp.58–67

Fletcher, J.E. (1989) 'Physiological Foundations of Intrapersonal Communication', in Roberts and Watson (eds), *Intrapersonal Communication Processes* (pp.188–202), New Orleans: Spectra

Gage, F. (2007) 'Brain Repair Yourself', *Best of Scientific American*, Dana, pp.121–31

Gordon, C. and Israel, R. (2002) *How to Think Creatively Using the 'TILS' 4 step technique*, Quicksilver, Miami, pp.18–9

Grainger, R.D. (1991) 'The Use and Abuse of Negative Thinking', *American Journal of Nursing*, 91(8), pp.13–4

Higbee, K.L. (1996) *Your Memory and How it Works*, Marlowe, pp.188–200

Iddon, Jo and Williams, Huw (2003) *Memory Booster Workout*, pp.8–10

Israel, R., Whitten, H. and Shafffran C. (2000) *Your Mind at Work, Developing Self-Knowledge for Business Success*, Kogan Page, pp.17–30

Kashdan, T.B., Uswatte, G. and Julian, T. (2006) 'Gratitude and hedonic and eudemonic well-being in Vietnam War veterans', *Behaviour Research and Therapy*, 44, pp.177–99

Korba, R. (1989) 'The Cognitive Psychophysiology of Inner Speech', in Roberts and Watson (eds), *Intrapersonal Communication Processes* (pp. 217–42), New Orleans: Spectra

Levine, B.H. (1991) *Your Body Believes Every Word You Say: The language of the body/mind connection*, Boulder Creek, CA: Aslan

McCullough, M. E., Emmons, R. A. and Tsang, J. (2002) 'The grateful disposition: A conceptual and empirical topography', *Journal of Personality and Social Psychology*, 82, pp.112–27

McGonicle, D. (1988) 'Making Self-Talk positive', *American Journal of Nursing*, 88, pp.725–26

North, V. (2001) *Get Ahead: Map your way to success*, pp. 58–91

Ouspensky, P.D. (1957) *The Fourth Way*, Routledge and Kegan Paul, pp. 43, 173, 314–15

Pearson, J.C. and Nelson, P.E. (1985) *Understanding and Sharing: An Introduction to Speech Communication* (Third Edition), Dubuque, IA: William C. Brown

Restak, R. (2006) *The Naked Brain*, Harmony, pp. 121–36

Shedletsky, L.J. (1989) *Meaning and Mind: An Intrapersonal Approach to Human Communication*, Bloomington, IN: ERIC Clearinghouse on Reading and Communication Skills [ED 308 566]

Small, G. and Vorgan, G. (2008) *iBrain: Surviving the Technological Alteration of the Modern Mind*, HarperCollins, pp.6–8, 20–2

Turkington, C. (2003) *Memory: A self-teaching guide*, John Wiley pp.17–26

Watkins, P. C., Woodward, K., Stone, T. and Kolts, R. L. (2003) 'Gratitude and happiness: Development of a measure of gratitude, and relationships with subjective well-being', *Social Behavior and Personality', 31*, pp.431–51

Weaver, R.L. and Cottrell, H.W. (1987) 'Destructive Dialogue: Negative Self-Talk and Effective Imaging', Paper presented at the Speech Communication Association Meeting. [ED 290 176]

Wood, A. M., Joseph, S. and Maltby, J. (2008) 'Gratitude uniquely predicts satisfaction with life: Incremental validity above the domains and facets of the Five Factor Model', *Personality and Individual Differences, 45*, pp.49–54

Wood, A. M., Joseph, S. and Maltby (2009) 'Gratitude predicts psychological well-being above the Big Five facets', *Personality and Individual Differences, 45*, pp.655–60

Wood, A. M., Joseph, S. and Linley, P. A. (2007) 'Coping style as a psychological resource of grateful people', *Journal of Social and Clinical Psychology, 26*, pp.108–125

Wood, A. M., Joseph, S., Lloyd, J., and Atkins, S. (2009) 'Gratitude influences sleep through the mechanism of pre-sleep cognitions', *Journal of Psychosomatic Research, 66*, pp.43–8

Wood, A. M., Maltby, J., Gillett, R., Linley, P. A. and Joseph, S. (2008) 'The role of gratitude in the development of social support, stress, and depression: Two longitudinal studies', *Journal of Research in Personality, 42*, pp.854–71

Zimmer, C. (2007) 'The Neurobiolgy of the Self', *Best of Scientific American*, Dana, pp. 47–57

Recommended Reading

Allen, Robert (2004) *Improve your Memory*, Collins and Brown

Amen, Daniel G. (1999) *Change Your Brain, Change Your Life: The break-through program for conquering anxiety, depression, obsessiveness, anger, and impulsiveness*, Crown

Amen, Daniel G. (2008) *Magnificent Mind at Any Age: Natural Ways to Unleash Your Brain's Maximum Potential*, Crown

Amen, Daniel G. (2006) *Making a Good Brain Great: The Amen Clinic Program for Achieving and Sustaining Optimal Mental Performance*, Crown

Bate, Nicholas (2005) *Get a Life*, Capstone

Begley, Sharon (2007) *Train Your Mind, Change Your Brain: How a new science reveals our extraordinary potential to transform ourselves*, Random House

Black, Octavius and Bailey, Sebastian (2006) *The Mind Gym*, Time Warner

Blyth, Laureli (2002) *Brain Power'*, Metro

Braverman, Eric R. (2004) *The Edge Effect*, Sterling

Brizendine, Louann (2007) *The Female Brain*, Broadway Books

Brown, Paul B. and Davis, Alison (2006) *Your Attention Please*, Adams Media

Buzan, Tony (1974 and 1999) *Use Your Head*, BBC Books

Buzan, Tony (1991) *Use Your Perfect Memory*, Penguin

Callahan, Roger (2001) *Tapping the Healer Within*, Judy Piatkus

Chernow, Fred B. (1997) *Memory Power Plus*, Prentice Hall

Cialdini, Robert B. (2008) *Influence: Science and Practice* (Fourth Edition), Pearson

Collins, Susan (1995) *Our Children are Watching*, Barrytown

Collins, Susan Ford (2003) *The Joy of Success: 10 essential skills for getting the success you want*, Harper Collins

Curry, Don L. (2004) *How Does Your Brain Work*, Scholastic

Dispenza, Joe (2008) *Evolve Your Brain: The Science of Changing Your Mind*, Heath Communication

Doidge, Norman (2007) *The Brain That Changes Itself: Stories of Personal Triumph from the Frontiers of Brain Science*, Penguin

Eden, Donna (1999) *Energy Medicine*, Jeremy P. Tarcher/Putnam

Felberbaum, Frank (2005) *The Business of Memory*, Rodale

Felgoise, Stephanie H. (2005) *Encyclopedia of Cognitive Behavior Therapy*, Springer

Feinstein, David, Eden, Donna and Craig, Gary (2005) *The Promise of Energy Psychology*, Jeremy P. Tarcher/Penguin

Fritz, Robert (1989) *The Path of Least Resistance: Learning to become the creative force in your life*, Random House

Gelb, Michael (1988) *Present Yourself*, Jalmar

Gordon, Conni (2004) *Oops and Ahas*, Gordon Trust

Green, Cynthia R. (1999) *Total Memory Workout*, Bantam

Hagwood, Scott (2007) *Memory Power: You can Develop a Great Memory: America's Grandmaster Shows You How*, Simon and Schuster

Howard, Pierce J. (2006) *The Owner's Manual for the Brain: Everyday application from mind–brain research*, Bard

Hyman, Mark (2008) *The UltraMind Solution: Fix your broken brain by healing your body first*, Simon and Schuster

Jensen, Eric (1994) *The Learning Brain*, Turning Point for Teachers

Kagan, Jocelin (2006) *Stand and Deliver*, Knowres

Katz, Lawrence and Manning, Rubin (1998) *Keep Your Brain Alive: 83 Neurobic Exercises'*, Workman

Le Messurier, Mark (2005) *Cognitive Behavior Training: A How to Guide for Successful Behavior*, Corwin

Leary, Timothy (2000) *Change Your Brain*, Ronin

LeDoux, Joseph (2003) *Synaptic Self: How Our Brains Become Who We Are*, Penguin

Levitin, Daniel J. (2007) *This Is Your Brain on Music: The science of a human obsession*, Penguin

Lundin, Stephen (2001) *Fish! A Remarkable Way to Boost Morale and Improve Results* Hyperion Books

MacDonald, Matthew (2008) *Your Brain: The Missing Manual*, O'Reilly Media

McPherson, Fiona (2000) *The Memory Key*, Career

Magee, Patrick (1998) *Brain Dancing*, BrainDance

Mandhayan, Raju (2004) *The heart of public speaking*, WLF-IDC Publishing House

Meshel, Jeffrey W. (2005) *One Phone Call Away*, Portfolio

Mukajea, Dilip (2005) *Brainfinity*, Oxford University Press

Nast, Jamie (2006) *Idea Mapping*, John Wiley

Newberg, A. and Waldman, M.R. *How God Changes Your Brain: Breakthrough Findings from a Leading Neuroscientist*, Ballantine Books

Newquist, H.P. and Kasnot, Keith (2005) *The Great Brain Book: An inside look at the inside of your head*, Scholastic

O'Brien, Dominic (2003) *Quantum Memory Power: Learning to Improve your Memory with World Memory Champion*, Simon and Schuster

O'Donohue, William (2009) *Cognitive Behavior Therapy: Applying Empirically Supported Techniques in Your Practice*, John Wiley

Osho (2005) *Body Mind Balancing, Using Your Mind to Heal Your Body*, St. Martin's Griffi

Papageorge, Andrew (2004) *Go Innovate!* Go Innovate Publishers

Pink, Daniel H. (2005) *A Whole New Mind, moving from the Information Age to the Conceptual Age*, Riverhead

Rackham, Neil (1988) *Spin Selling*, McGraw-Hill

Ratey, John J. (2002) *A User's Guide to the Brain: Perception, Attention, and the Four Theaters of the Brain*, Knopf

Restak, Richard (1988) *The Mind*, Bantam

Russell, Peter (1979 and 2009) *The Brain Book*, Routledge and Kegan

Samples, Bob (1983) *The Metaphoric Mind*, Addison-Wesley

Schulz, Mona Lisa (2005) *The New Feminine Brain: Developing your intuitive genius*, Free Press

Schwartz, Jeffrey M. and Begley, Sharon (2003) *The Mind and the Brain: Neuroplasticity and the power of mental force*, HarperCollins

Sousa, David A. (2006) *How the Brain Learns*, Corwin

Spirduso, Waneen (2007) *Exercise and its Mediating Effects on Cognition*, Human Kienetics

Stafford, Tom and Webb, Matt (2005) *Mind Hacks, Tips and Tools for Using Your Brain*, O'Reilly

Vitale, Barbara (1986) *Free Flight*, Jalmar

Wang, Sam and Aamodt, Sandra (2008) *Welcome to Your Brain: Why you lose your car keys but never forget how to drive and other puzzles of everyday life*, Bloomsbury

Wenger, Win (1996) *The Einstein Factor*, Prima

Whitten, Helen (2009) *Cognitive Behavioural Coaching Techniques for Dummies*, John Wiley

Wycoff, Joyce (1995) *Transformation Thinking*, Berkley Books

Zander, Benjamin (2000) *The Art of Possibility*, Penguin

Zeigler, Kenneth (2005) *Organizing For Success*, McGraw-Hill

Further Resources

For up-to-date information on Mind Chi and all training and products please see www.MindChi.com

Mind Chi Mentors

We are looking for either in-company or entrepreneurial trainers, facilitators, H.R. and training department specialists and fitness/stress and well-being instructors to conduct 'Mind Chi Matters' sessions and seminars all over the world. As a Mind Chi Mentor you will enjoy:

- increased income opportunity
- credibility by appearing on the official Mind Chi website
- lesson plans and tips to run effective Mind Chi Matters sessions
- access to the Mind Chi Mentor blog
- superb in-company ROI through increased employee motivation
- an official Mind Chi Mentor Certificate
- being a part of a global community to improve the quality of life
- experiencing the benefits of Mind Chi for yourself!

Contact us at www.MindChi.com for more details.

Mind Chi Matters sessions

Mind Chi Matters sessions may be run in-company, in a fitness centre or with any pre-existing group. The sessions are conducted by a qualified Mind Chi Mentor (verified by the Mind Chi website). The sessions may be held weekly, fortnightly or monthly and are conducted in eight session blocks. For the greatest impact it is highly recommended that the Mind Chi Matters sessions remain on-going, with new people joining as the word spreads. There is no limit to the number of people that may attend the sessions in any year. The Mind Chi Mentor may be either an in-house employee or an external consultant (as long as they are qualified). If the Mind Chi Matters sessions are conducted by an in-house employee, there is no charge per attendee and the only request is that every Mind Chi-er receives the *Mind Chi* book. (If the sessions are conducted by an external consultant, a fee will have been agreed that will include a book per attending Mind Chi-er.)

Mind Chi Coaching and keynote speeches

Mind Chi Mentors who are already certified coaches or experienced keynote speakers may add Mind Chi to their selection of skilled interventions.

Sample Pages

The following pages are for you to copy (or tear out) so you can have a working copy.

If you wish, you will also find a copy of these pages in a downloadable format from the website: www.MindChi.com

Included here are:

Mind Chi Questionnaire (from page 23)
Mind Chi Commitment letter (from page 29)
Mind Chi Basic 8 Step Routine Map (from page 43)
Mind Chi Basic 31-day Tracker Calendar (page 329)
Mind Chi Basic 31-day Tracker Matrix (page 330)
Mind Chi Applied 8 Step Routine (page 332)
Mind Chi Plan (from page 333)

Mind Chi questionnaire

To give you an idea of how you are presently functioning and how Mind Chi can be of assistance to you, please complete this short questionnaire. (There is an additional copy on page 23 and at www.MindChi.com)

Instructions: Use a scale where 0 = none/negative and 10 = high/perfect*

Questions   Now   Later
  1 How would you rate your energy throughout your work day?
  2 How much energy do you have at the end of a work day?   ....
  3 How well are you sleeping?   ....
  4 How would you rate your memory?   ....
  5 How would you rate your concentration?   ....
  6 How is your ability to make choices?   ....
  7 How clear is your thinking?   ....
  8 How positive are your 'inner thoughts'?   ....
  9 How would you rate your self-esteem?   ....
 10 How well are you managing negative stress?   ....
 11 How satisfied are you with your work/life balance?   ....
 12 How is your general health?   ....

What does this questionnaire reveal about how you are currently using your Mind Chi (mental energy)? Any response that is less than five needs your attention – now!

Name:_____ Date: _____

Dates: _____; _____; _____

Return after Mind Chi Basic and answer the questions again to note your progress.

*NOTE: This little comment pertains to all activities and is also a life philosophy!
We have used a scale of 0–10 because that is what most people find easiest to relate to. However, in workshops we prefer a scale of 0–100, as it provides a far greater level of refinement. (E.g. a 93 score versus a 97 on a scale of 0–100 speaks volumes that a simple 9 on a scale of 0–10 does not convey.) Please feel encouraged to use the 0–100 scale on any of the activities in Mind Chi (and in your life) if you would like to.

Dear Mind Chi Reader,

We want Mind Chi to be a success for you and we know that it requires 100% commitment to do **JUST eight minutes a day** for the next 28 days.

The only way that this will work is when you have:

- selected your real benefit
- rated it as very important in your life
- organized a time to do your eight minutes a day
- felt your heart beat a little fast with anticipation and
- signed this page with a witness who will help you hold yourself responsible.

We have your best interest at heart and that's why we created Mind Chi. However we must warn you that without 100% commitment you are probably wasting your time. That is the best advice we can offer before your start.

I, (your name) _____ , am making 100% commitment to complete the eight minutes a day for the next 28 days of Mind Chi Basic.

_____   _____   _____

Your signature   Witness   Date

Make it Mind Chi-easy!   Richard Israel   Vanda North

Mind Chi Basic 8 Step Routine Map

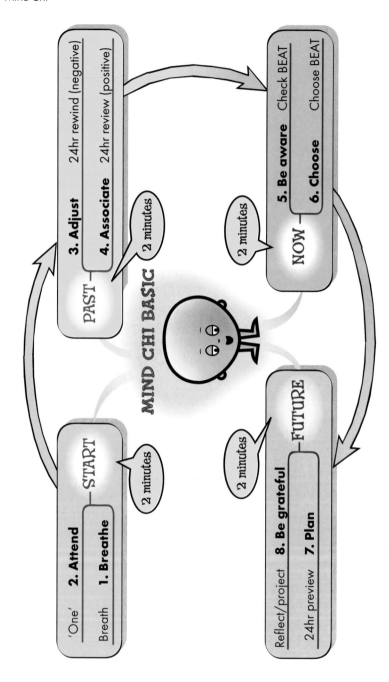

Mind Chi Basic 31-day Tracker Calendar

Monday	Tuesday	Wednesday	Thursday	Friday	Saturday	Sunday

Mind Chi Basic 31-day Tracker Matrix

	Breathe	Attend	Adjust ☹	Associate ☺	Be aware BEAT	Choose BEAT	Plan 24 hrs	Be grateful
1								
2								
3								
4								
5								
6								
7								
8								
9								
10								
11								
12								
13								
14								
15								

16	17	18	19	20	21	22	23	24	25	26	27	28	29	30	31

Mind Chi Applied

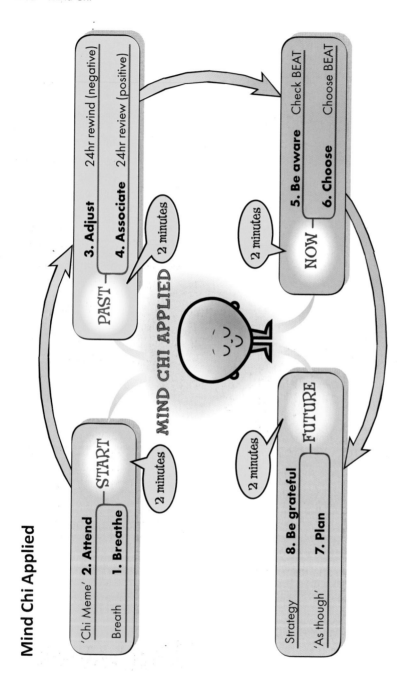

Mind Chi Plan

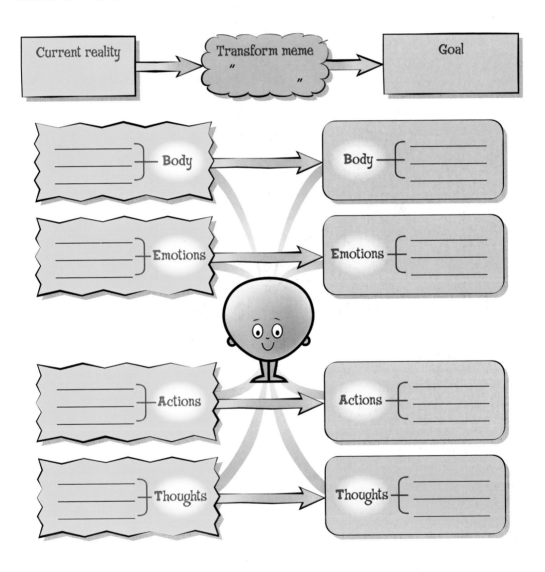

COVENTRY ARENA PARK LIBRARY

The beginning ...

Make it
Mind Chi
Marvellous!

Index